GETTING
OUT

GETTING OUT

YOUTH GANGS, VIOLENCE, AND POSITIVE CHANGE

KEITH MORTON

University of Massachusetts Press
AMHERST & BOSTON

Copyright © 2019 by University of Massachusetts Press
All rights reserved
Printed in the United States of America

ISBN 978-1-62534-427-4 (paper); 426-7 (hardcover)

Designed by Jen Jackowitz
Set in Minion Pro and Good Headline Pro
Printed and bound by Maple Press, Inc.

Cover design by Rebecca Lown
Cover photo by JakubPr, *Graffiti Wall*, Shutterstock.com.

Library of Congress Cataloging-in-Publication Data
Names: Morton, Keith William, author.
Title: Getting out : youth gangs, violence and positive change / Keith Morton.
Description: Amherst : University of Massachusetts Press, [2019] | Includes
bibliographical references and index. |
Identifiers: LCCN 2018051829 (print) | LCCN 2019000204 (ebook) | ISBN
9781613766767 (ebook) | ISBN 9781613766774 (ebook) | ISBN 9781625344267
(hardcover) | ISBN 9781625344274 (pbk.)
Subjects: LCSH: Gang members—Rehabilitation—United States. | Juvenile
delinquents—Rehabilitation—United States. | Ex-gang members—Services
for—United States. | Problem youth—Services for—United States.
Classification: LCC HV6439.U5 (ebook) | LCC HV6439.U5 M687 2019 (print) | DDC
364.4—dc23
LC record available at https://lccn.loc.gov/2018051829

British Library Cataloguing-in-Publication Data
A catalog record for this book is available from the British Library.

To Tou Pathoummahong,
who invited me into something short-term
and ended up shaping my life journey.

And to my wife, Kathy Morton,
who always leads with love and compassion.

CONTENTS

PERSPECTIVE TAKING

I promised to show you a map you say but this is a mural
. . .   .
Where do we see it from is the question
—Adrienne Rich, *An Atlas of the Difficult World*

I drafted the following reflection in 2010, two years into Rec Night, a youth program I helped run for eight years. This program and the many people involved in it are the inspiration for this book. I open with this reflection to suggest why youth involved in gangs and street violence matter to me, to share my point of view, and to invite you to consider how your perspective shapes the way you respond to the stories and arguments that follow.

Mary is a young Laotian American woman I met through Rec Night about three years ago. She's now nineteen years old and lives in Smith Hill (a neighborhood of Providence, Rhode Island)—though she has lived in four places in the past couple of years. She considers her mom, big sister, and godsister her only family. Her stepfather and she argue and fight. Her stepmother, on the other side, with her dad in North Carolina, "hates her." I believe this. Until recently, Mary fought a lot, has been stabbed and shot at, dropped out of school. She had a reputation on the street as "serious." Not a member, she nevertheless hung out with Laos Pride (LP) and could often be found at a small store behind the 7-Eleven at the intersection of Chalkstone Avenue and Smith Street. Her brother has been in and out of trouble since he was eleven and was a member of Laos Pride. He went to prison a couple of years ago for shooting two young men on Camden Avenue in July 2008, killing one of them. He was seventeen at the time and is now serving forty to sixty years at Rhode Island's Adult Correctional Institute. While Mary writes and visits him, she thinks of him as in many ways dead—his life seems over, and visiting him is also a reminder of the boundary that separates them.

The gaze of Mary's brown eyes is direct and fleeting, and she has long black hair, usually in a ponytail held by an elastic band. She wears flat-brimmed hats with authenticity stickers still on the brim, chosen to coordinate with her T-shirts and sweatshirts rather than loyalty to a given team or color. Her clothes are usually sized to make her shapeless. Both arms are extensively tattooed, including her family name and a memorial to her father that includes his birth date. Another tattoo is on one leg.

Maybe four years ago, Mary was introduced to the Institute for the Study and Practice of Nonviolence by Tou Pathoummahong, who was the inspiration for Rec Night. Tou, also Laotian, is an ex-gang member, turning his life around, who now works as a street-worker for ISPN. In his early thirties, he is an old friend of Mary's father—they even used to live together—and when Mary moved from Woonsocket, Rhode Island, to Smith Hill, her father asked Tou to help her out, which he does. For the past two summers—2009 and 2010—Mary had been in ISPN's Beloved Community Summer Jobs Program, painting a mural at Tides Family Services, and most recently doing office work at the Smith Hill Community Development Corporation. As part of her SHCDC experience, Mary also attended life-skills workshops a colleague and I ran, and I got to know her a little better. Tou and others at ISPN "keep contact" with her. They are always there for her, she says.

At the celebration marking the end of the 2010 summer jobs program, held at the Providence Place Cinemas, Mary was inspired by a friend who had been asked to speak to perform a talking rap for the audience about her decision to seek a more positive path than the one she had been on. It took five minutes by the clock of Mary standing mutely at the podium and looking at the audience of 250—which at one point chanted, "Mary, Mary, Mary . . ."—for her to share her words. Heather Gaydos, the job program's director and a strong supporter of Rec Night, stood by her shoulder the whole time, waiting. Afterward, I talked briefly with Mary about her rap, thanked her for what she performed, and asked for a copy. She handed me the copy she had brought with her. It read:

> I never thought I had the right potential, My only potential was chasing that dough, Never understand what was a violent or a drug free zone, Been around it so much them were the only things I know, It took me a while to figure out where I wanted to go, I used to have all these crazy negative thoughts, where I would think of doing something & hope I won't get caught, But we all know no one ever gets away, so I think twice about how I wanna end my day, Come home alive or mess around and get sprayed, No life is worth losing, So I mind my business and keep it moving, Then came summer of 09 was a new beginning to my life, where I started doing right, all the negativity started to fade away, Started to have more positivity day by day, Took the non-violence training, A year ago I wouldn't picture myself here but after two years I'm still remaining, Keeping myself steady & tryna get my message out to young youths, Let em' know the study & practice of non-violence isn't a lie, it's the truth.

Heather, also director of all youth programs for ISPN, is coteaching a course on the history of childhood with me at Providence College the fall following Mary's rap. Heather is one of the trusted adults in Mary's life. She asks Mary if she'd like to join the class for the semester; Mary says yes, comes a couple of times, and as we begin to historicize childhood, and to view it as a social construct, gets it right away, especially Henry Giroux's concept of youth who are treated as "waste." As we turn our attention to Max Van Manen's methodology of "hermeneutic phenomenology," Mary again gets it and proposes to Heather, and then to me, that she make her rap an object lesson for us. She suggests that in the next class we read her rap and then ask her questions about her life. We do this. After class she proposes that, for her to get to know the other eleven students as well as they have gotten to know her, and so that they can begin to explore their points of view and how that might shape how they hear her story, we start the next class with her asking them questions about their lives.

The conversation in class after we read Mary's words is quite extraordinary. It is extraordinary, certainly, because Mary's story is so complex, and hard and often scary, and because she is, for the most part, quite matter-of-fact about it all. It's extraordinary because the space that opens up is one of hospitality. The college students show sensitivity in their questions, Mary in her responses, each doing his or her best to really hear one another. It is also the first time Mary has shared much of her story with any but a couple of trusted adults from ISPN, and the experience is emotional and liberating—she remains in control of how much she shares, but she talks about her life and reveals herself as a deep and generous thinker. You can see tension leaving her face and neck and shoulders even as her eyes occasionally tear up.

Among other things, she talks about learning from her brother's experience how to tell the difference between people who are really there for you and those who just say they will be: how his gang, which he thought of as family and did violence for, abandoned him. People join gangs, she says, because they want acceptance, want someone to get their back, for reasons they can't articulate. Because they want love. But they don't visit, don't write her brother, hardly ask after him. He has learned, she says, that "you do your own time. Nobody shares it. You can't divide it up." And this summer (she doesn't share this last with the class), her life was threatened if she or her brother snitched out anyone else. Tou arranged for her safety—effectively putting out the word that she was protected. She talks about supporting a younger cousin, fourteen or fifteen, who is in a life similar to hers and sometimes suicidal. She says, "I tell him, 'You come into the world alone and leave it alone. And you have to look out for yourself, make your own life in between. You can't let others take that from you, tell you what it is going to be.' I tell him, 'You think you are stressed, but you aren't, really. It could be a lot worse, and people still get through it.' I tell him he has to be strong and find his own way. I tell him he can always talk to me." Earlier in her life, she says, she wouldn't have really gotten involved with him, too wrapped up in her own worries and without any sense of hope.

Her hope comes from Tou and Heather and other staff at ISPN. It comes from Rec Night and getting to know me and other volunteers. It comes from positive opportunities. And Mary's existential embrace of aloneness finds its paradoxical opposite in her appreciation of being with "positive people," of being given opportunities to work and help other people, to come to class and tell her story and draw out the stories of others. Mostly, she appreciates, and is good at, making meaning. And, as she might tell her younger cousin, she appreciates making her own meaning of her own life.

There is a great deal to think about in Mary's stories and in her presence in the classroom. But what really strikes me as I listen to her is how much her stories and voice sound like the stories I have heard of my father as a young person: moving so often, poverty, trying to take care of a train wreck of a family while still a child himself, dealing with a violent and abusive stepfather and stepbrothers, dropping out—or being kicked out—of school, a mother who was struggling and who used guilt to manage her world, a grandfather who both loved him and humiliated him. My father found support and structure, eventually, by joining the military as soon as he came of age and staying in for twenty years. But he never dealt directly with this history or his childhood trauma. He learned to compartmentalize and to tightly lock the door on the compartment containing all of these bad experiences, even as he financially helped support his mother, brother, and sister until their deaths. He taught me, through his example, that we are fundamentally alone, that life is hard and owes you nothing—you have to be hard and work, relentlessly, for what you want; there are no guarantees—it's always likely that what you care about or have worked for will be taken from you.

Mary says, "It's hard to believe, I know, but I want to be a cop someday." When my father joined the U.S. Air Force in 1950, he joined the military police. I hear this desire from so many youth like Mary or my father: they mistrust, often actively dislike, the police and authority, yet they want to be cops. Like troublesome students who want to become teachers so they can draw on their own experience and "do it right," Mary wants, as my father did, to keep safe the people she cares about. She wants to do it in a way that is consistent with what her experience has taught her about criminal violence—that sometimes it can only be met with "legitimate" violence. She wants to have the power necessary to make things right. At my mother's request, my father moved from policing into communications three years after I was born. The violence he was witnessing through police work magnified, rather than diminished, his sense of the world as dangerous and his anxiety about protecting us. He was proud of all the work he did throughout his life, and especially of starting his own small company at the end of his working years, but he always told me he would really have liked to have become a labor negotiator and mediator—reflecting his experiences working in the textile mills of Fall River between school and the military—protecting workers and negotiating resolutions to conflict.

I think Mary is a philosopher. She is a rigorous and honest thinker. I don't think she will become a police officer, or, if she does, I think it will be a transitional moment in her life to the something else in which she practices the deliberate making of meaning and uses that to connect with others.

My father never really dealt with his history. Even locked down, it made itself visible as attention deficit/hyperactivity disorder, as a need to be in charge and maintain control, as anxiety, as a capacity for anger that would surface abruptly, and occasionally, I imagine from my vantage point of fifty-two to his eighty years, as depression, none of it diagnosed. Much of this way of being he passed on to me and my sister, and it shaped our family and his life. He and my mother remained married until her death in 2014, but he has always been pretty much alone and is almost constitutionally incapable of just being with the people he cares about and who care about him. He wants to connect and doesn't know how. Despite his many successes, he worries that things are never good enough, dependable enough. The undercurrent of latent anger is more visible as he ages, rather than less.

I share, in a more muted way, some of these characteristics. For all of my community work, I also believe we are alone (though I find in compost a practical, spiritual metaphor for how much we are all intimately connected). Intimacy is difficult. I am dependable—but also controlling. I am pretty tough, physically but especially mentally—and I can use this to keep people at a fixed distance and can feel defensive and prickly in an instant. People will sometimes tell me that I have made them nervous or scared them—and I am always surprised and a little saddened that this is the face I must project. Certainly, my upbringing had its own challenges—moving all the time, the sense always that money and security were the most important things and that we didn't have quite enough, the mixed messages I got about fighting that resulted in my getting in a lot of trouble, early sexuality, friends who did get in serious trouble, and also resilience and compassion.

It is thrilling and heavy to watch Mary unlock the compartment where she keeps her shadows and to witness her beginning to make friends with them.

Mary's gift to me, in this class, is the realization that I like working with the youth at ISPN and Rec Night because I imagine their childhoods are something like my father's in so many respects, the ones that count: love and fear and relationship. I also see something of myself in them, and I get the chance to reach out to them as I wanted done for me. But the real insight as I listen to Mary in class today is that in working with these youth, I get to know a part of my father, to see our relationship from a life-affirming perspective, and, if I am lucky, to treat these youth the way I wish he had been treated so that he might have felt more at home in this world and had his love for others and ours for him more simply realized. It seems such a basic truth, but it has remained invisible to me for years, illuminated only now in the courage of Mary's voice.

I have come to believe through my teaching, research, and community engagement, and by reflecting on the way I live my own life, that our arguments about violence/nonviolence are ultimately arguments about power, fear, and love. Paradoxically, working with gang-involved youth and the people whose lives are affected by gang violence has made me more firmly committed to nonviolence—to not being governed by fear and choosing love and relationship over "othering" as a way of engaging the world. It seems to me the most sensible, practical, powerful, and life-affirming way to go forward.

ACKNOWLEDGMENTS

Books like this are not really written by one person. This book is composed of the stories and research and reflections of hundreds of people over tens of years. I hope it honors the community of meaning that inspired it. I have changed the names and identifying details of people in the book unless they are already part of a public record, and that makes it more important that I recognize some folks here and now. There would be no book without Tou Pathoummahong, whose street-smart vision inspired the youth program that launched this book. While I may be the author of record, *Getting Out* is a product of our combined strengths, and I am thankful that our collaboration has turned into a continuing friendship. Teny Gross, Heather Gaydos, and the entire staff of the Institute for the Study and Practice of Nonviolence stuck their necks out time and time again on behalf of the youth this book is about. Please know how much you are appreciated. Some of the best teachers I've ever had were ISPN staff. Most often they had come up just like the youth we were trying to support; and yet their generosity of spirit, hopefulness, and desire for a less violent world led them to teach me to see what I was looking at. Thank you David Cartagena, Ali Amoury, Jose Rodriguez, Dimke Edouard, Graig Bustillo, Ray Duggan, Tony

Kim, Ajay Benton, and so many more. And thank you also to the youth who schooled me and revealed their stories little by little—they are almost too numerous to name, but here are a few: thank you Mohamed, Matthew, John V., Trey, Jay, Tony, Charles, Meatball, Angel, Vothavong, Tina. And of course I want to shout out to the college and community volunteers who helped make our work real and to recognize several who imprinted their spirits on the work and on me: Chris Horn, Kris Karl, Sam Bergbauer, Griffin Rouse, Caitlyn Treem, and Peter Klein. Thanks also to Lieutenant Gannon of the Providence Police Department, who put the community in community policing. I'd like to thank my colleagues at Providence College as well. They supported our work in so many ways: providing release time, fund-raising, welcoming youth onto campus, volunteering, and supporting classes with strange titles like "Violence and Nonviolence in American Culture" that allowed me time and space to reflect on what I was experiencing and observing. A special shout out to Sal Monteiro, nonviolence trainer at ISPN, who has co-taught this course with me six times. (Talk about slow learners.) I also want to recognize Matt Becker and the staff at the University of Massachusetts Press for encouraging the writing of this book and so graciously seeing it into its final form. And finally, of course, I want to thank my home team, starting with my daughters Sarah and Brenna and resting with my wife, Kathy. You've all encouraged me to spend lots of time doing what I love, and I hope that I have returned that in kind. As the proverb says, "I am we."

GETTING
OUT

INTRODUCTION

Practice seeing the world as it is, in its genuine meaning, as interpreted by your most honest wits. Process attendant pain with others. Pay particular attention—honest attention—to young children. Resist writing off horrors and absurdities as normal.

—Jim Tull, *Positive Thinking in a Dark Age*

Getting Out—the title of this book—is intended as an invitation for each and all of us to "get out" of our usual ways of thinking about youth, gangs, and violence. "Getting out" points us to the kind of insight and learning that comes from what Bryan Stevenson (2014) calls getting "proximate": getting close to people we have been socialized to think of as "other," sharing our stories, and coming to understand our respective situations and contexts. "Getting out" of ourselves begins with the practices of relationship and compassion. It is also how we learn about the public dimensions of our lives as members of a diverse and pluralistic community.

"Getting out" reflects my wanting to know what I would see and what I would understand more fully if I put aside the prejudices, stereotypes, myths, and assumptions that shape most public discourse about youth gangs and instead spent time with them and used a lens of "making sense": the perspective that youth involved in gang and street violence are doing the best they can (as perhaps each of us is) to keep their heads up, given their situation, and attempting to do what they believe will be most meaningful in their lives, given their options.

This perspective invites a fundamental question: If I assume that youth involved in gangs and "on the streets" are doing what makes most sense to them, that they are seeking meaning, and that the life goal of all of us is to become more fully human, then how do I explain people being hurt by and hurting others deliberately, in ways that often appear to be self-destructive, antisocial, and intended to cause suffering? I use this book to explore this seeming paradox: how youth can come to believe it is in their self-interest to pursue what the mainstream culture—and often friends, families, mentors, and youth themselves—perceive as violent, self-destructive, and antisocial behavior.

Getting Out is organized to explore this paradox. The beginning chapters investigate what we mean by "gang," how the United States' fascination with violence shapes contradictory perceptions of gang, and how it is that otherwise ordinary youth can become convinced that participating in violence is a good option. The remaining chapters describe the "youth positive" approach that emerged over a period of eight years as I reflected with the participants in a program called Rec Night about answers to these questions. It then makes a case for nonviolence as a meaningful and practical alternative to violence for youth involved in the streets and the institutions that shape their choices. The concluding chapter summarizes my argument about how gang and street violence happen and are interpreted, makes a case for adopting a "youth positive" perspective, and suggests how we might reframe "success" when working to end gang and street violence. It also directs our attention to representative efforts currently under way to change the institutional context that so reliably produces gangs and street violence.

Thich Nhat Hanh, a Vietnamese Buddhist well known for his work as a peace educator, teaches a compassion meditation to people who have been victims of violence or injustice at the hands of others. "Close your eyes," he says, "breathe, and imagine the person who hurt you as a five-year-old. Imagine what must have happened along the way to let them hurt you as they did." He offers this meditation as an invitation to seeing those who have hurt us with compassion.

I will describe what I think it means to respond to gang-involved youth with compassion in a later chapter, but responding with compassion as the starting point for change is the essential point of this book: youth get into gangs and develop their capacity for violence as "an adaptation to circumstances," and stopping youth violence requires that we respond with compassion, not force, to help them unlearn, heal, and grow, even as we work to change the circumstances that made their adoption of violence seem reasonable. It is a process made immensely complicated when we recognize that people are often both victim and perpetrator and by the challenges of restorative justice—attempting to repair the sometimes irreversible harm that is caused by the choice of violence.

The bulk of this book is given to making a case for this perspective and offering some practical ideas for embodying compassion in work with gang-involved, gang-affiliated, and on-the-street youth. Recognizing how difficult, slow, and iterative this work can be, I describe the positive change that can happen when youth whose identities come largely from the street and their involvement in violence are engaged as traumatized persons whose perspectives and behaviors make sense and are "adaptive" under a narrow set of circumstances but "maladaptive" in nearly every other social context. I think it is obvious that succeeding in this is good for our collective public interest as well as for the lives of individual youth and the people who care for them.

The observations, reflections, and arguments I offer in *Getting Out* were largely inspired by my participation as coleader, from 2007 to 2015, of a modest weekly program called Rec Night. I was drawn into the program by Tou Pathoummahong and Heather Gaydos, staff members of the Institute for the Study and Practice of Nonviolence, based in Providence, Rhode Island. ISPN focuses on reducing gang and street violence through a number of intervention programs, including victim's services, and by training community members, including gang members, police officers, and teachers, in the principles and steps of Kingian nonviolence. They are unique in supporting both victims and perpetrators of violence. Tou, an ex-gang member, worked as a streetworker, getting directly involved to prevent, mediate, and respond to street violence. Heather coordinated programs for street-involved youth, including employment and training in nonviolence.

Each Monday evening for eight years, Rec Night would welcome seventy to ninety youth from the Smith Hill neighborhood and Chad Brown housing project of Providence, ranging in age from eight to twenty-four, into the local recreation center. The great majority of youth participating were male, and the culture of Rec Night was predominantly masculine. Our numbers reflected the data gathered by ISPN, where more than 85 percent of their program participants—gang- and street-involved young people—are male. While they were less visible, the girls and young women in the program—like Mary—were also profoundly affected by gang and street violence, sometimes as gang members or violent actors, but more often as victims of violence or by the choices thrust on them by their relationships to males involved in the streets. With notable exceptions, it was also the case that the young women more often responded to the trauma in their lives by internalizing their reactions, while the young men externalized much of their response. While both would carry anger, the boys and men would typically act out and become aggressive or violent, while the girls and women were more likely to drop into the background and become withdrawn, isolated, anxious, and depressed in response to trauma.

More often than the boys and men, the young women were or had been victims of sexual harassment or violence, and they were constantly negotiating boundaries among love and sex and violence. These boundaries, reflecting the values and assumptions of an aggressive, masculine (and sometimes "hypermasculine"), heterosexual culture, what some observers (Kivel 1999; M. White 2011; Messner, Greenberg, and Peretz 2015) have called "toxic masculinity," were even more fraught for youth who were gay or lesbian or somewhere in the process of figuring out this part of their identity.

Perhaps forty of the youth on any given night were gang involved, gang affiliated, or deeply involved in the streets. They were often from two different youth gangs and two or three street crews. The other youth were neighbors, friends, family. Most of the youth knew one another, and many went to (or had been to) the same schools. Street-workers from ISPN and community volunteers brought another eight or so "positive adults" into the mix. Starting in the second year, I began bringing ten or so students from nearby Providence College, where I teach, to join in. Rec Night became known in the community as a "safe space," a mostly neutral spot where youth would gather for basketball, board games, foosball, conversation, pizza, and informal connections to positive adults and other opportunities.

Tou had grown up in the neighborhood and been a member of Laos Pride, a local gang known for its ferocity, before moving along a path that led to his role as a streetworker at ISPN. His new job was to react to, intervene in, follow up on, and help prevent gang-related violence, particularly in his home community. As a streetworker, Tou wanted the neighborhood's gang-involved youth to have access to "their" rec center, from which they were routinely excluded; he wanted to show the youth that he could deliver something meaningful for them, that being positive gave him some juice. His goal was simply to keep them alive into their early twenties, the age at which many of them would drift away from street violence, and he wanted a simple mechanism for "keeping contact" and communicating with the large numbers of youth that he tracked. Informed largely by his vision, we used Rec Night as a hub for keeping contact and for informally connecting the youth who attended with jobs, programs, services, mentors, personal support, and activities like hiking, biking, and rock climbing. Mostly, though, it was a place they could just "be" for three hours a week.

Our approach began with the simple ideas that it would be harder to commit violence against someone you had played basketball (or other games) and eaten with and that it would take very little by way of building positive relationships with the youth to increase their resilience and amplify their reasons for walking away from violence.

I had met Tou in passing more than ten years earlier, when he was in his early teens and deeply involved in the streets. By the time he invited me to help with Rec Night, I knew the neighborhood, had been involved with the community for nearly twenty years, and was on ISPN's board of directors. I knew Heather, Tou's colleague, from other projects and respected her reputation as a fierce advocate of high-risk youth. They approached me because Tou needed political support to gain and keep access to the rec center. As a white, middle-aged college professor with access to mainstream institutions, I was able to offer Tou and Heather some of what they needed. A couple of months in, Tou and I began meeting weekly for lunch, using it as an opportunity to discuss specific youth or conflicts that were happening and reflect and strategize about next steps. We also came to realize over time the power of our conversations—what we were teaching one another and what it meant for us to develop a genuine, deep friendship despite our many differences of experience and perspective.

Over time, Tou and I, with the support of many other community members and an anonymous donor, developed Rec Night into a "deceptively simple" program. Rec Night was "owned" by ISPN, with Providence College's Feinstein Institute for Public Service as a lead partner, but it also received ongoing community organizing help from the Smith Hill Community Development Corporation. Use of the rec center space was donated by Providence Parks and Recreation. The district police lieutenant, who believed in community policing and David Kennedy's method of "interrupting" gang violence, worked hard to build a positive, ongoing relationship with us and the youth. The anonymous donor carried most of the program's modest budget (around $20,000 per year, which covered a large portion of Tou's salary, pizza, and supplies). Despite pushback from the rec center director, most local elected officials, including our city council representative and the command staff of the police department, proved sympathetic when they were needed. In addition to the twenty or so college students who volunteered each year, another fifteen to twenty community volunteers helped out on a regular basis, and for the first few years ISPN sent teams of three to five streetworkers to support Tou (this number declined as the perceived safety of the space grew and as cuts in federal, state, and foundation resources forced ISPN to lay off staff).

In addition to providing a safe place to be for three hours per week, we used Rec Night as a hub for checking in with youth and connecting them with other resources and opportunities that could help them grow in positive ways, a combination we came to call "youth positive," which I describe in the later chapters of this book. In many ways, Jane Addams's Hull House and Dorothy Day and Peter Maurin's Catholic Worker "houses of hospitality" were inspirations for our model: create a physical space based on deep, genuine hospitality in which all are welcome; provide opportunities for people to reflect together about whatever is on their minds; assume that people will begin to share their visions for their lives as their fear and stress decrease; and provide support as they pursue their emerging vision, however small or large it is. In other words, create a real community and make it genuinely inclusive.

Kingian nonviolence argues that the big goal is "building the Beloved Community," a concept so abstract and lofty that it can seem ethereal or impossible to imagine. We viewed Rec Night as a place to practice a concrete version of the Beloved Community: a place familiar with conflict and suffering and confusion but committed to inviting everyone to be a part of the community and help transform potentially destructive energy into constructive energy, much as compost changes waste into soil, a fundamental resource of living systems. Nonviolence and the Beloved Community, in other words, are not abstract, lofty, and ethereal philosophy; they are an invitation to a practical way of living in the world as it is with less fear and suffering, more opportunities to make meaning, and membership in a larger human community.

Over the years, I got to know many of the youth very well. Many of them attended Rec Night all the years it ran, and our familiarity with each other grew and deepened. I also developed and continue to teach courses that allowed my students and me to reflect on what we were observing and experiencing in the neighborhood and through Rec Night. Tou joined me in teaching one of these classes early on, and we created a number of roles that interested neighborhood youth could use to participate. Sal Monteiro, ISPN's director of training, also worked with me revising and teaching a course on violence and nonviolence that bridged some of the campus-community divide, and we continue to teach it on a nearly annual basis. Many of the insights, stories, and ideas I relate in this book come from the youth, my students, and Tou and Sal and their colleagues.

Midway through the first year of the program, as a way of shaping the public narrative about the program, and at Heather's suggestion, I began writing a weekly *Rec Night Update* that we emailed to all stakeholders, volunteers, and supporters. I would report what had happened on a given Monday, or in the community during the preceding week, and call attention to upcoming events and opportunities. These updates serve as one record of the program. In them, I also offered reflections on all that was taking place and shared scholarly, popular, and community resources that I thought people would find interesting. This practice, and the feedback that the updates received, combined with the action-reflection pedagogy of the dozen courses I taught, helped us clarify our understanding of the youths' lives and helped us articulate the method that we came to call youth positive.

Youth positive is, as I've said, deceptively simple: create a safe, hospitable drop-in space that is available on a consistent basis. The complexity lies in using this space to listen deeply to youth who are struggling to make sense of their lives and the violence they regularly experience and use what you hear to support them as they move toward and into options that let them engage in nonviolent, personally, and socially affirming ways of making meaning in their lives. Youth who have experienced violence, almost always as victim and perpetrator, do not share their stories easily, are often cut off from their feelings about what they have experienced, and are wary of adults who might want to change them. Relationships develop and stories emerge as you help cushion the impact of the violent, harmful decisions and experiences that inevitably happen to the youth along the way and are there to help them carry on.

Another way to view youth positive is to see it as a particular approach to mentoring that allows the youth to "self-organize" and make their own choices about their lives, while intentionally connecting them to larger communities of support that improve their options, help them grapple with the effects of past and current violence, help them become more resilient in light of the challenges they will face going forward, and consistently affirm them as persons. This approach is made very difficult by the continuing circumstances that led the youth into gang and street involvement in the first place and by the normative practices of youth development and gang intervention supported by such agencies as the Department of Justice's Juvenile Justice program.

Even as they are trying to change their lives, youth are often in chaotic personal situations, and the effects of these situations are generally amplified by the structural violence of racism and poverty with which they live. The violence and chaos in the youths' lives also contribute to a widespread public perception that they are "bad kids." Informed by this perspective, the dominant approach of programs that work with youth gangs is to eliminate the gang and control its youth members, most often by using behavioral modification methods that emphasize threats of punishment, value order and conformity, and offer high school completion (or GED programs) and low-skill work opportunities as carrots. As valuable as education and work are, they are insufficient to help youth. Stressed and traumatized youth predictably respond to threats of punishment with defensiveness, resistance, or withdrawal. So, Rec Night's emphasis is on "self-organization": encouraging youth to make positive choices, helping them have better choices, getting behind them when they begin to move forward, and acknowledging that they are in control of their own lives.

From a more theoretical point of view, youth positive is our effort to integrate concepts and theories of relationship, community, resilience, trauma, and positive psychology with methods of critical pedagogy and reflective practice to help youth name and examine their situations: the systems and histories that frame their options and choices and patterns of behavior. Often done casually, through conversation and over extended periods of time, this approach helps youth tell their own stories of who they are and move toward new ways of making meaning in their lives. It is, simultaneously, a first step toward developing a political consciousness and working toward social change.

Many of the questions I get when I make the case for youth positive are skeptical: How can you reward and care for people who have done heinous acts? Aren't people who regularly commit antisocial violence different from "us"—haven't they crossed a line where there is no coming back? Aren't they somehow mentally disordered? Shouldn't they be punished, and shouldn't we be protected from them? I am sympathetic to these questions because I recognize that the suffering caused by violence is real and can linger and ripple for a long time. There can be a grave imbalance when this suffering lasts even as the perpetrator of it develops and builds a meaningful, happier life.

My short answer, though, is that gang-involved youth are not "other." They are very much like most of us, making choices most of us would make in similar situations. They are our children, living in the world we created and have given to them as our legacy. Many of us forget or fail to see how our lives are connected to theirs, but I believe we are all responsible for the circumstances that make violence seem like a good option. The first chapters of this book unpack dominant cultural assumptions about gangs and violence to make this point.

That violence by and on youth in gangs happens on such a large, predictable, and consistent scale is evidence that something about our social systems "produces" this outcome. Meeting street violence with greater force, controlling and punishing people who are victims as well as perpetrators of violence, and expecting that the net amount of suffering will be reduced borders on the fantastical. Compassion and nonviolence, as embodied in ISPN, Rec Night, and youth positive, coupled with better options, are effective in helping individuals over time. The predictable effect of responding with greater force is that, at best, nothing changes. At worst, violence and suffering increase. It is nearly a cliché, but a true one, that damaged people do more damage. It is in all of our interests to help youth heal. I hope my fuller responses to questions like these throughout the book are adequate and persuasive.

Working with gang-involved youth is to be immersed in what Gandhi called a "constructive program": working directly to alleviate suffering while using the opportunity to develop an analysis of the historic, structural, and political causes of the suffering. As simple and often joyful as it was—safe space, conversation, access to positive people and opportunities—Rec Night was often a disheartening window into the chaos and systems effects made manifest in youth gangs. It increased our awareness of the intersecting, reinforcing, and confounding racial, economic, and social histories that make individual failure for this category of young people more likely than success. It is this awareness that leads me to argue, as do so many others who pay attention to youth violence, that while all of us have to live with the consequences of violence committed by youth gangs, youth gangs are a predictable product of the cultural and policy systems we have created at the national, state, and local levels. If we don't want youth gangs in the future, then we need to disrupt this system of social production and steer toward something better. Institutions, my sociologist friends tell me, are embodiments of values—vehicles for enacting what we believe and care about. Right now, our economic, educational, legal, and social institutions predictably result in youth gangs. Youth gangs are not accidents and not simply the result of individual youth making bad choices. And intervening with individual youth, while useful and necessary, will not solve the problem.

I believe it is this learning, and the relationships and emotional energy that accompany social, historical, and political analysis, that drives change for persons, local communities, and our more global systems. My belief, voiced by the Quaker theologian Thomas Kelly (1941), is that "individual experience leads to social passion, that the non-useful engenders the greatest utility." I close *Getting Out* by describing some cultural and policy changes that align with what we have learned from our experience with Smith Hill, Rec Night, and

ISPN. Like Rec Night itself, many of these policy changes—lowering the census of the RI Training School; banning the box; reframing police-community relations; training youth workers, teachers, and police to recognize and work with youth who have been traumatized; working for educational equity; instituting restorative justice practices in schools and courts; designing youth programs on principles of positive psychology—are deceptively simple, and the largest obstacle to realizing them is the resistance to change that comes from people who see the youth as "other" and as less than fully human and who believe that transgressions by youth must be met by force and containment.

Perhaps the biggest barrier to changing how we work with youth involved in gang and street violence is what Robert Jervis (1976) calls the "problem of the evoked set"—our tendency to see only what we are looking for and what conforms to our prior beliefs: "I'll see it when I believe it." Our tendency to see gang-involved and gang-affiliated youth—or, for that matter, any youth involved in the high-risk behaviors associated with this label—through a predetermined lens is one of the fundamental barriers to developing and enacting more successful strategies.

This book is intended as an invitation to look past the "evoked set" that influences how we view gangs and gang members and see more clearly the situations and persons for what and who they are. Drawing on systems theory and cultural history, and employing a combination of Paulo Freire's critical perspective and Max Van Manen's "hermeneutic phenomenology," I explore, with all the accuracy and compassion I can muster, what gang-involved youth I know and have known are experiencing and how they are making sense of their experiences; I share what I have learned from paying attention and listening carefully to people identified as gang members, as they describe and analyze their situations; and I use what I have gleaned from this practice to help us think more clearly and constructively about how personal and social change can and does happen.

I close this book by considering how to help drive broader cultural change that makes the violence of youth gangs a curious historical relic. At the heart of the argument offered is the idea that cultural change begins by recognizing the embedded cultural narratives—the source of our "evoked sets"—that shape how we interpret and act in the world and that we often mistake for reality, imagining and experimenting with alternative narratives, and internalizing a new way of thinking and being. Youth gang members are not other; they are doing what seems to make the most sense under the circumstances. Recognizing the violence they experience as traumatic and responding to them with compassion is more effective than responding with institutional force. Our shared goals are to become more fully human and live meaningful lives. It seems like a simple, commonsense perspective. Internalizing it and revising our values and perspectives accordingly is a pathway to changing our institutions. I try throughout to directly address the reasoned, realistic, and experienced voices that view the case I am offering as unsound, ungrounded, and naive.

I also use this book to tell stories and to reflect on the points in space and time where systems intersect with individual lives: how the structural violence of racism, poverty, and educational inequality become embodied in individual lives. Structural violence alone offers a necessary but insufficient explanation for why some youth join gangs and choose violence, while most in similar circumstances do not. The missing variable seems to me to be how individual youth experience direct violence—violence from adults, from peers, in their communities—and come to believe that the adults and institutions in their lives will not take care of them. Structural violence intersects with personal trauma, social isolation, anger, stress, fear, and the perceived failures of adults to make joining a gang seem like a good idea. I focus on this point of intersection, systems coalescing in the life experiences of individual persons, in order to ask what can be done to help youth enmeshed in these systems be less susceptible to the factors pressing them into violence, heal from the traumas they have experienced, and pursue more positive, life-affirming paths when it is difficult to change their material circumstances.

What would we do differently as persons and as a public, I wonder, if we recognized youth gangs as products of our culture's values, allowed ourselves to feel deep anguish when we recognized this, and used this anguish as inspiration to change our hearts, minds, and institutions so that youth violence became a rare exception rather than a commonplace?

CHAPTER ONE

THINKING ABOUT GANG//VIOLENCE

Thus the gang, itself a natural and spontaneous type of organization arising through conflict, is a symptom of disorganization in the
larger social framework.

—Frederic M. Thrasher,
The Gang: A Study of 1,313 Gangs in Chicago

There is no consensus definition of "gang," largely because the various stakeholders interpret the term differently and because any
meaningful understanding or definition is specific to a local situation. The term has a complex, layered cultural history, reflected in
its etymology, in contradictory public perceptions, and in patterns
of experiences of youth involved in gangs and the street. The ways
we understand "gang" reflects more about us, as observers, than it
does about any objective experiences of youth on the streets. In this
chapter I describe what I see as the most consistent assumptions
behind the use of the term "gang" in contemporary public culture
and reflect on what we might learn by testing our assumptions
against experience.

ETYMOLOGY OF "GANG"

"Gang" is an odd word, if you consider its history (*Oxford English
Dictionary*) and think about how it came to be applied to groups
of youth who are transgressing normative cultural boundaries. It is
both noun and verb. The first use of it as a noun dates to 825, and by
the 1630s its colloquial use had begun to take its current meaning:

"Any band or company of persons who go about together or act in concert (chiefly in a bad or depreciatory sense, or associated with criminal societies)."

The word "gangbuster" dates to 1930: "An officer of a law-enforcement agency who is known for successful (and often aggressive) detection of organized crime." This phrase is associated with intense energy: coming on "like (the) gangbusters: with great speed, force, or urgency; (hence) vigorously, successfully." Ironically, by 1946, "gangbuster" was beginning to be used to convey the idea of "an outstandingly successful person or thing; a winner, a hit."

"Gangbang," on the other hand, emerged by 1945 as slang for "an occasion on which several people (usually men) have sexual intercourse one after another with one person." And by 1953 it came to mean "something undertaken or experienced by a group of people, esp. a situation or activity characterized by high stress, intensity, or confusion." In 1969 "gangbang" appeared in R. L. Keiser's *Vice Lords* (1969), describing "a fight between rival gangs." "The social context of a 'gangbang' (gang fight)," Keiser wrote, "is considered by Vice Lords to be one of the most important social happenings in street life."

I wonder, as I think about the etymology of "gang" and contemplate its long years of use, how it got from "a way of going" to a group of people associated with violent criminal activity. Perhaps the most perplexing use is "gangbang," where the meaning is simultaneously sexual and violent. I think of love reduced to sex and sex reduced to violence: rape. "Gangbang" is a paradigmatic example of what it means to reduce a person to an object, to replace intimacy with alienation, and to replace relationship with violence. By extension, gang fights, like gang rape, are about force, objectification, domination, and humiliation.

Overall, then, "gang" has to do with groups of people who walk or travel together, and as these persons share visible characteristics and symbols they become increasingly "other." Their status is simultaneously minimal (their lives are forfeit) and mysteriously attractive: transgressive, violent, and unrepressed. It is an apt description of "gang" in the popular imagination: a modern-day "gang" travels together, represents a place, and is identified by colors, style, and hand signs. They "gangbang": fight and have sexual lives that are less civilized, more "real," and tear away the veneer of polite society. Gang members are often portrayed as having literally and metaphorically chosen a transgressive journey, and they occupy a liminal social status because of their perceived relationship with violence and sex. Labeling someone a gang member is a way of reducing them to an object defined by violence.

GANGS, CREWS, AND BOYS

Reality is more complicated and multidimensional than the word "gang" suggests. In Providence, Rhode Island, the place of most of my experience, there are gangs and crews and even more diffuse "boys." A gang has some sort of formal identity, recognized by others in the community as a discrete group. Some of these gangs are organized and structured in such a way that they will survive transitions in leadership and provide their members access to valuable resources such as a space to be and economic opportunity (even if it is part of the shadow economy), as well as identity, some security, and status. Other "gangs," or crews, are organized around one or two charismatic leaders, emerge out of specific situations and relationships, and are unlikely to survive a change in leadership. They are often less organized and are less likely to have consistent access to their own spaces beyond a street or block or section of a neighborhood. They may or may not participate in a shadow economy. They do offer security, identity, and support. "Boys" are just that—groups of young people, usually young men, who hang out together, watch each other's backs, and usually travel in small or large groups. They are often not involved in organized economic activity; they tend not to have a discrete space beyond a street or block that they share. Gangs, crews, and boys all organize around and are involved in violence. The people involved recognize a continuum of violence, from scuffles based on respect and disrespect to head-up fights and shootings. Choosing to carry a weapon—a knife or gun—is a big step. Developing a reputation as a "serious" person—someone who can fight and is a leader—is a mixed bag: it confers power but can increase risk by making you a more likely target.

The youth involved often only see the organized gangs, with membership, colors, economic activity, as gangs. Crews and boys are informal groups of friends. Police and other authorities, however, tend to see gangs, crews, and boys as gangs. Being seen associating with someone in a gang is often enough to get you on the police gang list. Young men out on the streets often feel they are labeled as gang members when all they are doing is getting by. Authorities responsible for policing youth (Giroux 2010) see boys as nascent gang members, crews as less effective gangs, and gangs as the enemy.

Paradoxically, then, "gang" is a social construct built by the ways that protectors of civil society view and define "gang" and "gang member" and by the ways youth understand the terms. These views are at odds with one another, and the differences matter because power is involved: civil society institutions such as schools, youth programs, police, and the judiciary wield enormous power in shaping the lives of youth. The ways in which they view, define, and respond to youth involved in the streets reflect the core values on which these institutions are built and direct the ways in which these institutions will respond to youth they see as gang involved. More often than not, that response is punitive. Institutional power also matters as we begin to recognize how race (racism) and class (poverty) are built into "gang," but made invisible when youth and their families and communities are blamed for individual and moral lapses in judgment. In this chapter, I describe several perspectives on "gang." The last of them is my story—what I have learned from the youth of Rec Night and Smith Hill, the Providence, Rhode Island, neighborhood that was home to Rec Night. The ways we name and define phenomena often suggest how we should begin to respond and contain the seeds of potential solutions. If we are serious about ending street violence by and on youth, then we need an understanding of "gang" that can more effectively direct our individual and collective responses.

BY THE NUMBERS

The great majority of gang-involved youth in Rhode Island live in three "core" cities of Providence, Central Falls, and Woonsocket, concentrating their presence. The 2008 estimate (Malinowski 2008) for Providence was 1,400 gang members and a dozen or so gangs in a city of 171,000; in 2014 (Reynolds 2015), police estimated that number had grown to 1,800 members and thirty-six different gangs, though only 400–500 of the members and twelve to fifteen of the gangs were considered "active." These numbers are likely overestimates because of the loose criteria that can get a person listed in the gang database kept by the police, including being seen with someone who is a known gang member.

Noting that the definition of "gang" and "youth gang" is slippery at best, the National Gang Center (2016) estimates that there were some twenty-nine thousand gangs and 850,000 gang members nationally in 2012. The National Drug Intelligence Center (2009) suggests that there are approximately 1 million gang members nationally and that 40 percent of them are juveniles, aged seventeen or under, which would place the total number of youth gang members at 400,000–500,000. Other estimates (Pyrooz and Sweeten 2015) place the number of gang members between the ages of five and seventeen at just over 1 million.

There appears to be no consistent methodology for defining and gathering data, and there is little reliable data on which to base any of these estimates. It is best to view the numbers with skepticism, using them as general indicators rather than precise estimates. One way of looking at it is that gang members make up approximately 0.3 percent of the total population of the United States. While small, the number of gang members in Providence constitutes 0.8 percent of the city's population, supporting the idea that gang involvement is geographically concentrated in urban cores.

The main problem in counting gang members is one of definition. They can be defined as members of "organized criminal enterprises," but this leaves out the great majority of persons that the criminal justice system, youth workers, and mainstream media view and treat as gang members. As John Hagedorn writes, "The best definition of gang . . . is an amorphous one: they are simply alienated groups socialized by the streets or prisons, not conventional institutions. . . . Young people, particularly armed young men, are everywhere filling the void left by weak, repressive, racist or illegitimate states" (2008, 31).

As Hagedorn also points out, public interest in gangs is almost exclusively focused on the violence with which they are associated. The Centers for Disease Control and Prevention (2012) has this to say about gang violence in a report that looked at gang homicides across five cities: "Consistent with similar previous research, a higher proportion of gang homicides involved young adults and adolescents, racial and ethnic minorities, and males. Additionally, the proportion of gang homicides resulting from drug trade/use or with other crimes in progress was consistently low in the five cities, ranging from zero to 25%. Furthermore, this report found that gang homicides were more likely to occur with firearms and in public places, which suggests that gang homicides are quick, retaliatory reactions to ongoing gang-related conflict." This report challenges the commonly held assumption that most gang violence is drug related. Despite public perceptions, the violence is unlikely to be directly associated with buying or selling drugs or other crimes in progress. The report suggests that people pay attention to gang violence because it happens to and is performed by youth (contradicting mainstream beliefs about childhood innocence), it happens suddenly, and it often happens publicly, generating ongoing and generalized fear. Gang and street violence are direct and intentional.

People also pay attention to gang violence because it is incredibly expensive. Ted Miller (2012), an economist with the Children's Safety Network, estimates that firearm injuries cost the United States $174 billion in 2010. He estimates the societal cost of a gunshot fatality at $4.7 million, $3 million of which is "quality of life"— the cost of pain, suffering, and loss of future life. Removing this subjective estimate from the equation leaves a direct financial cost of $1.7 million per gunshot death. The cost for someone wounded and admitted to the hospital averages $426,000; for someone who only visits the emergency room, it is $116,000. There were fourteen homicides in Providence (Malinowski and Milkovitz 2014) in 2013 and twenty in 2014. There were 110 shooting victims in 2011, 100 in 2013, and 92 in 2014. While most of these shootings were not directly related to gang violence, the approximate direct cost of gun violence in Providence in 2014 was $73 million, an average of $405 per city resident. In an average year in Providence, approximately one-third of these homicides, between three and five per year, and perhaps 40 percent of the shootings, are gang related. A low estimate, then, is that gang-related gun violence in the city of Providence costs somewhere around $29.2 million annually, excluding the costs of incarceration.

HOW MUCH VIOLENCE IS "A LOT"?

Another useful approach to thinking about gangs begins with asking what counts as a "lot" of violence. In 2007 Providence police said that one in five murders in the city was gang related, or three of that year's fourteen, and they noted that 59 people had been shot, up from 47 in 2006. In 2014 veteran *Providence Journal* reporter Bill Malinowski opened a story on street violence by writing that "there has been a constant drumbeat of violence in the capital city over the past three years with more than 100 shootings annually." Deeper in the article he wrote, "Three of the [city's] ten homicides this year are considered gang-related." Three homicides is three too many, but it is important to acknowledge that the other eleven in 2007 and seven in 2014 happened in the contexts of armed robberies and domestic and relationship violence. The State Police Uniform Crime Report data (2014, 48) reports between twenty and thirty-five murders per year in Rhode Island for the period 2008–14 and between eleven and twenty-five in Providence, with an average of seventeen. Three to five of these murders statewide are gang related in any given year and are concentrated in Providence and two other cities.

Context matters, however, and the statistics on youth dying by violence contradict mainstream perceptions of childhood. The Centers for Disease Control and Prevention (2015) estimates that approximately 90,000 youth aged twenty-four or less were murdered between 1999 and 2014, an average of 6,000 per year. Suicide was the cause of death for 74,000 youth in the same period, an average of 4,900 per year. The numbers flip for young adults twenty-five to thirty-four during the same fifteen-year period: an average of 5,800 suicides and 4,733 homicides per year. These numbers are disturbing because of the suffering they indicate and seem to demand a rational explanation: How can so many young people die by violence each year? While the great majority of these deaths are not gang related, gang-related murders are their powerful and dramatic symbol, simultaneously pointing to a social problem of epidemic proportions—the violent deaths of 11,000 youth and young adults each year—and locating its cause in "gangs," a simplistic caricature of the "other."

It is also important to recognize that violence is not distributed evenly across a city's population. A nineteen-year-old man I interviewed told me that six of his friends had died from gang-related violence. A young mother in her early twenties, who grew up surrounded by "knuckleheads" involved in "the streets," lost two brothers and the father of her son to gang violence; her current partner is incarcerated for a violent crime. Each of these people also told stories of growing up with violence and coming to believe early on that the world is a violent place. Both of them described symptoms consistent with reactions to traumatic stress, both of them worried about how they would be as a parent, and both of them were deeply concerned about what the future held for their children. In other words, as small as the numbers might be, street and gang violence is highly concentrated and has a deep, tragic, far-reaching, and long-lasting impact.

Here is what I think we can take from this all this data: by all counts, the number of gang-related homicides in Providence (and most of the country, with notable exceptions such as Chicago) is relatively low, but the violence is more likely to take place in public compared, for example, to homicides linked to domestic violence, armed robbery, or suicide; the age of the victims and perpetrators is lower than average, shocking public expectations of youthful innocence; and the violence often appears sudden, intentional, and shockingly extreme for the circumstances. The net result, as I will explore in the next chapter, is that gang violence is amplified in the popular imagination because it is public, extremely violent, and done deliberately by and to youth.

PUBLIC PERCEPTIONS OF GANGS AND GANG MEMBERS

Yet another way to approach "gang" is through the lens of public perception and cultural narrative. Formal descriptions of gangs and gang members tend toward some mixture of four perspectives: First are the personal narratives, memoirs, and ethnographies that introduce readers to life experiences and situations that are typically hidden from view. Some of the better-known examples are Piri Thomas's *Down These Mean Streets* (1967), Luis Rodriguez's *Always Running* (1993), Sanyika Shakur's *Monster: The Autobiography of an L.A. Gang Member* (1993), and Maria Hinojosa's *Crews* (1995). Josephine Metcalf's *The Culture and Politics of Contemporary Street Gang Memoirs* offers a useful analysis of this subgenre. "Contemporary gang memoirs," she writes, ". . . have been variously demonized as violent and sensationalist or, by contrast, praised as offering a pedagogic and preventative anti-gang stance. Such contradictory responses are reflected in the memoirs themselves. . . . Their narrative arc rests on conversion: the journey from violent young gang-banger, through punishment, on to political enlightenment and the renunciation of violence. The books emphasize both the frisson of violent gang exploits and the sober, salutary reflection of politicized and educated hindsight" (2012, 4–5).

A second, and currently dominant, literature has to do with policing gangs and gang violence and the technical challenges of identifying, containing, and eliminating gangs. This literature has exploded since the early 1980s, fueled by the War on Drugs, zero-tolerance policies in schools, and dramatically increased incarceration of poor, young, urban men of color. It might be characterized as social science–criminology literature. It tends to focus on crime prevention, delinquency, and poverty, and its emphasis is represented, with only a little exaggeration, in the title of Valerie Wiener's book of advice to teens and their families: *Winning the War against Youth Gangs* (1999). "Gangs as enemy" is reflected in an avalanche of shorter publications from sources such as the Juvenile Justice and Delinquency Prevention office of the U.S. Department of Justice and the National Gang Center, which collaborate on a "Comprehensive Gang Model" initiated in the 1980s. A representative title is their "Guidelines for Establishing and Operating Gang Intelligence Units and Task Forces" (2008).

A third strand offers what David Brotherton, in his masterful *Youth Street Gangs* (2015), calls a "humanistic" perspective. This approach has its roots in Frederic Thrasher's (1929) study of Chicago youth gangs in the opening decades of the twentieth century. It attempts to describe the point of view from which youth gang members see the world and to reflect on what can be learned from that perspective to address personal and social problems. Older examples of this perspective, such as Thrasher's, tend to normalize mainstream values and locate gangs as causes of social disorder even as they acknowledge the logic and validity behind the choices of gang members.

More contemporary examples of this humanistic perspective, such as Brotherton's, incorporate the histories that produce gangs and street violence and share a "critical theory" perspective. These include Elijah Anderson's *Code of the Street* (2000), John Hagedorn's *World of Gangs* (2008), Sarah Garland's *Gangs in Garden City* (2009), and Sudhir Venkakesh's *Gang Leader for a Day* (2008). These scholars use their observations about gangs and street culture to raise questions about systemic social problems such as racism, poverty, immigration, and inequality. Brotherton recognizes that the violence associated with youth gangs is problematic but concentrates his attention primarily on the social systems that predictably and continuously produce and reinforce this violence. Hagedorn adopts a similarly historical and critical perspective. "Gangs," he writes, "are shaped by racial and ethnic oppression, as well as poverty and slums, and are reactions of despair to persisting inequality" (2008, xxiv).

A fourth literature is found in a smaller number of works, such as Geoffrey Canada's *Fist, Stick, Knife, Gun* (2010), Cle Sloan's documentary *Bastards of the Party* (2005), Father Greg Boyle's *Tattoos on the Heart* (2010), Doug Magnuson and Michael Baizerman's *Work with Youth in Divided and Contested Societies* (2007), David M. Kennedy's *Don't Shoot: One Man, a Street Fellowship, and the End of Violence in Inner-City America* (2011), and Victor Rios's *Punished: Policing the Lives of Black and Latino Boys* (2011) and *Street Life: Poverty, Gangs and a Ph.D.* (2011). These observers combine elements of personal memoir and social history with a humanistic, critical perspective and use the resulting narrative to discover and describe a theory and practice of personal and social change.

GANGS FROM THE PERSPECTIVE OF EXPERIENCE

Empirical definitions and dependable numbers for describing gangs are elusive. Social and cultural biases stigmatize gang- and street-involved youth, while masking the circumstances that produce gangs. Focusing on social analysis can be helpful, but it suggests that the path forward is fundamentally political (changes in policy) rather than cultural (changes in how the mainstream culture perceives and values youth, leading to changes in policy). I find that approaching "gang" from the perspective of experience suggests a more promising way forward. Focusing on how youth involved in street and gang violence experience their lives, and on how I am experiencing them, allows me to discover and assess my core values, link individual experience to social change, and imagine new possibilities for change.

It may sound obvious, but a useful starting point is recognizing that youth gangs are composed of youth who have made the decision to have "gang member" as a part of their identity and have joined with others who have made a similar decision. "Youth" in this context is an elastic term, beginning as young as ten or twelve and extending into the early twenties, though in my experience most active youth gang members are young men between fourteen and twenty years of age. In Rhode Island, perhaps 250–400 gang-involved youth are actively involved in street violence at any given time, but they have a disproportionate effect, powerful enough to influence public perceptions of the "inner city" and safety and influence public policy around safety and security.

Individual youth are aware that their decisions to join a gang, or get involved in the violence associated with gangs, are significant, and they reflect on them strategically and ethically before, during, and after they are involved, even as they don't consider their decisions from the point of view of mature adults or civil society. Youth decide to get involved, typically around the ages of thirteen or fourteen, because they see it as a choice that makes the most sense and seems the most meaningful at the time. They have a sense that the institutions they depend on—families, communities, schools—see them as marginal and are unable to provide the conditions for their safety and growth. As Rachel Swaner and Elise White report, they become "involved in 'crews' or 'teams' which [are] largely geared around the acquisition of money and status and projection of an image of material success. While these crews might be nominally associated with more well-known gangs . . . most did not engage in criminal activity beyond occasional fights, smoking marijuana and public drinking—actions which they did not define as criminal" (2010, iii). While this description downplays the violence often associated with youth gangs, it accurately captures the idea that joining a gang is a way of gaining security, projecting status, and achieving success.

While many youth experiment with gang involvement and fade out in a short time, it is my experience that for those who stay on and become known as part of a crew, or as a junior in a more highly organized gang, developing a capacity for violence is a significant part of gaining and keeping status. This capacity for violence is not an end itself as much as a way of signifying a more complex identity that is being built around an emerging worldview: the world is a violent and often dangerous place.

"Gang" is also a culturally gendered term. While young women can be and sometimes are gang members, and can be violent, the capacity for violence associated with "gang" is an exaggerated expression of behaviors culturally associated with maleness and is the basis for the concept of "hypermasculinity" or "toxic masculinity." Ex-gang member Eldra Jackson III describes it this way: "As a gang member, I immersed myself into a world of toxic masculinity. I saw victimizing others as not merely a choice but a right. If I wanted something, I took it. If someone was in my way, I knocked them down" (2017). Violence, though, is a cultural attribute of what it is to be "male" and not an innate biological reality. "Not testosterone per se," notes Richard Rhodes, "but the patriarchal preference for subjecting males to violentization, and their physical advantage in achieving early successful violent performances, explains why men are more likely than women to be seriously violent" (2000, 320).

At Rec Night, the social or public identity of girls and women was defined less by their personal capacity for violence than by their relationship (distant or close) to boys and men who were gang members or violent actors. With occasional exceptions, including Mary, the young women at Rec Night tended to claim power with choices they made about public presentations of their sexuality, expressed visually and verbally. This could include how they dressed, the language they used, with whom they spoke. Often, their choices were framed by what got the attention of the boys and men around them—and their intention to invite or discourage that attention. Most often, the real audience of the girls and young women wasn't the males at all but other girls and women: being desired by males, especially the "serious" males, was a source of status and power. While their choices were being framed by the boys and men, the ways they responded to those choices were being evaluated and judged by the other girls and women present: With whom were they in a relationship, and how much power did that person have? How much of their "self" were they giving up to establish or keep a relationship? The ongoing "performances" of gendered identity and the negotiations around power that they produced were a constant source of conflict at Rec Night and on the streets. Buried inside all of the complexity, and refracted through their experiences of violence, was a vulnerable wish shared by most of the young men and women. The intense relationships that regularly flared up made visible how much they wanted to be fully and intimately seen and loved.

Youth gangs, then, are a systems effect. There is no singular or simple cause, but there are patterns of experience that, when they align, predictably result in the formation of a youth gang or an individual decision to participate in a youth gang or street crew. Systems theorists suggest that the best way to discover a system is by looking at one or more significant results and working backward from there to discover what contributes to the result—subsystems, feedback loops, sequences, inputs, and outflows. They also suggest differentiating between the intended results and the actual results of a system and paying attention to the latter as evidence of what is real.

The literature on youth gangs (Brotherton 2015; Hagedorn 2008; Thrasher 1929; Rios 2011; Ross et al. 2016) suggests that they result from a confluence of challenges in economic circumstances, family dynamics, access to caring adults, educational equity, housing stability, institutional racism, and the breakdown of the systems intended to provide them with physical and emotional security. As Brenda Gebo and Erika Bond argue, it is nearly self-evident that "policy that aims at reducing gangs must address the basic social and economic circumstances in which they arise: the ecology of place" (2012, 5). It is important to note, however, that these social and economic systems elements are only correlated with youth gangs and not predictive in any causal way. Far more youth experiencing these challenges do not join gangs or become involved in street violence than do join gangs. In my experience, there is nearly always an additional systems element that serves as a catalyst: the lived experience of violence that does not seem to have an end—chronic bullying, being targeted for exploitation, and domestic violence being the most common.

Once a youth begins to actively explore street and gang violence, feedback loops come rapidly into play, amplifying a particular way of looking at the world and a way of being in it: the world is a dangerous and violent place, and navigating it is easier if you are perceived as dangerous and violent. It is a "self-reinforcing" feedback loop and plays into a great many developmental tasks regarding identity, belonging, meaning, and purpose. Many youth experimenting with gangs test and then reject this perspective and seek alternative pathways to make meaning in their lives.

For youth who stay involved, the new "system" of gang and street violence they have entered is a world apart from the conventions of civil society. This parallel world is shaped by constant threats of violence and geographic isolation as turf becomes more important and the danger of "slipping" elsewhere increases. It can lead to social isolation as schools and other institutions label them and kick them out. It is a high-stress way of living. Youth I know talk about spending much of their school day thinking about how they will get home safely or about "putting on their street face" before they walk outside their home or their neighborhood.

SMITH HILL: LEARNING FROM YOUTH

I first began thinking about gangs and gang members in a deliberate way in the mid-1990s, shortly after coming to work at Providence College. I had recently been hired as a faculty member to help establish its Feinstein Institute for Public Service and design a new major and minor in what we called public and community service studies. These initiatives were based on a service-learning pedagogy and were designed to educate students through an action-reflection process of community engagement, formal reflection, and leadership development.

As an institute, we decided early on to build a "core" relationship with the Smith Hill neighborhood of Providence, which abuts the southeast corner of the campus. Smith Hill, just two-thirds of a square mile, has somewhere between six and seven thousand residents. It is ethnically and racially diverse and economically poor;

its poverty correlates with race and ethnicity. Smith Hill also has a young population, with one-third of its residents under the age of eighteen. Forty percent of its children live in families that fall below the federal poverty line (RI Kids Count n.d.).

A less obvious feature of the neighborhood's history, which I'll say more about in the chapter on violence, is that it has been and continues to be home to significant numbers of immigrants—many of them exiles and refugees—and their families: Irish fleeing the famines of the 1850s, Jews fleeing the pogroms of the late nineteenth and early twentieth centuries, Armenians who survived and fled the genocide that took place under cover of World War I, black families moving north during the Great Migration of the 1940s and '50s, Cambodian and Laotian families in the aftermath of the Vietnam War during the 1970s and '80s, Central American refugees fleeing civil wars in the late 1980s and '90s, and more recently refugees from civil wars in Africa and the Middle East.

One powerful symbol of this diversity is the neighborhood's Harry Kizirian Elementary School (known as Camden Avenue Elementary until 2001). Named after the son of Armenian refugees who grew up in the neighborhood, won a Medal of Honor in World War II, and became postmaster general, the school was built for 400 students in the early 1970s. When I first visited the school in 1994, it had nearly 750 students. Their families were from more than thirty countries and spoke more than twenty-five first languages. If you graduated from Harry Kizirian in 1994, I was told by the principal, you had only a 50 percent chance of finishing high school.

In the middle 1990s, Smith Hill was also a neighborhood with a long-standing reputation for violence and drugs, and the city's police considered Goddard Street, a residential street a little over a mile from campus, one of the roughest streets in the city. Goddard Street was then home to a community of Laotian refugees who had arrived in the aftermath of the Vietnam War. It also had easy on-off access to Interstate 95 and downtown Providence, and most of the drugs sold on the street went to people who drove in from the towns and suburbs ringing Providence.

I spent hours riding through and walking around the neighbor-hood, going to neighborhood meetings, talking informally with people on the streets and in diners. Our institute was committed to an "assets" (Kretzmann and McKnight 1993) approach to com-munity engagement, and I joined with staff of the Smith Hill Com-munity Development Corporation and the Smith Hill Community Center to sift through all we had heard. We drafted two lists: what residents were most concerned about and the potential assets they and we had for addressing those concerns.

The big three concerns (then and now) were youth violence, economic opportunity, and vacant houses and lots. Among the immediate assets were youth, vacant lots, and a lot of neighborhood people willing to contribute small amounts of time and money to help get things moving. We looked for a strategy that could direct these resources toward youth development and economic oppor-tunity, even on a tiny scale, and maximize our leverage. Over the next six months we organized a ten-thousand-square-foot vegetable garden in the park behind the elementary school, we linked the gar-den to the school's curriculum, and we hired eight neighborhood youth to run it. The youth were paid a stipend (initially donated by neighborhood residents) and split what they earned from selling their produce to local restaurants and markets.

The youth gardeners represented the neighborhood: a mix of young men and women; white, black, Latino, and Southeast Asian. Several of the youth were gang involved or gang affiliated. Initially, the garden was heavily vandalized by sixth to ninth grade boys who thought we were invading their space. We viewed the vandalism as an opportunity to surface some of the neighborhood's issues and as an opportunity to engage the youth doing the vandalism. Our goal was to transform destructive conflict into creative energy. The part of the story relevant here is that the youth doing the vandalism were juniors and members of a new youth gang, Laos Pride, a gang that became synonymous with Smith Hill street life over the next decade. One of the youth was Tou Pathoummahong, who ended up as a streetworker for the Institute for the Study and Practice of

Nonviolence and in 2007 initiated Rec Night, the project around which much of this book revolves.

Those of us organizing the garden listened to stories from the youth gardeners and from their neighborhood critics. We watched elders, often unemployed women with limited English proficiency who had immigrated from Southeast Asia, come out of their houses to show these unskilled urban youth (youth they already knew and often avoided) how to grow food. Intergenerational relationships improved just a bit. We got a handle on the vandalism.

The garden ended abruptly in 2001 when the city decided to renovate the park and build a new recreation center literally on top of it. Ironically, the city cited the neighborhood's renewed energy and interest as reasons for building the center, even as they erased the vehicle that was the primary organizer of that energy. It wasn't until 2015 that another community garden was built in the park.

My experience with the garden motivated me to begin paying attention to youth gangs in Smith Hill and Providence. Our first year, one of the gardeners was involved with Laos Pride. Alex's friends would play basketball or hang out on the court next to the garden while he worked in the hot sun, taunting him with jibes about selling out, being an "Asian nigger," and making less money than he would selling weed. He stayed with the program three seasons. At the time, I was most struck by his silence, by how little he said about his situation, the taunts, or why he wanted to do this kind of work. Looking back, I'm most struck by his persistence, his commitment to gaining access to a life that was off the streets and his ability to ride out the taunts of his crew.

As I learned about the neighborhood and the youth gangs that were part if it, I often found it hard to sort out fact from urban legend. Federal, state, and local police had begun ramping up the rhetoric in the early 1990s, increasingly demonizing gangs as a major public threat. There was little or no distinction between the "organized criminal enterprises" of highly organized adult gangs like the Latin Kings or Hell's Angels and local, neighborhood-specific street crews that were organized around one or two charismatic leaders and would disintegrate when that leader left or people aged out. The *Providence Journal*, the local newspaper of record, developed what seemed to me a formulaic way of writing about gangs and street violence: basically, "it's happening again in those neighborhoods because of these bad actors; tsk, tsk, tsk." It wasn't until reporter Bill Malinowski published an award-winning series on the gangs of Providence in 2008 that the paper would sometimes adopt and publish fuller, more complex, and real stories about gangs and gang members.

The federal War on Drugs was also gaining traction at this time, and the basic architecture of what would become the school-to-prison pipeline was being put into place. Neighborhoods like Smith Hill were painted in the media and by public agencies as "inner-city" sites of violence and drug dealing. Schools were adopting zero-tolerance policies for weapons, violence, or drugs, and nearly all of the gang-involved youth we met in Smith Hill had been suspended or expelled. The schools had begun having "school resource officers" on site, police officers who often wanted to be a positive influence in the lives of the difficult students but were under enormous pressure to protect all the other students and staff from the "bad kids."

On the other hand, the youth gang members we met every day were willing to be engaged. Their lives and aspirations were complex and often contradictory, and they described the tension they felt between their dreams and their behaviors. They wanted to be artists, musicians, small business owners, police officers; they wanted to travel, to own a car and a house someday. They wanted better relationships with their families. They wanted to visit their family's country of origin as part of an identity quest. If they were slow to trust adults, they valued and sought relationships with "positive people." This didn't often result in their dramatically changing their lives or paths, but it became clear that they were youth before they were "gangsters."

At the peak of the garden project, as many as three hundred residents would turn out for potluck dinners at the elementary school; neighborhood youth flocked to the garden and the surrounding park and enjoyed their time with the gardeners and Providence

College volunteers. We had testimonies from scores of community residents—and especially youth—about the positive things they wanted for themselves, the people who mattered to them, and the neighborhood as a whole. We knew that, in the face of rising public criticism that blamed teachers and teachers' unions for failing schools, the principal and most of the teachers at the elementary school were dedicated, hardworking, and engaged in the community. We could see that family members of the students—including those who were gang involved—most often cared about their success, even as they were struggling with their own lives.

The public narrative about the neighborhood crashed into our observations about day-to-day life in Smith Hill. Each contained some truth but also masked significant portions of the reality in confusing and paradoxical ways. Hidden from sight was the fact that otherwise ordinary youth were ending up as members of youth gangs and getting involved in street violence. Hidden from sight were the institutional systems—poverty, racism, social and personal marginalization—that contributed to the social production of youth gangs and gang members. And hidden from sight was the fact that the majority of neighborhood youth, living in similar social circumstances, were not getting involved in gangs or street violence. It became clear that most observers were looking for what writer Chimamanda Ngozi Adichie has since called a "single story": a simple, linear explanation that reduces the complexity of lived experience to a singular concept or, worse, a caricature.

The realities of people's lives, of community and youth violence, and the ways individual youth experience that violence are composed of multiple, complex stories that are sometime contradictory or paradoxical. There is no simple story to be told about social systems "causing" gangs and gang violence or about family negligence or the failure of personal responsibility driving youth into gangs. Many youth experience the pressures and weight of oppressive systems without ever joining a gang or deliberately committing violence against another person. The institutional systems of racism, poverty, and marginalization are, in themselves, what a logician would call "necessary but insufficient" conditions for explaining how gangs and gang membership are created.

I'll offer a fuller explanation in the next chapters on violence and what sociologist Lonnie Athens calls "violentization" (2003), but it seems to me to be the case that certain experiences, happening to young people who are also in contexts shaped by poverty, racism, and marginalization, come together to make joining a gang and practicing violence seem like a good idea—something that makes sense. That final ingredient, more often than not, is the youth's direct experience of physical and emotional violence—something that happens to him or her or to people they care for and that goes unchecked by the institutions that they expect would protect them: the adults in their lives at home, school, out in the community, or wearing uniforms and badges. It matters if the youth call the local police "the Occupation" and the gang unit "the jump-out boys," because of their practice of driving up on "suspicious" youth, confronting them, and driving away.

There is another part of Alex's story that stays with me. Alex's family had come to Providence through Thai refugee camps and Stockton, California. He had two younger siblings. His mother did not speak much English. His father, struggling with his own demons, was often violent, drank a lot, and was inconsistent in his financial support of the family. Alex was a solid, if unremarkable, student at a local public high school, an aspiring artist, and a dependable, hard worker on the garden. Alex periodically sold weed—marijuana—to support his family. He had personal rules about not selling it to anyone younger than sixteen, about not selling any harder drugs, about selling only when his family was in financial crisis. One evening he was picked up by police for dealing and sent to the RI Training School, where he ended up being held for several months.

The same evening Alex was picked up, an eighth grade student in a small Massachusetts town about thirty minutes north of Providence went to a school dance. Earlier that afternoon she had stolen a package of mail-order prescription medicine off the porch of an elderly neighbor. She brought pills from this package to the party, and she and ten or so of her friends ingested them before going into the dance. Eight of the students ended up being transported to the local hospital and having their stomachs pumped. The next evening, a special town meeting was held at the school, led by a panel composed of the principal, the police chief, and a social worker specializing in adolescent drug use. Parents packed the room. How could it happen here? How can we protect our children? The girl who had stolen the drugs appeared before a judge a day later. He sentenced her to counseling and strongly recommended a similar path for the other girls.

It is always dangerous to make too much of a single example, but Alex and his friends knew the story of the girl, which was on television and in the newspapers. They made the connection. In one instance, drug-related behavior of an inner-city Asian American youth was criminalized. In the other, involving white, suburban, middle-class youth, it was medicalized. Because the circumstances of race, class, and geography were different, the two events were understood to mean divergent things in court and in public opinion.

As John Hagedorn (2008), Henry Giroux (2010), and others point out, our social institutions—laws, courts, schools particularly—characterize some transgressive, antisocial behavior as criminal and similar transgressive, antisocial behavior by a different category of person as a product of ignorance, confusion, pain, or mental illness deserving of therapy. Too often the determining variables seem to be race or ethnicity combined with economic class. In other words, naming, criminalizing, and creating institutions to contain and punish gang violence play a role in institutionalizing gang violence.

If poverty, racism, and marginalization based on identity, such as Alex experienced, are forms of structural violence, and are experienced on a consistent basis, then direct physical and emotional violence adds to the burden. If no "good" authority is available to offer real safety, then the youth experiencing violence typically decides he or she will have to take things into their own hands and finds him- or herself trying to cope simultaneously with the effects of racism, poverty, marginalization, and direct violence. More often than not, a youth will internalize a view of him- or herself based on what this situation teaches them, and it teaches them that the world is a place defined by structural and personal violence. From this perspective, it makes sense to only trust your friends and to use violence to protect yourself and "your people" as necessary.

Once marginalized and labeled as a bad kid, it also begins to make sense that the punishments of suspension and expulsion by schools, surveillance and arrests by police, and being kicked out by parents who don't know what else to do cease to have much deterrent behavior. These negative experiences inside civil institutions fold seamlessly into other experiences of violence, proof that you will be violated regardless of how hard you try. You lose your sense that compliance makes any difference, you "man up" and take your punishment when it comes around, and it is a short step to get involved in the violence and off-record economy that come with being a gang member.

For youth who join gangs at twelve or thirteen, just as they are beginning middle school, it takes a while to figure out that the protection, friends, and money that go with belonging to a gang or crew come at a very high cost: You inherit the beefs of all the members of your crew, so you are involved in much more conflict; you end up geographically isolated because it becomes difficult and dangerous to travel outside your neighborhood. You are usually labeled and kept under surveillance by schools and police; this combines with the stress of getting to and from school safely and contributes to declining attendance and academic performance. Self-medication with drugs, alcohol, and sex numbs feelings. Tattoos, a criminal record, and increasing reactivity to anything perceived as "disrespect" make finding employment difficult. It can be incredibly isolating.

Living this way also teaches youth a very deep but limited understanding about how power works. Power is equated with force, and force, they believe, has only two sources: physical violence and money, both of which can be used to make other people do things they wouldn't otherwise choose to do. Personal challenges and alternative ways of thinking about power—power as relational or shared or available to everyone—are dismissed as naive or perceived as threats, as disrespectful, as inviting escalated responses to minimal provocation. Orders from bosses, constructive criticism from teachers, requests from neighbors are filtered through this lens of force, making it hard to keep jobs, stay in school, or have healthy, loving relationships.

In other words, said one youth I talked with, "it pretty much sucks being in a gang," but it is also the one place support exists. Not surprisingly, a number of the older youth I know talk about "putting on their street face" when they leave the house or tell stories about staying inside and not going out much in order to avoid conflict. They talk about wanting to change their lives and then sabotage the opportunities they find.

One nineteen-year-old member of a youth gang I know, highly motivated to change his life, got a part-time job when a youth worker advocated for him with a community-minded small business owner. The youth showed up on time but would sometimes start work "a little high, just weed," and his friends began dropping by the store. His boss asked him to be straight when he came to work and to tell his friends not to come by and visit. But he was getting high to "take the edge off" and be mellow when he worked. He didn't know how to tell his boys they weren't welcome without causing a rift. He interpreted his boss's instructions not as simple requests or as steps toward revising his life, but as evidence his boss didn't have a clue and as disrespect. When his boss repeated the directives a little more forcefully, he told his boss to "keep your fucking job" and walked out. His boss made the decision that he would no longer try to employ "youth like him."

An Asian American woman in her early twenties I got to know as she was about to graduate from college described the double or triple life she had led as a high school student. Her father, a war refugee, drank enough alcohol that it was affecting his health, and he was sometimes violent. A part of her believed that being a "good girl" would help him do better and result in his caring more for her. Entering high school, she was an honors student and would go on to become a first-generation college student. For the first two years of high school, though, she became the girlfriend of a high-status member of a local gang. She "became a party girl," drank and smoked weed, skipped school. She would leave the house each morning dressed as the "good girl" and change into tight, low-cut clothes. She became sexually active. She wanted to feel good, to have some status and power of her own, and her relationship with her father initially normalized her boyfriend's violence. Teachers, friends, positive adults in her life pointed out the divided life she was living. A personal health scare and her father's rapidly declining health became a moment of choice. Ultimately, she chose to do well in school and work nearly full-time to pay off health bills, gradually withdrawing from life with her boyfriend and his gang. She maintains a very complicated kind of double consciousness, though, recognizing that her authentic self incorporates her experiences both on the street and in the institutions associated with conventional success.

Worldviews, expectations, communication, and fair effort are difficult to negotiate and change.

VIOLENCE UP CLOSE

Five months before I started at Providence College, in February 1994, a fourteen-year-old boy from Smith Hill was robbed and beaten on his way home from high school. The "immediate" aftermath of this event took eight years to unfold. The incident found its way into the courts when Providence police left information about the victim where reporters could find it, and the *Providence Journal* published the youth's name in its crime log. The victim's mother then sued the City of Providence, arguing that the police disclosure violated confidentiality protections for minors and contributed significantly to her son's endangerment and post-traumatic stress. Ms. Grieco eventually won a $30,000 settlement.

The attack is described in the court's decision regarding an appeal by the city and is worth quoting at length:

On the afternoon of February 14, 1994, Grieco's fourteen-year-old son, "John," was traveling home after school with two friends. While walking on Felix Street in the Smith Hill section of Providence, the youths were approached by more than twenty young Asian males, seemingly gang-affiliated, who, using threats and intimidation, intended to rob John and his friends. While attempting to flee, John fell to the ground, and was beaten by these frenzied youths, who were enraged by the boy's empty pockets. Battered and bruised, John made his way home where he found his friends reporting the incident to his grandmother, who, despite John's pleas to heed the threats of the gang and keep quiet, called the Providence Police Department (department). An officer arrived at the Grieco home, interviewed John, and completed a standard report of the assault that was characterized as a "robbery-strong-arm" incident in the police report. Without the knowledge or consent of the Grieco family, this police report would soon become public information, causing further trauma for John. By notable travel of this report into a media-accessible box at the Providence police headquarters that included all recent incidents on file, Rhode Island's primary newspaper, The Providence Journal (Journal), gained access to John's identity, home address and the details of this crime. On February 18, 1994, John's true name and address, and the specifics of the assault, appeared in the "Providence Police News" section of the Journal.

At John's request, Grieco did not seek immediate medical treatment for his injuries, but kept a guarded watch over him until, four days after the attack, he had adequately recovered, both mentally and physically, to return to school. On the day John returned to school, his teacher expressed sympathy about the incident and John learned that on that very morning, his harrowing story had been circulated to the public in the Journal. As a result, John was not only forced to relive the attack, but also was subjected to a wholly new fear that the gang would return to his home and seek revenge. John's fear was well-founded. The day after the article appeared, several young Asian males began loitering outside John's home, and then threw rocks in the direction of the Grieco dwelling. Grieco called the police once again that week to report these latest disturbances. Unable to overcome his guilt about these threats and fearful for the safety of his mother and siblings, John and his family fled their home and remained at their grandmother's home in Cranston for the next seven to eight months. The family never permanently returned to their Providence residence. Further, John has never fully recovered from his fear and anxiety. A psychiatric evaluation, done approximately six years after the incident, revealed a diagnosis of post traumatic stress disorder. (Supreme Court of Rhode Island 2003)

The language of the decision represents both the objective reality of violence by a youth gang in a community and, in the narrative composed from the factual evidence, a broader cultural perspective about gangs and victims. The appeal is concerned with the ages of the perpetrators and victim; offers an implicit definition of "gang" and its association with age, gender, neighborhood, race, and crime; uses adjectives like "seemingly," "frenzied," and "enraged"; and associates the circumstances of the attack with the neighborhood and the neighborhood with vicious, random violence. It also points to subsequent events and the eight years they took to unfold, describes the lifelong consequences of traumatic violence for the victim and his family and friends, reveals the clumsiness of a system intended to serve and protect, and is infused with the emotional resonance of fear, insecurity, and anguish that frame public perceptions of the inner city and gang violence.

Public perceptions of Smith Hill and youth gangs have not really changed in the years since. A casual search of the *Providence Journal* database I did in May 2012 using the terms "Smith Hill," "gang," "Laos Pride," "Asian Boyz," "Young Bloods," and "YNIC" (Young Niggas in Charge) yielded the following headlines:

"Police: Violent Feud between Asian Gangs in Providence Continues," February 21, 2012

"Providence Gang Member's House Shot Up," January 24, 2012

"Rival Gang Dispute behind Gunfire in Smith Hill," December 29, 2011

"Providence Man Gets 6 Years for Drug Trafficking," December 15, 2011

"Youth Tied to Laotian Gang Gets 40 Years for Murder," January 15, 2010

"Providence Juvenile Arrested with Loaded Gun," March, 19, 2009

"Trainee for Streetworker Program Is Arrested," November 21, 2009

"Gang Leader Gets More than 18 Years on Drug Charges," October 23, 2009

"Asian Gang Member Gets 11 Years on Drug, Gun Charges," September 3, 2009

"Police: Gang Member, 15, Arrested with Loaded Guns," July 28, 2009

"Update: Sidewalk Bump Spurs Latest Providence Killing," July 1, 2008

"4 Laos Pride Members Arrested after Shooting," June 11, 2008

In one of the more notorious acts of violence in the neighborhood, a June 2008 "sidewalk bump" led a sixteen-year-old Laos Pride member to shoot and kill nineteen-year-old Jeffrey Lopez and wound his friend Carlos Javier. Neither victim had been involved in a gang or street violence. The shooter was sentenced to sixty years in prison. This shooting continues to ripple throughout the neighborhood—affecting all of the families it touched and informing or justifying continuing violent conflicts between different groups of people. The difference between 1994 and 2008 is that, for better and worse, I now know some of the context and a number of the actors behind these headlines.

Talking with neighborhood residents and with staff of community-serving public and private agencies over the past decade, I have heard over and over again that a central problem faced by the neighborhood is youth violence, and in many of the stories I hear echoes of the experiences of "John Doe" Grieco and Jeffrey Lopez. Some residents, those focused on personal responsibility and morality, view street violence as a root cause of much that is wrong with the neighborhood: its poverty, its inability to attract development resources, its poor schools, the rapid turnover of residents, racism. They argue that youth violence itself contributes to the breakdown of neighborhood institutions and prevents good things from happening. They want gang members policed and shut down and order restored. They blame gang-involved youth for per-petuating the worst stereotypes of the inner city.

Others residents put forward immigration, declining family values, and failed personal integrity as causes of youth violence. A third group of residents views gang-involved youth with sympathy, understanding them as victims and symptoms of one or more social pathologies: poverty, unemployment, poor schools, unstable living situations, racism, broken families. The majority of those arguing "social decline," however, blame immigrants, make a case for the fraying of the moral fabric, and argue that the youth and parents have to simply take more responsibility and try harder. Underneath all of these perspectives is a shared analysis and feeling: youth violence was and is one of, if not *the*, leading problem in the neighborhood, and it is closely linked to the turbulence and decline of Smith Hill.

It has taken me a long time to begin to come to my own under-standing of youth and gang violence in Smith Hill and to begin to be able to tease out the complexity of facts, assumptions, and inter-pretations that collectively define it as a phenomenon. In brief, my insight is simply this: the youth doing the violence that concerns the community are best understood as persons making understandable decisions in knowable situations. Gang members, or youths shoot-ing other youths, in other words, believe that they are doing the right thing under the circumstances. They believe that their circum-stances justify certain courses of action, and they argue that others, who would punish them, don't understand their circumstances. They are often very clear about the ethical choices they are making, the tension between the world as they wish it was and the world as they experience it.

This is different from saying that a gang member or youth committing an act of violence, such as beating and robbing John Doe Grieco or shooting Jeffrey Lopez, is doing the right thing or is doing something that he or she believes is socially acceptable.

Violence, from my perspective, even if understandable, is never the right thing, and my experiences of the past twenty years have only affirmed this belief. But I have also learned that the path toward any workable solution begins with perspective taking: mine, yours, the youths', institutional agents', neighborhood residents'. It can be challenging to do, but changing patterns of behavior and the social systems that produce such violence requires imagining, for example, that attacking John Grieco made sense to the attackers, for reasons they never shared and that are not even hinted at in the court documents.

If I begin with this assumption—youth are doing what makes sense to them, what fits with their sense of "right"—then a number of paths begin to open up: I now have something to inquire about, a conversation to start. Describe to me what you are doing; explain to me (or us) how and why your worldview makes sense to you; explain to me the feelings and history and thoughts that led you to this place. I also end up engaged in the practice of what Jane Addams, a pioneer of community development, called "social ethics." An ongoing interpretation and argument about how your behavior affects me and my behavior affects you, social ethics is, Addams argued, the basis for democracy and a process of democratic change. It is relational and entails "we." Everyone, even those with whom we disagree, must be at the table if a better way of living together is to be found. As the basis for grassroots democracy, social ethics looks past "two sides," allowing for multiple narratives: there are a lot of perspectives, values, and interests in play with the simplest of issues, and a highly charged issue like neighborhood violence brings many of them to the surface.

What I take from my observations about youth and gang violence in Smith Hill is that the problem of youth violence is simultaneously personal and social. There are multiple interpretations colliding with one another, and the current social framework in which these collisions are taking place serves primarily to reinforce and justify each player's judgment that his or her interpretation is the right one. It reinforces a process of justification rather than opening up a genuine search for understanding or a solution.

I began to wonder what I would notice if I asked how a "reasonable" response to a sidewalk "bump" could lead to a youth-on-youth murder. Why would a youth—someone acting out of their interests—fire a gun at the house of another youth? How could the youths who jumped "John Doe" Grieco believe that they were doing the right thing? I began to wonder, as well, how the friends and grandmother believed they were doing the right thing. How police officers and news reporters believe they are doing the right thing. How teachers, trying to do the right thing, could be tone-deaf to the effects of trauma on their students. How presiding judges believe they are doing the right thing. How, if everyone is trying to do the right thing, can the outcomes be so unrelievedly, so perpetually, bad for everyone involved and for the community as a whole?

The most important thing to come out of this collective exploration, this perspective taking and reflection, is the insight that most of the people involved see everyone who is not "us" as "other." Gang members and perpetrators of youth violence are not exotic "others"; police officers are not "other." Residents, workers, educators, college students are not "others." The challenge is discovering how we are, in fact, a "we."

The other thing I think I've learned, mostly from the gang-involved youth I've come to know, is that the success of this process of interpretation, of not seeing someone else as "other," begins with a leap of compassion: a willingness to feel and engage the pain another person feels and to try to alleviate it. This is no small task given the realities of direct and structural violence, our deeply embedded justifications for our own perspectives and interests, and the common belief that compassion or empathy is a kind of vulnerability and so a sign of weakness. Positive change in a democratic culture comes not from the combat of interests who lose and win but from the transformation and growth of everyone involved. And it is often a painful process.

REC NIGHT AND YOUTH GANGS

The first group of thirty or so youth to participate in Rec Night were Laotian American males ages twelve to twenty from the Smith Hill neighborhood of Providence, Rhode Island, and one Hispanic male in his early teens who ran with them. Most, but not all, of the participants were juniors or full members in Laos Pride, a gang based in Smith Hill. Most of the OGs, the older members of Laos Pride, dropped by only intermittently. The rest of the youth were relatives and friends.

Rec Night was started in December 2007 by Tou Pathoummahong, a onetime LP member then in his late twenties. Tou worked as a streetworker for the Institute for the Study and Practice of Nonviolence and believed that the rec center was a community resource and belonged to the neighborhood's marginalized and excluded youth as much as to anyone else. The youth weren't allowed in for a variety of reasons: they had broken rec center rules, argued with other participants, or hollered at the director and called him names and intimidated him. The center director had drawn a line in the sand, enforcing rules and looking for reasons to kick out the "bad kids." This same line had been drawn by the same director when Tou was in his middle teens, and it had made him feel even more isolated and devalued. Tou thought that getting access to the rec center would show the youth that he was serious about supporting them and that he had some political "juice." He thought that having access to the rec would give the youth something to lose if it was handled right. And he thought it could be a safe place for the youth each week, a place where they could let their guard down for a few hours and where he could check in with them.

The first time I met the youth at the rec center, all I knew was that some were LP and some were not. I saw ordinary boys and young men on their way to adulthood. They wore jeans and T-shirts and shorts and sneakers. When they were off the court they wore flat-brim ball caps. There was a lot of blue and no red. Most had one or more tattoos—a few had 1216 (L and P are the twelfth and sixteenth letters of the alphabet) tattooed in a visible place, but the favorite designs were Asian dragons and names of loved ones. They said hi, invited me into their basketball game, and didn't talk much. They were checking me out, and I was doing the same, while we all tried to mask our curiosity and sense that we were being judged and found wanting. Some young women—sisters, cousins, and girlfriends— came in and out, sitting on the bleachers or shooting around a little. That was it. Their backstories came in bits and pieces over time.

The program ended at nine, and most of the youth drifted away— home, out to a friend's. Tou was careful to give a few of them rides because he was concerned for their safety: because they were known to attend the program and because it ended at a certain time, anyone who was looking for them could be waiting nearby. This is what was different. The youth held themselves and walked a little differently than they had inside the gym. They walked or drove away in small groups—no one went alone. Being outside, on the street, meant they were always scanning their surroundings, had made decisions and prior arrangements about ways to protect themselves. They didn't try to make themselves invisible, but neither did they do anything to call attention to themselves.

This portrait is, I think, representative of youth gangs and youth gang members. They are adolescents and young adults. They could be any youth in any gym in America. They did not seem aggressive, they didn't swear more or less than other teenagers, and they liked to tease each other. What set them apart—what I was conscious of the first time we met—was the violence that defined and occupied a sig- nificant portion of their lives. They were much more likely than the average urban youth to commit or be harmed by intentional violence. Part of their identity was an "us" that gave them membership and kept everyone else at a distance. They were known to the police, who gathered information on known gang members and their associates.

Here is a slightly different story about the murder of Jeffrey Lopez: The spring after Rec Night began, two Latino youth were walking south on the sidewalk of Camden Avenue, just down the block from the rec center (and the elementary school). A group of LP juniors and friends was hanging out in front of a house. Someone was bumped; two shots were fired. One shot killed Jeffrey Lopez, and the second wounded his friend Carlos Javier. The lead in the first story reporting the shooting read, "A decision by two Smith Hill teenagers to walk through a pack of Laos Pride gang members cost one of them his life, the police said" (McKinney 2008). The shooter, who was sixteen years old at the time of the murder, pleaded guilty and was sentenced to sixty years in prison, with twenty years suspended, to be followed by twenty years of probation. His sister, who was thirteen at the time and may have introduced the gun into the situation, was charged as an accessory. She carries around a sense of guilt and trauma that has not lessened to this day. The shooter, his sister, and others hanging out on the sidewalk had been coming to Rec Night.

This is the tragedy and paradox that invite our careful attention: How could an average teenager make the choice to shoot at another teenager, knowing there was the possibility of killing him? How could the series of choices that led up to this moment have seemed like the right choices? It can be tempting to seek a simple explanation—spur-of-the-moment impulse, bad parenting, bad choice of friends, kid had something wrong with him, a monster, access to guns—but the reality is that the shooter was an ordinary young man. Jeffrey Lopez was an ordinary young man.

How could the shooter be provoked by a sidewalk bump to shoot at another youth? It's much like the urban myths of youth killing each other over pairs of sneakers: a person who would do this is inhuman, not normal. Their perspective and values are unfathomable to civilized, good people (like us!). Except it's never about the sneakers, and it wasn't about the bump. It was about respect, or perceived disrespect, and it was about exercising and taking away power. It was about access to a gun—a symbol of mortal power. A more fruitful course of investigation begins by asking about the backstory and circumstances that led the shooter to believe that what he was doing made sense at the time.

LISTENING

Laos Pride did have some "OGs," original gangsters, including Tou, who had created the gang in the early 1990s. By 2008 the OGs were in their late twenties to early thirties and were known for being hard and violent and sticking together. But the larger number of LP members were LP juniors and their friends. They were teenagers. Many had stopped attending school, but an equal number were still in school to varying degrees. Two LP juniors, until they were kicked out for fighting, had been in the top 10 percent of students at the city's college-prep high school. Nearly all of them had problems at home. For some, the problems were a consequence of their decisions about drinking, smoking weed, cutting school, wearing colors, and fighting. But for many of the youth, problems at home precipitated their resistant behavior and decisions to run the streets with a gang. Some of the youth were physically strong and knew how to fight with their bodies. Most of them were relatively small, physically unremarkable, and did not know how to fight with their fists very well. Most of them were either fearless or fronted fearlessness. They did know how to use and had access to weapons—bats, chains, knives, machetes, firearms—and were willing to use them in certain types of conflict situations. Many of them smoked a lot of weed; a few used harder drugs, especially acid and cocaine, "recreationally." Most of them drank a lot, with Hennessy cognac the beverage of choice. Most of them were sexually active at an early age. Nearly all had been physically and emotionally traumatized multiple times. They all knew someone who had died on the streets and knew a number of people who had been badly hurt in street violence. They did not believe the adults they knew could keep them safe.

All of them had learned to be violent, and they had learned the companion story: they couldn't depend on adults or civil society institutions to care for them. Stories of violence took up much of the air time—debates about strategy and preparation and ethics peppered in among anger, reactivity, adrenaline, and machismo. And a closing refrain in many of the stories was, "That's just how it is on the streets."

Those of us leading Rec Night reflected constantly with the youth to understand what it would mean for them to thrive, in their terms; we paid a lot of attention to their environment; and we thought about how to most simply and sustainably create positive change in this system. Our experience suggests that the process of change for youth begins by creating a genuinely safe and hospitable environment, one that depends on what systems theorists call "self-organization" and a desire to cooperate, rather than on rules and force for order and safety. (Over eight years of working with the youth, we had only one brief fight at the Rec Center.) The program moves forward by building relationships between the youth and a network of positive, caring people, and this is mostly done by informally drawing out and listening to their stories and helping them to reflect on the meaning and possibility embedded in those stories. For those working with the youth, this means learning to see the violence in the lives of the youth as meaningful and measuring the alternative of nonviolence only by its potential for creating more and better meaning. The biggest hurdle, as youth consider shifting from violence to nonviolence, cuts to the heart of this. "I get nonviolence. It makes sense," a number of youth have told me over the years. "I want to do it. But if I do this on the streets, it will get me killed." This is the threshold that strategies for change must meet.

Talking with youth about the violence in their lives—listening to them deeply—helps many of the youth discover that the violence they live with is evidence they are leading a "divided life." They begin to see that street violence is a systems effect and trace its dynamic based on their own lived experiences, and they use the idea of its opposite—nonviolence—to shed light on some of the key tensions in this contradiction: fear and security, anger and love, force and cooperation, selfishness and compassion, inclusion and exclusion. Rec Night offered youth involved in violence a place to reflect on the divisions in their lives and to receive and give support to others embarked on similar journeys. It introduced the youth, program leaders, and volunteers to the public dimensions of these personal experiences and invites reflection on the logic of youth gang violence: this violence is experienced by individuals, but it is "produced" by systems. The "alternative reward" Rec Night pointed toward was quite simple and seemingly invisible: stay alive, do more of what is meaningful and life affirming, live a good life, and, if it makes sense, join with others in advocating for change.

YOUTH IN DIVIDED AND CONTESTED SOCIETIES

The majority of these perspectives—etymology, numbers, the bulk of the literature on youth gangs, experience—describe how the larger public views and interprets "gang" and why they associate "gang" with criminality, social disorder, and physical and sexual violence. I have come to believe that gang involvement is more usefully understood by seeing it through the eyes of youth who stay involved for an extended period of time, and I have come to recognize that their experiences have more in common with the lived experiences of youth described in Doug Magnuson and Michael Baizerman's *Work with Youth in Divided and Contested Societies* (2007) than with youth in the mainstream culture of the United States. Magnuson and Baizerman's edited collection of reflections by youth workers focuses on communities enmeshed in civil and international conflicts, such as Northern Ireland, Serbia, Burundi, South Africa, Iraq, Syria, and Gaza. It is a bit startling, at first, to imagine that the life experiences of gang-involved youth in the United States have more in common with the life experiences of youth in current or recent conflict zones than youth in the United States who live within the boundaries of civil society. Nonetheless, it is a useful and accurate way for people who have not experienced ongoing violence to begin imagining what it is like to live in a context defined by perpetual threat, constant stress, and chronic if unpredictable violence. The youth in these divided and contested societies are affected, as are members of youth gangs in the United States, by "poverty, displacement, loss of parents, hunger, search for status, peer pressure, and desire for revenge" (Lancaster 2007, 18).

The large insight that emerges across all of these perspectives is captured by Siobhan McEvoy-Levy. Though she is writing about youth she interviewed in Belfast, her analysis seems to apply globally to youth who become involved in gangs. "As these dialogues show," she observes, "violent behavior and prejudiced and divisive attitudes and speech emerge in the context of collective and personal trauma, negation of rights and lack of security, political and economic marginalization, and collective narratives of loss and threat" (2007, 101).

Direct experiences of trauma, the belief that adults and civil institutions cannot be counted on, and immersion in stories that convey the truth of these experiences create a context in which joining a gang or choosing violence makes sense.

McEvoy-Levy goes on to note, "Sectarian or ethnically homogeneous social groups, armed groups, and gangs . . . offer physical protection, group solidarity, cultural and/or religious identification, moral and political education, self-esteem, honor, economic hope, voice, engagement and excitement" (ibid.). In other words, not only does membership make sense because it seems to offer security, but it also offers opportunities to find and make meaning. It simply seems like the natural thing to do. Taken together, "these factors suggest youth policies should monitor the rights and security of young people and address their recreational, community service, participation, economic development and training, and narrative building needs" (101–2). Ending gang violence begins not with a declaration of war but by ensuring the safety of, protecting the rights of, and listening to the youth involved.

The observations and reflections of McEvoy-Levy and her colleagues helped me learn how to listen to the youth members of gangs or crews that I came to know through Rec Night. The youth of Rec Night share a belief that the world is a violent place and that developing their personal and collective capacity for violence is necessary to their survival and success. Like the street-involved youth of Northern Ireland, "they have learned . . . that the use of violence can be a legitimate and effective way of resolving conflict" (Harland 2007, 179–80).

This belief in the foundational reality of violence seems to be characteristic of much youth violence across the globe, largely because, as Ken Harland points out, "many of the youth struggle to identify realistic alternatives to violence" (180). This struggle matters because, "while young people may not wish to be violent, they may be fearful of the consequences of not being violent in certain circumstances." They have to decide whether to use violence, often in the moment, in the spaces they inhabit: schools, streets, neighborhoods, cities. Lying behind the decision to embrace violence is the nagging expectation that things will be even worse without it.

As McEvoy-Levy and Harland note, it is not the experience of direct violence alone that makes joining a gang or crew seem like a good idea. It is the companion belief that the available social institutions cannot, at best, provide security or, at worst, view the youth as the enemy. It can be hard for people who trust the power and authority of civil institutions, including police, schools, and government, to imagine what it is like to fear them. The Black Lives Matter movement (n.d.), inspired by the death of black citizens at the hands of police, offers one example of this perceptual divide. "When we say Black Lives Matter," the organizers write, "we are broadening the conversation around state violence to include all of the ways in which Black people are intentionally left powerless at the hands of the state. We are talking about the ways in which Black lives are deprived of our basic human rights and dignity."

One of the most compelling descriptions of this institutional divide is found in Michelle Alexander's *New Jim Crow*. Discussing "gangsta" culture, she asks, "Are we willing to demonize a population, declare a war against them, and then stand back and heap shame and contempt upon them for failing to behave like model citizens while under attack?" (2010, 170). She quotes Ronny, aged sixteen: "Shit don't change. It doesn't matter where I go, I'm seen as a criminal. I just say, if you are going to treat me as a criminal then I'm going to treat you like I am one, you feel me? . . . I grew up knowing that I had to show these fools [adults who criminalize youth] that I wasn't going to take their shit. I started to act like a thug even if I wasn't one" (181). In other words, mainstream social institutions and their processes of cultural production, more than the youth themselves, are deeply implicated in creating, marginalizing, and demonizing youth gangs and their members.

Alexander concludes, "There is absolutely nothing abnormal or surprising about a severely stigmatized group embracing their stigma. . . . Psychologists have long observed that when people feel hopelessly stigmatized, a powerful coping strategy—often the only apparent route to self-esteem—is embracing one's stigmatized identity. . . . Indeed, the act of embracing one's stigma is never merely a psychological maneuver; it is a political act—an act of resistance and defiance in a society that seeks to demean a group based on an unalterable trait" (ibid.). Putting people in positions where they either give up their identity and power or embrace their stigma is one of the more powerful processes by which mainstream institutions participate in the construction of youth gangs, establish narratives about what a gang and a gang member are, and establish boundaries that position gangs and gang members as "other."

Adopting violence as a strategy for survival and resistance, Alexander notes, is "inherently self-defeating and destructive," but she concludes that "gangsta love" is a corollary to black power or gay pride for "young men trapped in the ghetto in an era of mass incarceration" (182).

Looking at gang violence through the lens of a "divided and contested society" brings a profound cultural paradox into focus: the public simultaneously works to eliminate this violence and turns its back on the causes of that violence because it is "those" youth who are perpetrators and victims: poor, of color, and geographically isolated in inner cities. Hagedorn (2008), Brotherton (2015), Garland (2009), and others note the association of race with the composition of "gangs" and the "inner cities" of which gangs are a symbol. Their analysis points, as Hagedorn suggests, to questions about the institutions and systems that predictably "produce" gangs and gang members: the small value these institutions place on the lives of youth who become gang involved and the dynamics of structural racism that place the entire blame on the moral failure of individuals who become gang members. Brotherton writes, "In the United States it is self-evident more than twenty years into the so-called War on Drugs how important the state has become for the creation and perpetuation of gangs. Gonzalez . . . argues that cultures of control . . . and government through fear . . . initiated by successive elites constitute a new form of class and racial hegemony. In other words, it is domination through the means of criminalization, and in this the gang has been an important symbol against which to organize both materially and ideologically" (2015, 23). When it comes to youth gangs, the "color-blind" neutrality of civil institutions is, in practice, profoundly compromised and deeply implicated in their creation and dehumanization.

It is also the case that adults working with youth in divided and contested societies and adults working with gang-involved youth, such as ISPN's streetworkers, share common challenges and goals: the work can be objectively dangerous, it requires knowledge of youth and social contexts far outside the assumptions and normative understandings of civil society, it requires modifying or inventing alternative youth development institutions and strategies, and it entails a long process of unlearning and relearning to "turn [youth] from latent spoilers to peace builders" (Kemper 2007, 45).

As I'll explore in the next chapter on violence, youth gangs and gang members inhabit a curious symbolic space in mainstream American culture. They are vilified, criminalized, marginalized, and scapegoated as threats to social order, and they are romanticized as rebels, as symbols of resistance to the oppressive weight of social structures that produce and reproduce inequalities of race, wealth, and opportunity. "Gangsta" culture is a big seller in fashion, music, and movies, even as police and judicial systems at local, state, and federal levels approach gang culture with an equal and opposite reaction, casting gangs as a leading cause of violence and punishing gang members with increasingly harsh laws and sentencing guidelines that treat them as thugs, as people who are no longer fully human, and as cancers to be permanently removed. Both perspectives, fascinated by the violence associated with "gang," treat members of youth gangs as cultural symbols and commodities rather than as the youth, community members, and citizens they are: adolescents, teenagers, and young adults, persons with complex identities and histories.

CHAPTER TWO

VIOLENCE, CONSIDERED

Violence is as American as cherry pie.

—H. Rap Brown, Student Nonviolent Coordinating Committee

LEGITIMATE AND ILLEGITIMATE VIOLENCE

Truth be told, most policymakers, police officers, voters, and community residents are not very interested in the lives of youth in gangs. They are concerned, rather, with the violence associated with youth gangs and the ways that this violence disrupts the larger community, contributes to a heightened sense of insecurity and fear, and consumes public resources via policing, prosecution, medical care, incarceration, and insurance.

Youth gang members are often described as transmitters of violence and the public goal as the elimination of gangs as a way of eliminating the "disease." As ethnographer Dwight Conquergood wrote in "The Power of Symbols," "Gangs are depicted in public discourse as malignant microbes, perpetrators of an 'epidemic of violence.' Gangs are referred to as a 'plague,' 'pestilence,' 'scourge,' 'cancer,' 'virus,' 'blight,' 'disease,' 'infestation,' and described as 'parasitic.' Particularly the imagery of spreading infection and metastasizing cancer conjure fear of deadly contamination. . . . The moral panic provoked by portraying gangs as carriers of epidemic violence poisons cross-class relations and polarizes society. Metaphors of disease, hygiene and quarantine reinforce the boundary between

56

sanitized suburb and dirty inner city, and underpin reactionary laws and policies" (1995).

Even as violence is framed as a disease and gangs as the vector in the public imagination, there is a second discourse in the popular culture of the United States that is fascinated by and celebrates gang membership and violence, presenting it as more "real" than everyday life, as a form of resistance to oppression, and as ritualized drama that illuminates and reflects on commonly held beliefs about the centrality of violence in human society and the boundary between legitimate and transgressive violence. "One does not have to search very hard," write Kenneth Hardy and Tracey Laszloffy, "to find examples of how we, as individuals and as a society, are able to simultaneously condemn violence as a matter of principle but act in ways that support violence in practice" (2005, 20).

Such contradictions around powerful, complex symbols often point to larger unresolved tensions in a culture. If the tensions are important enough, they appear regularly in the stories people use to explain themselves and the world they live in, and over time some of these symbols become cultural metaphors. The more powerful of these metaphors are called "strong metaphors" (Ortony 1993), and they serve to contain and normalize, rather than resolve, cultural contradictions. These metaphors help us to believe that these tensions and contradictions are natural, and they often point toward courses of action that allow us to live with the contradiction. "Gang," I think, operates as a strong metaphor in American culture. It contains and seems to make sense of a contradiction that tells us something about the broader public culture of the United States and its simultaneous fear of and fascination with violence.

Anthropologist Mary Douglas argued in her classic *Purity and Danger* that social order is threatened by "the existence of an angry person in an interstitial position . . . and this has nothing to do with the particular intentions of the person" (1966, 102). The metaphor of "gang" positions gang members as angry persons in interstitial positions—angry people inhabiting a wavering borderland that separates civil society from the social chaos of savage violence. The public views youth gangs and gang members as dangerous not only because of the physical threat they represent but also because they reveal how easily the veneer of civil society—our implicit social contract to use reason and law rather than force and violence as the basis for social relationships—can be peeled away. And, in the other half of the metaphor, youth gangs and gang members focus attention on the contradictions between publicly stated "American" values of equality and the rights to pursue life, liberty, and happiness and ongoing systems of poverty and racism that predictably result in marginalization and violence. We celebrate unfettered freedom and resistance to injustice.

In the United States, legitimate violence—violence sanctioned by the state—is viewed as an unfortunate necessity, as a method of protecting personal and public boundaries, as an effective element of social control. It is the tragic necessity on which civil society depends and a major source of cultural regeneration. Cultural observer Gil Bailie calls this kind of violence a "brutal act done in the name of civilization" (1994, 79). We express, in our mainstream cultural narratives and in our public institutions, the belief captured by Stephen Carter in his *Violence of Peace*: "Peace, ironically, sometimes requires battle" (2011, xi). And we believe in the silver lining of violence: committing or surviving it is potentially transformative, opening dimensions of self and world that would otherwise remain unknown (Bailie 1994; Douglas 1966; Drinnon 1980; Slotkin 1973).

The "illegitimate" violence of gangs simultaneously justifies the use of legitimate violence and invites us to recognize that the distinction is socially constructed, changeable, and contested. Gang violence is a metaphoric vehicle for assessing the stability of civil society and imagining what we would do if it failed. We believe gang violence must be contained and order maintained, and we consider how much violence will be required to accomplish this. We also wonder: Would we have the mix of courage, strength, smarts, and brutality necessary to survive the collapse of social order? Are some or all of us potential gang members? Or are we sheep rather than wolves?

This context and the problem of existential identity the metaphor surfaces animate, for example, huge, popular genres of mass media storytelling, including detective shows and gang-focused shows such as the television series *Sons of Anarchy* (Sutter 2008–14) and *The Wire* (Simon 2002–8). The scope and meaning of legitimate violence is a question deeply rooted and constantly revisited in the cultural narratives of the United States.

Despite the perennial and predictable destruction caused by violence, our public institutions present it as a reasonable and necessary reaction to threat and harm and embrace it in the belief that the proper use of violence will interrupt, and somehow reverse, the circumstances that invite it. Popular culture narratives in fiction, journalism, and film are fascinated with the boundary where civil society niceties begin to disintegrate and violence becomes necessary if order is to be restored and maintained. More often than not, the endings in these stories portray violence as tragic, redemptive, and regenerative. The deep structure of these stories about violence demarcates the boundaries of acceptable, legitimate violence— violence intended to prevent further violence—and presents this "good" violence as the period at the end of the sentence, a punctuation mark signifying the resolution of conflict and the end of the story. Order and meaning have been restored.

Inside these narratives, we do not object to violence in itself but object to violence performed by someone perceived as a cultural "other," who transgresses the boundaries of civil society and threatens to return us from social order to social chaos. In mainstream narratives, this is illegitimate violence—destructive violence that threatens civil society. Not surprisingly, the "other" is most often linked directly to identities based on race and class: the other is black, Latinx, or Asian and poor, or wealthy through illegitimate means. This identification of the "other" is further confirmed in a handful of symbols: tattoos, flat-brim hats, hoodie sweatshirts, sagged jeans, slang, and a swaggering walk. Any young man of color, displaying (or "representing") any of these symbols, especially if he is in or near an economically poor location, becomes this "other," and the burden is on him to prove that this is not the case. This is also, in metaphoric terms, the moment when we can begin to witness the limits and contradictions of legitimate violence.

Recall vigilante George Zimmerman's 2012 killing of African American teenager Trayvon Martin in Sanford, Florida. Zimmerman tried to justify his violence as regenerative, necessary for restoring social order in a declining neighborhood, performed against a young black man in a hoodie who was the threatening "other" responsible for the decline. This interpretation was undermined as word of Zimmerman's personal aggressiveness and the history of racial violence rocketed into the picture. Nevertheless, the courts found Martin's murder to be legitimate based on Florida's "stand your ground" laws. If Zimmerman felt threatened, he was justified in protecting himself, and the outcome, while tragic, was legitimate.

The day the verdict was announced in Zimmerman's case, Attorney General Eric Holder, an African American man, tried to explain the difference between the legal and social meanings of Zimmerman's violence: "It shook an entire community," he said, "drew the attention of millions across the nation, and sparked a painful but necessary dialogue throughout the country. Though a comprehensive investigation found that the high standard for a federal hate crime prosecution cannot be met under the circumstances here, this young man's premature death necessitates that we continue the dialogue and be unafraid of confronting the issues and tensions his passing brought to the surface" (Department of Justice 2015).

It is disingenuous, at best, to suggest that Martin's "premature death" sparked a dialogue about racial violence: it was, rather, the latest evidence of an ongoing pattern of violence in a long and unresolved history. It surfaced this question: Was Martin's the tragic murder of another black teenage boy in a long history of racial violence sanctioned by white institutions or the unfortunate but understandable result of a legitimate effort to restore and maintain social order? The contradictions surfaced by Trayvon Martin's death remain so deep and painful that they raise fundamental questions about the distinction between legitimate and illegitimate violence made by the state and our public culture.

As another example, call to mind the 2014 shooting death of Michael Brown by a local police officer in Ferguson, Missouri. Like Trayvon Martin, Michael Brown was initially presented by police and media as "other": a physically large, young, black man; living in a poor, transitional neighborhood; and suspected, without evidence, of low-grade criminality. A grassroots movement calling attention to a larger pattern of police violence against young black men coalesced, and protesters gathered for weeks in Ferguson, becoming a catalyst of a national Black Lives Matter movement. Again, the officer was found to be justified in the shooting death. The organizers of the protests called attention to the unrelenting consistency with which Brown was presented as "other" and argued that young men like him should not have to prove that they are not "other" in order to be secure in their persons and treated as citizens with equal rights and protections under the law. The Black Lives Matter movement called—and continues to call—attention to this unjust burden, again challenging the legitimacy of public institutions that would justify this kind of violence by its representatives.

Martin's and Brown's deaths allow us to glimpse, at least partially, the contradictions of race, class, and violence contained in the "strong metaphor" of "gang" by which their killers—a civilian vigilante and a police officer—attempted to justify their deaths. Neither Martin nor Brown was a gang member, neither was known to be "on the streets," and neither had a court record of violence. Yet the formal and informal efforts to justify their deaths began by calling attention to the way they looked—male, black, dressed in symbols associated with the street, from economically poor neighborhoods. In the heated public debates about the meaning of these deaths, institutions at the heart of civil society—the police, the judicial system, and the media—felt it appropriate to begin by asking if Martin or Brown was associated with gang and street violence.

One insight we can gain from the way the public debates unfolded is that Martin's and Brown's deaths could have been more easily justified if they were just a little more "other," known for being violent, were associated with a gang, or carried a gun. It is worth pausing to consider the ethical standard this suggests. A second insight is that, on balance, our mainstream institutions—mass media, courts, police—tip the scales in favor of reactive violence when it is intended to maintain social order. Finally, we can see how these same institutions are formally indifferent to the social upheaval and human suffering that inevitably follow when the contradictions contained in the metaphor of "gang" come into view. The difference between television, movies, fiction, and real life is that in real life, the boundaries between legitimate and transgressive violence are not clear and an act of violence is not the end of the story. The meaning of violence is socially constructed, and violence is always destructive and only rarely regenerative. Violence as it is experienced has no neat end, and its ripples reappear over and over again in the lives of individuals and public discourse.

The greatest danger contained in this metaphor of gang, with its simultaneous repudiation of and empathy for gang members, is that it predicts what Gil Bailie warned about: a "growing sense of moral symmetry between the criminals and the cops . . . the tendency of violence to erase all difference between the adversaries while at the same time enflaming the passions and causing the level of violence between them to escalate" (1994, 63). Acts of violence are not conclusions. They are only waypoints in the ongoing negotiation of interpersonal and social relationships, competing interpretations of meaning, and continuing conflict.

The deaths of Trayvon Martin and Michael Brown suggest just how powerful this strong metaphor of "gang" is in our collective imaginations and give us some insight into what happens when the strong metaphors on which a culture depends begin to fall apart, allowing the contradictions they contain to come into plain view. Acknowledging the contradictions destabilizes the culture, puts social relationships into play, and challenges the authority of current institutions. This is the danger that Mary Douglas was pointing to, the disruptive potential of an angry person in an interstitial position: these persons can crack open the assumptions, values, and institutions on which our personal and collective identities depend.

Once we step inside the strong metaphor of gang, no longer see gang members as "other," and begin to empathize with their situation and relationship to violence, we can begin to ask very different questions: What would lead an otherwise ordinary young person to choose a path of violence that places them consistently outside the margins of civil society? How and why do they become angry persons at the crossroads of powerful cultural boundaries?

CONTOURS OF VIOLENCE

A partial explanation is that the anger and violence associated with gangs emerge from the life experiences of gang members, who believe that their violence is a necessary part of responding to the options they are given. An equally powerful dynamic is that they become located in a cultural narrative about violence that turns them from persons into symbols, from persons into gang members. Youth gang members become what the broader culture believes them to be. Youth thinking about joining a gang are acting out, in an exaggerated form, the mainstream belief that peace requires violence, but they are othered and perceived as threats to peace. Youth in gangs believe that performing violence is a way of restoring order and control and have the expectation that it will allow their lives to be more meaningful.

Violence can be difficult to define in a precise way. Alain Richard offers as a useful starting point the idea that violence refers to "situations and actions originating with humans or human structures coupled with foreseeable physical, moral or economic harm, degradation, death or destruction to humans, or creation" (1999, 13). Violence can be physical or "discursive"—words. It can be committed or received as threats that elicit fear or acts that force a reaction. It can be internal or interpersonal—between persons. It can be structural—systems of oppression and privilege that seem invisible yet reliably produce and maintain poverty or racism, as Eduardo

Bonilla-Silva describes in *Racism without Racists* (2003). Violence can range from minor experiences to the catastrophic. Continued small experiences of violence, such as bullying or racial slurs, that are sometimes characterized as "microaggressions" (Sue 2010), can cause profound physical or psychic wounds. Their impact is not, in fact, "micro." When determining if something is violent, we find ourselves thinking simultaneously about continuums of intensity, specific situations and relational contexts, and histories. Violence often seems to establish its own logic of growth; its root causes can seem embedded in unique personal and historical circumstances, obscuring broader patterns of cause and effect. While it seems always to involve perpetrators and victims, violence ripples out across time and space and regularly becomes its own justification.

This said, I have come to think of violence in this way: violence is whatever separates us from ourselves, other people, or the natural world. When we commit acts of violence, we are acting in ways that violate our wholeness and core integrity, making ourselves responsible for things beyond our control, holding on to anger and blame, and exaggerating and dwelling on our faults. Violence done to us damages relationships of self to self and self to other. It can cut us off from larger communities of belonging and can cut us off from our "self," physically, emotionally, or spiritually.

I believe the violence we commit, even if we believe it is justified, divides us against ourselves, distancing us from what Martin Buber called the "thou-ness" of our selves and our victims. Betrayal, beating, murder, and torture require perpetrators to suppress compassion and humanity, tamp down emotions, and move away from wholeness. Deliberately hurting someone else for the first time is ethically and emotionally difficult, and every culture has a rich literature of stories describing what it is like to do so or, as Stephen Crane's Civil War novel *Red Badge of Courage* explores, fail to do so. Historian Dave Grossman (2009) estimates that fewer than 20 percent of soldiers in combat during the Civil War actually fired on the enemy: most were unable to overcome the psychological barriers to taking another human life.

In addition to committing violence against ourselves and other people, we regularly commit acts of separation from the natural world, only rarely considering that our relationship to the earth is, in fact, a dimension of our humanness. As the nineteenth-century French philosopher Jean Anthelme Brillat-Savarin quipped, "Tell me what you eat and I'll tell you who you are" (1825). There is growing evidence (Pollan 2002; Wohlleben 2015) that trees feel, that fungi comprise a "nervous system" in particular ecologies, that animals think and communicate. Industrial farming methods, clear-cutting, habitat destruction, mountaintop removal, discharging heat and waste into rivers and estuaries, open-pit mining, even climate change might be looked on as forms of violence against the natural world. A friend once described gardening—especially weeding—to me as "the selective murder of plants." Aldo Leopold, who introduced millions of readers to the concept of ecology in his *Round River*, wrote, "One of the penalties of an ecological education is that one lives alone in a world of wounds" (1993, 165).

At the heart of violence, then, is relationship. My belief that relationship is essential to understanding violence is deeply influenced by Thich Nhat Hanh's concept of "interbeing." He writes:

> If you are a poet, you will see clearly that there is a cloud floating in this sheet of paper. Without a cloud, there will be no rain; without rain, the trees cannot grow; and without trees, we cannot make paper. The cloud is essential for the paper to exist. If the cloud is not here, the sheet of paper cannot be here either. So we can say that the cloud and the paper inter-are. "Interbeing" is a word that is not in the dictionary yet, but if we combine the prefix "inter-" with the verb "to be," we have a new verb, "inter-be." (1987, 53)

Violence requires that we forget or ignore or damage our interconnectedness—our minds and bodies, our social relationships and networks, our shared environments.

Nonviolence, which I will explore at length in a later chapter, is the opposite of this damage to relationship: it is the practice of recalling, learning to see, repairing, and encouraging relationship. Youth affected by violence as perpetrators or victims or both become disconnected from themselves and from the people around them. They shut off their feelings and learn to minimize compassion for themselves and for others. Trapped as youth gang members are by the possibility of being attacked if they "slip" and let down their guard, their social and physical world becomes smaller and smaller over time. They internalize their separation, becoming violent toward themselves and the world around them.

While this generalized definition of violence as whatever separates us from ourselves, other people, or the natural world may seem too sweeping to apply to specific situations with precision, it does produce a useful insight as we contemplate the violence associated with youth gangs: suffering is what we call our physical and emotional reactions to the destruction of relationship.

Our own suffering is fully an experience, something that only later might be described through words—an intense pain, a great disappointment, an emotional catastrophe. Suffering reminds us of the limitations of words and challenges the modernist and postmodernist conceit that we know the world through words and ideas. It reminds us that behind all words lies a mysterious whole of experience, of which words are the imperfect ghost, reflection, or description. "A major preoccupation in the Western tradition," write Arthur Kleinman, Veena Das, and Margaret Lock, "has to do with the incommunicability of pain, its capacity to isolate sufferers and strip them of cultural resources, especially the resource of language" (1997, xiii). To suffer intensely is to be fragmented and isolated and unvoiced. It is an experience of disconnection in ourselves and in our social and ecological relationships.

We can also begin to discern patterns of suffering that are caused to classes of people by the willful or inadvertent agency of other people: slavery, racism, poverty, neglect, abuse. It is useful to distinguish between particular biographies of suffering and suffering caused by what Paul Farmer calls "structural violence." "While certain kinds of suffering are readily observable—and the subject of countless films, novels and poems—structural violence all too often defeats those who would describe it" (1997, 272). We regularly encounter the consequence of structural violence, social suffering, out in the world. Kleinman, Das, and Lock describe it as the "devastating injuries that social force can inflict on human experience" (1997, ix). They note that the impact of these social forces is magnified in disintegrating communities.

Evidence of this kind of "structural violence" is discovered by studying patterns of social suffering and asking what produces them: Why is poverty so consistently correlated with one or more social identities, such as race? Why is domestic violence enacted disproportionately by men against women? Why does enforcement of drug laws result in mass incarceration of people of color? How does public education funded primarily by local property taxes result in what author Jonathan Kozol (1991) calls "savage inequalities"? Structural violence happens when we do not recognize how one thing is connected to another or when we determine that elements of a system are not connected or can be treated differentially. Structural violence becomes visible as we practice an ecological way of seeing relationship.

Approaching violence through the lens of relationship is also a starting point for exploring what violence means in cultural terms—the stories we tell about it, how central a role it plays in these stories, how we frame the stories we tell about it, the "strong" metaphors on which the stories are built, and what the stories are intended to teach about violence as a part of the world in which we live. Somewhat surprisingly, this line of inquiry suggests that youth gang members and those involved in street violence share in the dominant cultural narratives of violence, differing only in how they express the beliefs and values embedded in the metaphors. Viewing "them" as "other" obscures this commonality.

Most cultural narratives about violence in the United States are concerned with a fundamental social question, revealing a preoccupation that borders on obsession (Slotkin 1973; Armstrong 2014). What do we do when evil, in the form of violence, appears and threatens our peaceful persons, communities, or environment? How should we react? It is a problem of fear, reframed as a question of social ethics, and it is revisited over and over in the literatures, music, and aesthetic products across the diversity of lived experiences that make up contemporary U.S. culture.

Most often, the stories through which we explore our relationship to violence also suggest a solution, and the combination of dilemma and solution becomes a deep part of widely shared worldview: violence must be met with violence if civilization is to endure. And so we are given a paradox (Carter 2011)—peace requires violence—as the bedrock of a widely shared cultural creation story in the United States.

This paradox is not unique to the United States, but the ways we frame, tell, and interpret it are part and parcel of our public culture, reflecting cultural perspectives that emphasize individual rights and self-defense. It shapes the ways we define, isolate, and punish transgressive "others." We can find some evidence of our public understanding of violence by placing national and regional homicide rates, statistics on gun ownership, and shifting attitudes about the death penalty in a global perspective. Much of the rest of the world looks at the way violence is framed in the culture of the United States; associates this framing with data about the high rates of gun violence, murder, and incarceration; and concludes that ours is a deeply violent worldview (Adler and Denmark 2005).

At the heart of this deep cultural narrative—peace requires violence, and successful violence depends ultimately on individual character—is a widely held belief that serves as additional evidence of a common worldview, shared by most citizens of the United States, across ideological boundaries (Armstrong 2014; Pinker 2012). It is the belief that violence is a fundamental and innate dimension of being human: consistent throughout history and prehistory, a capacity everyone is born with. We believe violence is woven into the DNA of our species as an irreducible and largely unchangeable building block.

Exploring our cultural preoccupation with violence, the cultural mythology that we have developed from it, and the practical implications of this mythology (Shore 1996) is somewhat beyond the scope of this book, but I want to consider it briefly to suggest why our broader culture is so fascinated with gang violence, because I believe doing so offers some insight into the origins and dynamics of gang violence in the United States.

One representative and useful expression of our cultural fascination with violence is the 1985 movie *Pale Rider*. Produced by and starring Clint Eastwood, an iconic actor whose career reflects a fascination with the paradox of peace through violence, *Pale Rider* was the highest-grossing western of the 1980s, the same period in which the War on Drugs and the move toward mass incarceration were beginning to surge. The title of the movie references the four horsemen of the Apocalypse, drawn from the book of Revelation in the Bible.

The story line is simple: A frontier town is terrorized by the (all-male) ranch hands of a ranch owner who believes he can use violence to take whatever he wants whenever he wants it—people, money, land. The conflict comes to a head when one of the ranch hands threatens a young woman, the daughter of a settler, with sexual violence. The civilized settler fights back ineffectively, the violence escalates, and the frontier town prepares to stave off an attack from the rancher's men. Many of the settlers flee rather than fight, because the ranch hands are good at violence and they are not. A stranger known as Preacher rides into town on a pale horse. He decides to get involved and uses his exceptional understanding and skill with violence to organize the residents, kill the ranch hands, and save the girl and the town. Then he rides away. The settlers have been initiated into the world as it really is: they have to acknowledge and contemplate the froth of violence just below the veneer of civilization, and as peace-loving people they have to accept that their existence depends on violence. They are thankful for the Preacher and equally as happy that he leaves.

Violence is also the theme of Eastwood's similarly popular *Gran Torino* (Eastwood 2008), a movie well liked by many of the Southeast Asian youth who attended Rec Night. In this movie, a disintegrating social order is the setting and the mystery that drive the movie. A residential neighborhood is sliding into urban decay, signified by the arrival of Southeast Asian immigrant families and, with them, street gangs. Eastwood plays a retired, widowed Marine, a misanthropic, self-reliant white holdout whose main emotive expression is anger. He discovers a Southeast Asian teenage boy, who lives next door, trying to steal his beloved Gran Torino as ordered by the gang (hence the title). Rather than punish the boy, Eastwood befriends him, with the intention of mentoring him in the values of hard work and respect for family, education, and duty. In Eastwood's imagination (as character and director), he is simply restoring a traditional and foundational neighborhood value of elders mentoring youth, something lost in the chaos of economic decline and familial dislocation.

Predictably, the local street gang again violates the youth, the youth's family, and Eastwood. In the end, Eastwood's character sacrifices his life to save the youth and his family: a blood sacrifice of redemptive violence that validates the core values of family, community, and loyalty, peace through violence if we are willing to sacrifice enough. It is worth noting that ultimate sacrifice by a white male hero with war experience is required to restore order, a task beyond the capacity of both the new immigrants and the soft, privileged whites who have fled the city and abdicated their responsibility.

It is this narrative structure about the destructive and redemptive potentials of violence that frames much of the public perspective on youth gangs and ongoing efforts to eliminate them: youth gangs are sources of danger, they are symbols of a decaying moral order, they threaten to disrupt social order, and they are represented as a social "other" disconnected from the larger web of communal relationships and civic values.

As Richard Slotkin (1973) and Gil Bailie (1994) have pointed out, the foundational stories of U.S. culture teach that blood sacrifice is necessary to restore order—and so there is honor in going to war with what threatens us. This is what Eastwood's characters do in *Pale Rider* and *Gran Torino*. The experiences of small groups of dedicated people willing to use violence to protect the community against the destructive violence of gangs are also a consistent theme on popular television shows over the decades, such as *Hill Street Blues* (Bochco and Kozoll 1981–87), *The Wire* (Simon 2002–8), and *Gang Related* (Kouf 1997; Morgan 2014). How far can those who use violence on our behalf go? Should they be constrained by rules that don't apply to the enemy? However these shows answer the question, all of them explore the ethics of containing and eliminating gangs as the source of social disorder.

Bailie traces the logic of the expectation that blood sacrifice is necessary to social order to Heraclitus, a pre-Socratic Greek philosopher who died in 475 BC: "For Heraclitus, the *logos* of violence was an ordering principle that was generated by disorder itself. Once in play, the *logos* turned chaotic and destructive violence into socially stable and hierarchically differentiated social systems" (1994, 241). That is, it is our deeply rooted cultural belief that violence is generative and regenerative—that we perform it in order to restore order.

Our cultural concern with the ethical dilemma presented by the paradox of violence as a path to peace arguably extends into a broader public perspective on national and global politics that cuts across the mainstream of both Democratic and Republican politics: the perception that the peaceful community of the United States survives in a violent world only because our capacity for violence far exceeds that of any potential enemies. Tracy Kidder's nonfiction *Strength in What Remains* (2009), for example, considers personal, national, and transnational violence as he traces the story of Deo, a survivor of genocide in Burundi and a migrant to the United States. Deo works with international health-justice activist Paul Farmer. Reflecting on his experiences, Deo quotes Peter Uvin, a scholar of Burundi and the surrounding region who discusses "structural violence": "In societies where rule of law is close to nonexistent and security forces are neither effective or trusted, small groups of people willing to use violence can create enough chaos and fear to force everyone into making violent choices" (2008, 201). The capacity of the U.S. police and military to contain these small, violent groups is what saves the country from chaos. It is a familiar public narrative, playing out in Afghanistan and Iraq and begging resolution in Syria.

While social order nearly always wins, media representations of gang violence simultaneously convey a contradictory counternarrative: gangs are symbols of resistance in communities targeted for violence by the dominant culture, and they are blood sacrifices intended to restore order to the dominant culture. This counternarrative helps drive well-known, commercially successful movies about gangs as far-ranging as *West Side Story* (Robbins and Wise 1961), *Colors* (Hopper 1988), *Boyz n the Hood* (Singleton 1991), and *Menace II Society* (Hughes and Hughes 1993). Each of these examples, from quite different perspectives, explores the same question: Is gang violence, in part, a failed or vestigial effort to generate personal and social order through destructive violence? If we recognize this, isn't there something honorable and tragic in gang violence when all is said and done? And what do we do once we begin to recognize the paradox that members of youth gangs are trying—and failing—to use violence to restore some control and order to their worlds?

Many contemporary stories considering gang violence also note the narrowing of the ethical distinction that separates gang members from police officers, a theme in *Colors, Hill Street Blues,* and *The Wire,* for example. Discussing Rodney King, the 1991 Los Angeles riots that followed his brutal videotaped beating by police officers, and the shifting perception community members had of the police, Bailie considers what happens when those allowed to practice "legitimate" violence (usually in the name of maintaining order and the authority of the state) begin to lose their moral legitimacy: "The growing sense of moral symmetry between the criminals and the cops corresponds to what [René] Girard speaks of as the doubling effect of violence, the tendency of violence to erase all difference between the adversaries while at the same time enflaming the passions and causing the level of violence between them to escalate" (1994, 63).

The growing sense of moral symmetry—or even a reversing of moral valence—creates a context for soaring tensions between police departments and poor communities of color, whenever police violence results in injury or death to a community member, as with Eric Garner, Freddie Gray, or Sandra Bland. The doubling effect of violence creates a sense of moral symmetry, simultaneously delegitimizing all violence and justifying violence on all sides. Once moral legitimacy is lost, violence can offer no way out.

Gangs, then, are something to honor and despise and always something to fear. They are metaphors in which we can find our own beliefs and doubts about the meaning and legitimacy of violence. Readers and viewers are fascinated by stories of gangs and gang violence because they explore a deep cultural concern (will I have to resort to violence to protect our peace, as part of the dominant order or as a victim of that order?) and consider questions of honor and transgression as they are distilled in experiences of violence. What would I do if I was forced into making violent choices? We are simultaneously attracted and repelled, sympathetic and alienated.

While I have said only enough to indicate the shape and depth and continuity of this strong cultural metaphor, what matters here is how common and continuous this narrative form is, how natural it seems, and the familiarity of the fundamental ethical question it poses in our understanding of ourselves. What do we do when we are confronted with evil in the form of violence that threatens our identity or existence? Are we justified in turning to violence? And if we do so, how does this change us?

Experiencing and internalizing this paradoxical view of ourselves as peaceful and violent is our journey from innocence to wisdom, from childhood to adulthood. We unconsciously accept as a given that this journey will take place, and we turn most of our attention to considering what we want to be like when we have completed it.

TARGETING GANG VIOLENCE

Youth gangs and gang members are positioned as the enemy in the popular culture of the United States and as the source of social disintegration. They are defined in ways that allow them to be treated by more aggressive, hostile standards than ordinary citizens. Because race and class are factors in how gangs are defined, this treatment ends up disproportionately targeting economically poor black, Latino, and Southeast Asian youth. Hollywood films such as *Fort Apache, the Bronx* (Petrie 1981) and *Colors* (Hopper 1988) amplify the idea of communities with gangs as "frontiers" defined by violence, make gang members the equivalent of "Indians" in 1950s westerns, and show police officers as a military force, appropriating an older violent racial narrative used to justify westward expansion (Drinnon 1980) into a new social context.

The updated narrative structure goes something like this: peace requires violence, a scapegoat must be killed in order to restore our community to itself, gang members and gang violence are "othered" and positioned as being outside the mainstream community and culture—gang members are scapegoats. This is, I think, the underlying justification for the emergence of a surveillance, policing, and punishment approach to youth gangs and street violence over the past twenty years (Giroux 2010). As Michelle Alexander points out in *The New Jim Crow*:

> The hypersegregation of the black poor in ghetto communities has made the roundup [of black youth/men] easy. Confined to ghetto areas and lacking political power, the black poor are convenient targets. . . . It is not uncommon for a young black teenager living in a ghetto community to be stopped, interrogated, and frisked numerous times in the course of a month, or even a single week, often by paramilitary units. . . . The militarized nature of law enforcement in ghetto communities has inspired rap artists and black youth to refer to the police presence in black communities as "The Occupation." (2010, 122–23)

Many of the youth I know in Providence also call the police "the Occupation," often with an ironic nod to the larger social discourse, and more often tell stories of the "jump-out boys," the heavily armed, abrupt paramilitary gang unit that drives up on them, jumps out, and confronts them, seemingly without cause, on a regular basis.

As Bailie points out, though, this kind of violence has a doubling effect and diminishes the moral distinction between legitimate and illegitimate violence. Youth gangs and gang members are resisting "the Occupation" and the structural violence that it represents and demonstrating a willingness to make a blood sacrifice to restore order on their terms. It is an understandable goal of much of gang violence. The moral symmetry that results becomes a context for perpetual war.

This counternarrative, in which the mainstream order is the threat, is lived out daily by gang-involved youth. One young man I know was the youngest in a large family, with several older brothers who were gang involved. He was not involved in the streets, and his brothers were supporting his plan to "stay straight" and finish high school. Right around his fifteenth birthday, as he was beginning ninth grade, police officers stopped him and one of his brothers and forced them to the ground so they could be questioned. The youth told me that the officer told him they knew his family, knew he would be like his brothers, and had their eyes on him. He was traumatized, became depressed, and began skipping school as he tried to understand how the police could see him the way they did. It took him a long time to accept the reality that they hadn't, in fact, seen him but had instead seen a symbolic enemy. Several months later, he had mostly pulled out of his depression but carried with him a new understanding of what "other" people saw when they looked at him. He slowly made a resolution, again with the support of his older brothers, "to stay straight," but he no longer recognized the moral authority of civil institutions.

Another young man I know, who had been affiliated with a youth gang, posted on his Facebook page that he was not doing well. I asked him, also on Facebook, if he was okay. He messaged me privately. His brother had been shot in the head a couple of days earlier. I had not made the connection. His brother would heal, but the young man was preoccupied with finding out who had shot his brother. He messaged me a couple of days later, saying that he thought he knew and that I probably knew one of the people involved. He wasn't sure what was next, but he was feeling enormous pressure to retaliate. A week later, he said he had decided he was "done with all that." He had no expectation that he would engage with the police to catch the shooter and framed his choice solely around his personal decision to use, or not use, blood violence.

For both youth, stepping out of the old narrative of regenerative violence and into a new one of nonviolence was a step into uncharted territory that raised questions of survival, justice, and identity. The only practical alternative to regenerative violence, articulated by both young men and taken up in the chapter on nonviolence, was to recognize and change the entire narrative. Instead of allowing themselves to be defined by externally imposed expectations that restoring peace required violence, they focused instead on concrete actions that emphasized reintegration and relationship, on "interbeing," on connectedness, on community. They asked mentors to support their efforts to become whole, rather than divided against themselves, and to open pathways by which they could reintegrate into social institutions such as schools, sports, family, community service, and work.

Their counternarratives suggest that we should approach communities experiencing gang violence not with our concern for containing and eliminating violence that threatens social order but with a concern for the ways in which the youth have become othered and the ways in which we, the larger community, are implicated in this separation. This shift in perspective is, I believe, the key to reducing gang violence.

The way that youth gangs form follows the dominant cultural narrative: The youth recognize that direct, discursive, and systemic violence are visited on them all the time. They are physically hurt, bullied, and demeaned (even by those charged with their care, like teachers or police) and live in poverty. The youth conclude that they need to defend themselves and the people they care for and that their best recourse is violence—to others and to themselves. They understand, from experience, the reality of violence beneath the veneer of civilization and believe that the veneer has been stripped from their lives. I have heard a thousand times over, "That's how it is on the streets." Like the settlers and neighbors in Eastwood's stories, members of youth gangs must overcome their innocence and naïveté if they are going to survive, they depend on leaders to initiate them into the realities of violence, and once they have begun the journey they are changed forever.

We are fascinated and compelled by gang violence and repelled and afraid of it in equal part, I think, because it supports our culture's perception that the veneer of civilization is thin. Youth gang members remind us simultaneously of the violent rancher, whose violence is destructive, and the "pale rider," whose capacity for violence is redemptive. The destructive aspect of gang violence is evident in damage to individual youth, to the people directly and indirectly hurt by gang violence, and in the larger community that is threatened. The positive aspect of gang culture and violence is that it provides a way of resisting what most threatens its members. The most horrific aspect of gang culture is that these young people are changed beyond recognition by their journey into violence and become a threat to the rest of us. We glorify and condemn their capacity for violence, participating in a cultural paradox that has deep meaning for all of us. As Gil Bailie reminds us, our culture is deeply concerned with "the underlying anthropological dynamic at work: *a brutal act done in the name of civilization,* an expulsion or execution that results in social harmony" (1994, 79). Bailie also observes, "By fits and starts . . . gangs are experimenting with home-made versions of the 'all-encompassing, absolute rationale for sacrifice and destruction' which is the oldest known recipe for generating social solidarity" (61).

Gang violence scares us not only because of the potential for physical harm but also because it raises the specter of a failing social order: If violence results from fragmenting social order, and is intended to be generative of restored social order, what are we to make of gang violence? It contributes, on the one hand, to the dissolution of social order. It also suggests that the social order is in itself profoundly unstable because it is built on a foundation of violence.

Russian author Leo Tolstoy, in his 1886 *The Kingdom of God Is Within You,* an early voice of Christian nonviolence, challenged the common perception of violence as regenerative and necessary to maintaining social order. "That the social order with its pauperism, famine, prisons, gallows, armies and wars is necessary to society; that still greater disaster would ensue if this organization were destroyed; all this is said only by those who profit by this organization, while those who suffer from it—and they are ten times as numerous—think and say quite the contrary." From Tolstoy's point of view, state violence was as often a tool of oppression as of order, and we recognize the truth of this perspective in public discourse about gangs.

Gangs are a cultural metaphor, and gang violence is a cultural paradigm. They are sites of fascination and reflection. They invite our affirmation of the resistant and regenerative energy embodied in the gang as a new social form. They are a threat to a desired social order and an unmasking of oppressive structural violence. Some part of us tends to believe that violence always churns just below the surface, and gangs serve to justify this belief. And gangs, youth gangs in particular, invite us to consider how this journey into violence would affect us. Are they members of our community, or are they other? Are they like or unlike the rest of us?

I share Paulo Freire's perspective that the members of our society we describe as marginalized are not, in fact, marginal. "The oppressed," he writes, "are not 'marginals,' are not living 'outside' society. They have always been 'inside' the structure which made them 'beings for others.' The solution is not to integrate them into the structure of oppression, but to transform that structure so that they can become 'beings for themselves'" (1970, 53).

As much as the larger cultural narratives of gang violence marginalize gang members, positioning them as threats to social order or victims of structural violence, it is more promising to recognize that gang members and gang violence are not marginal but are a part of the larger community to which we all belong. This invites us to pay attention to a very troubling reality: the way in which our shared cultural system produces youth gangs. It invites us to begin by considering the lives of individual youth who are drawn into youth gangs, the impact of these gangs on the social dynamic of their immediate communities, and the process by which youth become capable of deliberate physical violence.

Stepping deeply into this recognition that members of youth gangs are members of our community, are "inside" society, helps us to see that they are a reflection of who we are as a whole. It allows us to recognize that youth gangs don't exist in order to be used as blood sacrifices for the restoration of social order. Before they are gang members, the youth are persons with the potential and right to grow up as whole persons and realize their potential as whole human beings. This is the subject of the next chapters on violentization, youth positive, and nonviolence, which explore in some detail how youth can become capable of transgressive violence; how choosing street violence makes sense; the potential of responding to youth as persons traumatized by violence with compassion, affirmation, and opportunity; and nonviolence as a practical alternative to violence.

Asking this question—how do ordinary youth choose a path of transgressive violence?—directs our attention past the symbol and toward the whole of a youth's lived experience. What we discover, as we begin to pay attention, suggests that the solution to the violence embedded in youth gangs lies in caring for the youth as persons who are struggling, and often failing, to find a workable path toward wholeness. It invites us to reach out to individual youth in a spirit of hospitality and compassion and to consider how we have collectively arrived at a system of social institutions and processes that so predictably produce youth gangs and violence.

CHAPTER THREE

VIOLENTIZATION (AND TRAUMA)

We treat our children so badly that, in the end, they have no means
of expression except through violence.

—Henning Mankell, *Italian Shoes*

BECOMING VIOLENT

I was returning from a morning walk and settling in to work on this
chapter when I got a call from a friend telling me that Isaac, a longtime Rec Night participant now in his early twenties, had been shot
the night before. His forearm was shattered, he was hit in both feet,
and he had driven himself to a local hospital. He was having surgery
that morning. A friend of his, who had also attended Rec Night, was
shot in the leg. My friend said that Isaac told her they were picking
up two younger friends when a shooter ran up on their car and fired
around twenty shots. Only Isaac and his friend were hit. When I
talked to Isaac the next day, he said, "They aired out the car. I feel
lucky to be alive." Isaac says he was at the site of this recent shooting
to informally squash some beefs and get some of the younger guys
to calm down. I believe him, though there is undoubtedly more to it
than this.

Isaac has been on the streets for a long time. He has a reputation as a fighter, a serious person, a hustler, very smart. This is the
second time he has been shot. He has also been stabbed and given
two serious concussions with baseball bats. He is one of the Rec
Night participants I got to know quite well. He was receptive to and

participated in nonviolence trainings and work programs through ISPN, he made himself a positive presence at Rec Night, he participated in several classes I teach, and for a couple of years we met inconsistently but with some frequency for coffee or lunch. He is smart and curious. I visited him at the Adult Correctional Institute when he was incarcerated for eighteen months on a gun charge. I have watched him work to be a good father to his daughters.

Isaac came to the United States at age ten as a refugee from a civil war in another country. His mother moved him and his brother into a housing project in Providence and got him enrolled in a local elementary school. One of his new friends got his hair braided in cornrows by another youth and ran off without paying the agreed-upon six dollars. Later that afternoon, as Isaac and some friends were hanging out, the young stylist showed up with some of his older friends, juniors in a local gang, and they stabbed Isaac's friend, who died of his wounds.

Isaac told me that he made a decision in the weeks following to be a person who would protect his friends and family. His mother had told him they would be safe in their new country and situation, and he realized it was not true. He looked around for role models and guidance, paid attention to what he thought worked, and ended up starting a crew with his friends. As they got older, their conflicts got bigger and extended into an expanding geographic area.

As I think about how people choose and learn violence, I also think of Joey. Joey was thirteen, the oldest of two brothers. Their mother had brought them to Smith Hill from Central America, and their father had left the family a short while after their arrival. They were barely scraping by financially and conscious of the fact that, in an economically poor community, they were thought of as poor. A man in his late teens or early twenties began harassing Joey's mother whenever she walked down the street by their apartment. As the oldest son, Joey believed it was his job to protect his mother. He had come to this idea partly because of his beliefs about what it was to "be a man," but also because he spoke English, his mother's English was limited, and he often had to translate for her. He was used to her depending on him. Joey dropped by Rec Night one evening and told me, "I hit a guy with a rock today." He looked at me for my reaction. I asked for more details and then asked why. He explained about his mother being harassed, about trying to protect her from this guy. When the guy started bothering his mom on the street again, ignoring Joey's and his brother's requests to stop, Joey picked up a softball-size rock and hit him hard in the head from behind, knocking him out. Telling me about this, Joey was both proud and shaken. He clearly wanted to know if he'd done the right thing, if it was something he should do again. As we weighed the possibility that this older guy would retaliate, Joey looked across the room at a group of older boys, a neighborhood "crew." "You see how they get each other's back?" He was thinking about asking to join the crew or start one with his friends.

While it was not the only reason that Isaac and Joey decided to become involved in a youth gang, the pattern of their stories is one I have heard with great consistency over time: each of them wanted to protect himself and his friends, especially the people he loved; he wanted to be a good person, and this meant being willing to sacrifice for his family and friends; he believed that the adults who should have been protecting everyone—parents, teachers, police, community members—had failed, leaving it on him and his friends; and the truth he had learned was that the world is a violent place and that you have to fight violence with violence in order to get by. Each of them heard calls from adults to "behave," stop fighting, get off the streets, resolve conflicts through talk, and pursue the carrots of finishing school and getting a job as evidence that the adults were out of touch or hypocritical or both. They said they already understood these things and would be doing them if it were that easy.

Digging a little more deeply, Isaac is describing the effects of a life context of violence. He was a child in a war zone and then a refugee. His mother practiced survival before and after coming to the United States and carried her own traumatic experiences with her as she cared for her family. Isaac's sixth grade class was in an overcrowded school that had many students in economic and social circumstances similar to his. As he tried on a new, more aggressive persona, he was punished; he resisted even more and was soon labeled a "troublemaker." He left school in ninth grade. He didn't see himself as a troublemaker, exactly, but as someone whose reality was profoundly different from the world projected by civil institutions like schools. He lived according to different values and ideas about what was right, grounded in his experience. Even as he recognized and often wanted to cross back over this divide, he would explain, "It's just how it is on the streets." His friend's death had opened his eyes to this new reality.

Joey's life experience parallels Isaac's. He was trying to care for a brother and mother; he was dealing with the long-term emotional and economic impacts of dislocation, domestic violence, and abandonment. He was struggling academically in school and developing a temper that reacted aggressively and immediately to any form of disrespect. Like Isaac, he was on his way to being labeled a troublemaker, seen not as a kid to be helped but as another young man "lost to the streets." Most of the advice Joey got from adults seemed impossible to follow or based on ignorance: it emphasized his personal responsibility to change his behavior, while doing virtually nothing to improve the circumstances in which he lived.

I was in the gym at Rec Night, talking with a colleague visiting from another campus, when Anaya came up and gave me a brief hug. "I have news," she said. "I'm going to have a baby!" I had known Anaya for three years. She had just turned eighteen, had just graduated from high school. She was a tall, broad-shouldered, physically strong person and had not had a steady relationship. She had grown up in a chaotic family situation, experienced sexual violence, and been bullied on the streets. She had developed alternating strategies for contending with her life, by turns aggressive and violent or withdrawn and quiet. She had been kicked out of school several times, but teachers and staff sympathetic to her warmth and genuine desire to graduate from high school had helped her to achieve her dream. She was the first person in her family to get her diploma. Anticipating the baby, she focused on the prospect of having a person she could love unreservedly and who would love her unreservedly in return.

Anaya had had several sexual partners in the months prior. She had viewed it as a way to establish herself and get power: she believed it communicated that she controlled her sexuality and she decided with whom to share it. It was a way to exercise power over the young men who "wanted her" and over the young women who were threatened by her sexuality and her physical strength. Her sexual activity was, at the same time, a response to her persistent depression and an expression of her deep desire to be cared for and loved. She hoped that the intimacy of sex would lead to love and that love would lift her out of her situation. It didn't, and the young men and women around her turned the tables on her, labeling her easy, a slut. Her emotional vulnerability made it easy to "get over" on her. Anaya's reactions were again divergent and constantly shifting back and forth: aggressive and physical one week, withdrawn and depressed the next. She put most of her hope into imagining the mother she would be to the child she was carrying. As Anaya's pregnancy started to show, her mother used it as a proxy for other conflicts they were having. She kicked Anaya out of their house, saying, "You want to act like an adult, go be an adult." Homeless, scared, and depressed, Anaya couch-surfed, worked at a part-time job, and eventually started writing bad checks, leading to her arrest; she had her daughter while out on bail and awaiting her trial.

I also think of Jose Rodriguez. Now in his early thirties, Jose grew up in Providence's Smith Hill and Olneyville neighborhoods. He has been in and out of prison multiple times, starting with the Training School at age eleven. I have known Jose for the past six or so years as a staff member at ISPN and a student in College Unbound, a new, innovative college for working adults. He currently works with ISPN's Victim's Services department. Jose's involvement with ISPN and College Unbound introduced him to local playwright Holly Jensen, and in the summer of 2016 he opened a one-man play about his life, written with her coaching. He called the play *I Won't Love You If*. The play explores his entrance into and efforts to exit from violence, a journey we have talked about a number of times. While the details of Jose's story are unique in significant ways, his story suggests patterns of experience and meaning similar to those of Isaac, Joey, and Anaya.

Jose says he learned by the time he was six or seven that he would have to take care of himself: an absent father and intentional humiliation and rejection by his mother taught him that all love was conditional and that he failed to meet the minimum conditions, that he was unlovable. Jose began to experience a disconnect between his reality and the mainstream institutions such as schools of which he was a part. In his play he says, "I learned not to feel." He locked down all of his emotions for years. He became a drug dealer and gang member and had a reputation for serious violence. As a youth processing all of this emotional chaos and the everyday realities of needing to feed and clothe himself, he resolved that he would do everything necessary to take care of himself. He looked around to see who was successful, what was working, and learned from older youth on the street how to be violent. He developed a reputation as fearless and explosive. He figured his life wasn't worth much and it didn't really matter if he lived or died, so he might as well take risks that would build his reputation. He was suspended and expelled from schools and then quit. He came to see material symbols of wealth—especially high-end cars—as proof of his worth.

While there is much more to Jose's story, including finding his voice and working to heal the relationships and communities he once harmed, it is the story of how and why he became violent that interests me here. Like Isaac's, Joey's, and Anaya's stories, Jose's is characterized by a resolution to protect himself, a failed desire to be loved and lovable, a realization that the adults in his life would not or could not care for him, success in using violence to have power and make meaning, and an awareness that he lived in a reality based on fundamentally different perceptions and values than those of civil society.

VIOLENTIZATION

In Rec Night's second year, I invited Lonnie Athens, a sociologist whose lifework has been the study of violence (Rhodes 2000), to visit Providence and speak with my students, ISPN staff and board members, and Providence and state police. Athens's theory of "violentization" (Athens 2003; Rhodes 2000) became a central part of how I understood violence and youth gang behavior.

Athens's research method is phenomenological: gathering stories and evidence that grow out of people's experiences, observing patterns in them, and then describing the patterns in ways that allow him to theorize and test his ideas against other experiences and evidence. As Athens explains it, "violentization" is a pattern of experiences that can lead to a worldview built on the belief that the world is unjust and inherently violent and that being able to meet violence with violence is an essential part of being a successful adult. Athens argues that this pattern is common to all (in his view) persons who become capable of deliberate physical violence against others. His research draws on hundreds of hours of interviews with people convicted of first-degree murder and is based on a "symbolic interaction" theory and method familiar to sociologists. Athens's explicit focus on power and domination as core elements of human interaction has led him to articulate a specific form of symbolic analysis that he calls "radical interaction" theory. "In radical interactionism," Athens argues, "the spotlight is always placed where it belongs—on the emergence, maintenance, and change of intra- and interinstitutional dominance orders . . . on the exercise of domination both within and across all major societal institutions" (2007, 156–57).

A critical assumption of Athens's explanatory model, which I share and which underlies much of the argument in this book, is that persons develop their worldviews, the ways they interpret their experiences and make meaning, through their interactions with the world and especially other people. Athens argues that people who become capable of deliberate violence consistently find themselves in certain types of experiences; have certain types of interactions with other people; go through a relatively predictable emotional, psychological, cognitive, and social process as they explain to themselves what is happening; and have a relatively limited number of options as they consider what they will do with their new insights about themselves and the world. One of those "options" is violence.

Athens argues that people develop the capacity for deliberate violence against other persons over four stages: brutalization, defiance (called "belligerency" in his earlier work), violent resolution, and malevolence. The "stages" are not necessarily linear; most parts of the process can be and are repeated or revisited multiple times without advancing to the next stage, and people who move in the direction of becoming violent often retreat from it, sometimes overwhelmed and struggling and other times because alternative paths open up. Athens notes that relatively few people complete the entire process of violentization and graduate into a "malevolent" worldview in which violence becomes an end in itself. The process is consistent, though, for those who do become persistently and deeply violent, and it helps us to recognize a pattern in stories like those of Isaac, Joey, Anaya, and Jose. Perhaps the most important insight afforded by Athens's work is that most gang- and street-involved youth are not ultraviolent; they are not "malevolent" and do not see violence as an end in itself. Rather, they resolve to use violence when it is necessary to have power, develop and exercise relevant skills, and recognize that there is real value in being seen as a "serious person."

"Brutalization" is a harsh word. People—especially youth—typically experience this stage in the form of bullying, an experience common to children, youth, and adults across all social strata. The "subject," Athens says, is first forced into "subjugation" by a member of his or her primary group—by friends, family, classmates, teammates, or neighbors, for example. Not all bullying is the same; what matters is the type of bullying. In *violent subjugation,* Athens observes, the subject must comply with an order or face physical or verbal force, up to and including violence. When subjugation is *coercion,* the violence ends on submission. When it takes the form of what he calls *retaliation,* the violence does not end on submission, and the authority figure continues with the violence to gain long-term submission or respect. Athens says retaliation denies the subject the "precious luxury" of "choosing when to end the assault by submitting." Isaac's, Joey's, Anaya's, and Jose's childhood stories are full of moments when they were brutalized (and experimented with brutalizing others), and it is a dominant feature in Jose's stories of his childhood and youth.

Bullying can also entail *personal horrification,* in which the subject experiences the violent subjugation of a member of his or her primary group—"mother, sister or brother or a very close friend." This builds conflict in the subject, as she or he begins to feel guilt behind their helplessness. In Isaac's story, personal horrification took an extreme form with the murder of his friend—and the fear, helplessness, anxiety, and anger the murder provoked in him and his friends. Isaac not only experienced these responses himself but also had to watch them unfold in his friends, and he had to relive them whenever he saw some of the violent actors out in the neighborhood. Joey was repeatedly placed in a position where he had to watch his mother be humiliated, while his little brother looked on. His mother's harassment provoked fear, anxiety, and the feeling that he should do something, along with intense feelings of shame at being unable to do so. Anaya instrumentalized her sexuality, trying to use it a tool of domination, only to find that she had lost control of her situation.

Finally, and quite commonly, bullying is inflicted as *violent coaching:* someone appoints him- or herself as a coach who insists that the subject must defend her- or himself, depend only on him- or herself, and that it is their "personal responsibility [to fight] which they cannot evade, but must discharge regardless of whether they are a man or a woman, young or old, large or small, or what their prior beliefs . . . about hurting others may have been" (Athens 2003, 8; Rhodes 2000, 120–21).

The means of coaching vary, and there may be more than one coach at a time. Coaches can practice *vainglorification,* which "glorifies violence through storytelling," or *ridicule,* which "promotes violence through belittling and derision." And some coaches simply use *coercion,* "threaten[ing] novices not with psychological punishment, as in ridicule, but with physical punishment." The coach might say,

"Stand up and fight, or I'll beat you myself" (Athens 2003, 9; Rhodes 2000, 122).

I have seen all of these happen, most commonly in the form of what I think of as "direct" coaching, often combined with threats. Many of the gang-involved youth of Rec Night told stories about this kind of coaching. Typically, a parent or older family member would tell them they had to deal with a situation in which they were being bullied by fighting back. This order would often be reinforced with threats that, if they didn't fight back, they would get something worse at home. Often, they were also told they had to win the fight and that the more aggressive they were willing to be, the better their chances of winning.

This threat would often be linked to a second form of coaching, a version of Athens's "vainglorification." One or more people the youth looked up to would recognize that they were being bullied and (often after telling them that they had to fight) tell them stories about being faced with the same dilemma. They would talk about how they had decided to take control of the situation, how they had used violence to gain control, and how much better they felt afterward. Almost always, these stories contained an explicit moral: faced with this type of situation, you have only two choices—fight back or be a punk. If the youth wanted to keep the respect of the storyteller, there was only one choice. In many instances, the stories would be followed up by an offer to teach the youth how to fight, and more often than not—especially if the youth's peers were watching—the offer would be accepted.

Isaac, Joey, and Anaya all had multiple experiences of personal horrification—in Isaac's case culminating in the murder of his friend. All were coerced multiple times. All received violent coaching from friends, older youths, and adults around them. Jose was also coached—and when he was drawn into selling drugs, it was the symbols and narrative of seizing control and having power through violence that drew him in.

The second stage of violentization Athens describes as "defiance," in which people respond to brutalization by "making the decision to take personal responsibility for stopping it. They ask themselves,

'Why have I not done anything to stop my own and my intimates' violent subjugation?'" The subject's "problem finally becomes fully crystallized in his mind," Athens writes. "The subject understands clearly for the first time that he must find a way to stop people from brutalizing him. . . . It is *as if* the subject . . . has only now heard what his coach had been telling him all along: Resorting to violence is sometimes necessary in this world" (2003, 10–11; Rhodes 2000, 126).

Athens makes this moment of resolution a stage in itself, rather than a threshold between stages, because the dilemmas of identity and ethics it presents take time and effort to process. As Geoffrey Canada writes, "It takes years of preparation to be willing to commit murder, to be willing to kill or die for a corner, a color, or a leather jacket" (2010, 35).

Deliberately choosing violence is difficult and fraught; crossing to it is a liminal journey into a reality that operates according to an alternative set of assumptions, values, and logic. "For the brutalized subject to determine for the first time in his life to attack other people physically who unduly provoke him, with the serious intention of gravely harming or even killing them," Athens writes, is a "deeply emotion-laden resolution" (2003, 12–17; Rhodes 2000, 126). This second stage is one in which the subject imagines committing violence, considers the strategic and ethical questions embedded in the possibility, and tries on the identity of being a person who could choose to be violent.

The first steps from defiance or belligerency to action, Athens writes, are couched in provocation and precaution. "The brutalized subject resolves to . . . use serious violence—but with an important qualification: he resolves to use serious violence only if he is seriously provoked and only if he thinks he has a chance of prevailing" (Rhodes 2000, 126).

The first "mitigated violent resolution"—the decision to deliberately use serious violence—marks the end of the second stage and sets up the subject to begin "violent performances." This qualified resolution is the liminal threshold—a way of explaining to oneself the need to do what is necessary, while simultaneously holding on to the idea of oneself as a good person who is not innately violent. Given the subject's relative inexperience with violence, however, it can be difficult to gauge how much violence will be necessary, and the subject worries that he may not be equal to the task ahead. It is a moment of fear, anxiety, and stress.

Again, Isaac's, Joey's, Anaya's, and Jose's life stories align with defiance and belligerency. Each had to ask him- or herself hard questions about who they were: Could they do this? How would they do it? What would be the consequences? And who would they be once they had done it? In all four cases, the emotional earthquakes happening under the surface were accompanied by changes in affect and behaviors: they became unruly, resistant, angry, in a word belligerent, difficult, and defiant.

The responses of others around them as they became defiant—avoidance, criticism, punishment—tended to result in escalating resistance and a hardening resolution, because it was interpreted by Isaac, Joey, Anaya, and Jose as further proof that no one could change their situation except themselves. Teachers, for example, told them they needed to submit to authority and do as they were asked or told. When they resisted, the pressure to submit would be increased, and they would resist more. Isaac, Joey, Anaya, and Jose, though, were not intentionally defiant—they were not trying to be "bad kids." They were simply trying out their new way of protecting themselves from further trauma, interpreting the well-intentioned admonishments of teachers, parents, and others in authority to behave better as a form of coercion and as a recipe for further victimization. They were imagining resistance and fighting back and dealing with the stress of not knowing if they could commit violence or if they would be successful. They were trying on and exploring the meaning of a new, defiant identity that was based on their lived experience.

In the third stage of "violent performances," Athens writes, the subject acts on her or his resolution and builds confidence in his or her own violent performance, typically by repeating them. Athens makes clear that it takes more than a resolution to be violent, because actual violence is frightening and dehumanizing and entails the risk of losing. The subject who makes a first violent resolution wants to be sure that if and when he is called on to engage in violent acts, he will be able to do so and that there is some probability of an outcome other than "irretrievable loss and further subjugation." The stress is significant enough and the threshold meaningful enough that Isaac, Joey, Anaya, and Jose can each recall, months and years later, their first deliberate violent performance or decision to use sex as a form of dominance.

Failing to be violent when it seems necessary, or failing when violence is attempted, can have devastating consequences, as Anaya experienced when her sexual partners and other youth turned the tables on her. Newly pregnant, she found herself struggling to reconcile her experiments with violence and sex with the newly available social identity of "mother" and all that it entailed. It was not the outcome she had planned.

Another youth, Scott, was sixteen, a short, solidly built white guy who repped Eminem. He always had a backpack with him and in it the possessions that were his talismans: A notebook of rhymes and poems and paragraph-long stories. A gold chain. Food. One time, a knife. Another, a pellet gun. His size 8.5 Jordans finally fit—for his birthday, a bunch of people at Rec Night had collected money to replace the size 6.5s he had outgrown. Scott cut his hair just so—tight, with a fade. He chose his clothes carefully as well: designer, or label, fitting just right. And he was always clean.

Other than some of the volunteers from Providence College, Scott was often the only white person at the rec center. This was true in some of his classes at school and on his block. He tried to steer around the violence of the crews that lived near him. His family was as poor as a family can be without becoming homeless—and his poverty was an ongoing subject of ridicule from some of the rougher youth in his neighborhood.

Scott was always looking for a balance point: being tough and aggressive without actually fighting, appearing unafraid. He wanted a rep strong enough to earn respect, but didn't want to, or couldn't, cross too many lines to get it. He sometimes carried a knife or pellet gun for show, but I don't think he ever used either one. Humor was hard for him—using it to deflect aggression was a "soft" path requiring a self-confidence or self-deprecation that he never found. Scott became a rising junior in high school, in an industrial arts program, and wanted to go into construction. He wrote out raps and poems, his thoughts, and carried them with him everywhere. He told people he was a rapper. Every week for two years, on the way to pick up pizza for Rec Night, we renegotiated what he was going to pay me to buy my truck when he got his first real job.

One warm summer evening as Rec Night was ending, Scott was called out by a member of a neighborhood crew as a fake rapper—a "weak white wannabe." He found himself in a spontaneous rap battle with an audience in the dozens. He was crushed, buried in a torrent of wounding words. Humiliated. He squared up, began to walk away, and then tried again to spit some rhymes. He was buried, again, and the crowd laughed at him. This time he just walked away, trying to keep up his front.

Scott tried hard to protect himself. He had an older brother who coached him with stories, threats, encouragement, and skills. Scott opted instead for music, figuring it was an equalizer and that rap battles could substitute for physical battles. Some of the older, kinder youth in his neighborhood advised him to just make himself invisible. The bullying continued, however, in a strange dynamic: Scott would be bullied, physically or musically, and since he didn't back down, the aggressors would offer him a little respect and begin to ignore him. Scott couldn't leave it alone, though: he wanted acceptance, and he wanted real respect. He kept creating conditions for conflict, then failing to follow through. He wanted people to notice and value his sensitivity and creativity, but the only method he knew for getting any of this was to aggressively demand attention: He would start a fight, flash a weapon, try to organize younger kids into a crew. He would rap a new song in public, calling out other local musicians. And he would get beaten, again.

This window, when a youth is trying on their identity as a fighter, as someone who will fight back, is a moment of primary intervention. It is here that the process of violentization can be most effectively interrupted. The youth want to do the right thing, and the best way to engage them is by helping them process the ethical and identity conflicts they are experiencing. They need empathy, attention to their stuckness, and real alternatives that can help them solve their dilemma. The bullies and threats will still be in their homes, on their blocks, in their schools, and in their neighborhoods, and their material circumstances may prove intractable. What can they do?

The first violent act, which Athens calls the *violent personal revolt,* is typically directed at a "protagonist [who] is always a current subjugator of the subject or of a loved one of the subject," and the subject requires top levels of provocation: "actions that purposely and cruelly antagonize the subject to the point of tormenting him" or "actions that place the subject or someone about whom [he] cares in imminent danger." Since the subject "is seeking to thwart either his own or a loved one's violent subjugation, his act is one of outright defiance against a perceived evil oppressor. If the subject wins, oppression may cease, but he understands that if he loses, his oppression may become far harsher. Such a defeat could discourage the subject from continuing on the path of violentization, or could deepen and escalate his belligerence and confirm him/her in that path" (Rhodes 2000, 129–30).

Where Isaac, Joey, Anaya, and Jose made clear choices about violence and came up with strategies they could act on, Scott kept failing. He was not respected. He continued to be bullied for his poverty, but also because he would not accept his "place" as someone with low status. He could not act successfully on his violent resolution, and when he attempted to do so, he failed and his subjugation became, at least temporarily, worse. He wasn't welcome to join a local crew. This took its toll over time. Scott began drinking and smoking a lot of weed; it got so he was high much of the time, and he began selling weed to pay for his own. He was robbed several times. He became deeply depressed, dropped out of a school he had actually liked, and stopped attending Rec Night. A year later, I saw him on the street. He still carried his backpack. He was destitute, panhandling in front of a local pizza place. He said he was sleeping on his grandmother's couch. He talked about being a rapper. He said he was thinking about getting and carrying a gun. While Scott had failed in his "violent personal revolts" and seemed to be losing ground, he continued to believe that carrying out a successful violent act was the way to change his life.

Athens also argues that "a notable violent performance will not *by itself* have any lasting or significant impact on the subject. For lasting impact the subject needs to comprehend the full significance of his success." The meaning of the violent act needs to be determined and shared socially, reinforced as not only effective but as the right thing to do. "The job of impressing the subject with the full significance of his successful violent action," Athens writes, "is gladly performed by other people who, for whatever reason, always seem to take a perverse interest and pleasure in violence—all the more so when they know the offender or victim." Within a relatively short period of time, the subject develops a reputation as "serious," "dangerous," or "crazy," and their reputation becomes generally known. This is where Anaya's strategy fell apart, as the people around her changed the meaning, and so the power, of what she was doing.

Isaac completed this third stage of violent performance as he was transitioning from elementary to middle school. He continued to fight with his fists and with weapons. He learned early on that in conflict situations, the person who went on the offensive first and escalated the conflict most rapidly—"from zero to a hundred in no time"—gained a useful edge. He learned that fighting skills mattered and sought out older, more experienced people who could coach him in boxing and wrestling. He used his ability and intelligence to organize a crew and claim a geographic turf as "theirs."

In another example, a group of ten or so neighborhood boys in their early teens began forming a street crew, led by a couple of boys who were quite taken with their growing reputation as fighters. They would call out other youth and go "heads-up" with one-on-one fights or start fights with other crews. Someone affiliated with the crew would video the fight, and it would be posted on social media soon after, accelerating the pace by which the fighters became notorious and thought of themselves as "serious." Occasionally, one of them would pose with a weapon or compose a rap about the outcome of the fight—a kind of performative violence intended to publicly project and establish their new identity. And then they would come to Rec Night, paradoxically thinking of themselves as full, supportive members of the safe space.

Joey told me his story of the rock because it was his first deliberate violent performance. He had been in scuffles with other kids, and generally presented himself as unafraid and tough, but until this moment he did not think of himself as a person capable of violence. When he hit the man harassing his mother with a rock and dropped by Rec Night to talk about it, he was asking himself, and me, if he was in fact someone who did this kind of thing, if he was violent. He was proud and shaken, pleased and ashamed, ready to embrace this new "adult" self, and unsure he wanted to or could sustain it. How I and others he trusted responded would have a significant impact on how he interpreted what he had done. We talked about the likelihood that his violence would prove successful: end the harassment and not lead to retaliation. Joey thought out loud about his options. The safest path, to him, lay in assuming that the dude would come back and hunt him down. The logic was simple: "Otherwise everybody will know he's a punk." He said he would have to be ready—maybe have a bigger rock, he said, laughing. Really, though, he thought he would have to carry a knife or be with some friends who would back him up. He looked over at his adolescent friends, weighing them in his mind. On the other hand, as far as retaliation went, Joey said that the man had been beaten by someone half his size and he thought that retaliating against a smaller, younger enemy would backfire and make this man a punk even if he won: he had already lost so much reputation that there was no way he could win. Still, it would be good to be prepared.

Did he want to be someone known for this kind of violence? This question was complicated by Joey's rejection of the domestic violence he had witnessed before his father left: he never wanted to be "that" person. What did his mother think of what he'd done to the dude? Could he think of ways to de-escalate the situation while staying safe and caring for his mother?

In the final stage of violentization, which Athens calls *virulency,* the subject discovers the advantage of being "famous," even if the fame is notorious. He becomes, says Athens, "overly impressed with his violent performances and ultimately with himself in general. . . . Filled with feelings of exultancy, he concludes that since he performed this violent feat, there is no reason why he cannot perform even more impressive violent feats in the future. The subject much too hastily draws the conclusion that he is now invincible. Most people will not disabuse him of his arrogance, for to them he is 'dangerous.' Thus, he is permitted to continue in his 'vainglorification'" (Rhodes 2000, 133).

It is at this stage that the subject "now firmly resolves to attack people physically with the serious intention of gravely harming or even killing them for the slightest or no provocation whatsoever. . . . He has suddenly been emboldened and made venomous at the same time. . . . The subject is ready to attack people physically with the serious intention of gravely harming or killing them with minimal or less than minimal provocation on their part." It is only at this point, Athens argues, that "he is ready to become an ultraviolent criminal" (ibid.).

In the first months that he attended Rec Night, it was as though Isaac was surrounded by a magnetic force field. He would walk into a crowded gym, and the crowd would part ahead of him as he juked along. Everyone knew him, gave him respect, wanted to be liked by him. He got your back. He was for real. He was serious. And Tou, as streetworker and organizer of Rec Night, worried a lot about him: Isaac was getting so known that he was being called out by people who wanted to make their reputation or who felt their reputation was being threatened. He was so good-looking and charismatic that girls liked him a lot—and he was having a lot of beefs because of this. He was too smart for his own good—always playing, always hustling some angle: Tou believed he would inevitably piss off the wrong people. In fact, as Tou taught me, this is the profile of a youth gang member most at risk of being attacked and badly hurt or killed: smart, fearless, good-looking, athletic, physical, charismatic, and someone who has developed an internal identity and public reputation based on a capacity for deliberate physical violence against other people.

As Isaac got older, he began to recognize the costs of his notoriety, and it would periodically send him spiraling into despair and depression. He was perpetually a target. The stress was exhausting. He got concussions that resulted in short-term memory loss and hand tremors that took months to clear up; he was afraid this would become permanent "next time." He struggled with the likelihood that his life as it was would be his life forever. He wanted to read, travel, go back to school, get a meaningful job, have a family he could love and that would love him. All of this seemed out of reach. In other words, Isaac hovered somewhere between violent performance and virulency. I believe he came to live a divided life: an interior self, shared very rarely, that differed profoundly from his notorious identity as a gang member and leader.

As we talked about his being shot in the arm, I asked Isaac if the shooters who had hit him and his friend would continue to look for them. He paused. "No. They were after the other guys and didn't know who they were shooting. But they are lucky I'm out of that life. I won't go after them. But you know they better not come after me again." Not retaliating was a major concession on Isaac's part—and a vulnerable, complex expression of ethics and identity as he continued to weigh the place of violence in his life.

Unlike Isaac, who had chosen an identity based on his capacity for violence, Joey chose an intermediate path. He and his friends agreed to be a "crew" and look out for one another. Joey and his friends did not want to be violent, though, and resolved that they would only fight under certain conditions. Joey's friends respected what he had done, and he liked his new reputation. On the other hand, he was afraid that he would lose what little support he had from caring adults, and he had adults he respected telling him that he could choose other paths. He continued to test what William

James called the "cash value" of his thinking, constantly clarifying the amount of provocation he would require to become violent and describing the necessary conditions that would allow him to be nonviolent. His new self-identity had to allow him to take care of the people he cared about, the adults had to do their part and be real with him about his situation, and he needed support in order to heal from the effects of the traumas he had been and was experiencing. In other words, Joey hovered on the precipice between socially acceptable and socially unacceptable violence. The older he got, the narrower the ledge would become and the longer the fall would be if or when he came to the attention of the police.

My best guess is that Joey, like the great majority of youth gang members I came to know, will remain someone who only chooses violence under what he sees as severe provocation. His biggest risk is that he will be obligated to back up his friends when they have conflicts. The result will be that he fights more, not less; that the fighting will become more dangerous as he gets older; and that the outside world will care less and less for the finer distinctions informing his violent choices. Once he is through puberty, he will be viewed by the representatives of civil institutions as violent, his violence will be interpreted as criminal, and he will be labeled by civil society as fully "other."

Joey wants a life that is pretty normal by mainstream standards, though: to graduate high school, develop a marketable skill or knowledge base that will earn him a living, find a girlfriend he can fall in love with, remain close with his family and friends, own a car and maybe buy a house. He is smart enough to mostly keep off the surveillance radar of schools and police and is open to support. With opportunities, access to an expanded network of positive adults, and some luck, he will make it to his early twenties and leave the street behind. These are the same things Anaya wants.

There is another other youth I think of when I weigh the accuracy and utility of Athens's description of violentization as it applies to youth gang members. I met Carlos when he was eleven years old. He loved the Red Sox, the Patriots, the Celtics. Even the Boston Bruins.

These were the teams of his favorite uncle, and Carlos had promised him that they would be his teams, too. Carlos is Dominican American. His uncle is well over six feet tall, tattooed, and a slab of muscle. Everyone told Carlos his uncle looks like his dad, whom Carlos doesn't remember, and that Carlos looks like both of them. Carlos has small scars on each cheekbone and small scars on the corners of his forehead and chin. He has a natural swagger to his walk, a way of collecting himself before he sets off. People talk to him, and he cocks his ear to them and then turns and makes direct eye contact. There is no backdown in him at all, and he seems, almost always, completely self-possessed.

When a stray paintball splashed my white truck with black paint outside the rec center, Carlos was horrified and waited for me to retaliate. Instead, we got a bucket of water, and he washed the paint off the truck in the parking lot of the rec center. Carlos wouldn't let me do the work, doing it himself with his crew. It was a generous gesture of respect: I was one of his people, and he was worried that others might misinterpret my nonretaliation as weakness. At twelve years old, he was using his status to define mine, even as he tried to understand my perspective.

A time came when Carlos spent every day chilling on his front steps or on a picnic table outside the rec center in the afternoons and evenings. He had been suspended from school for two weeks and kicked out of the rec center; he was allowed in the rec center only for our program. Carlos didn't really understand his punishment, although he accepted it. He did swear at the director of the rec center, but the director had disrespected him in front of everyone. He said the teacher kicked him out, and it didn't make sense to him. Yes, he hit another student in class with a closed fist, but he was only doing what needed to be done—"dusting up" a kid who was in his face, disrespecting him in the hallways, and then hiding behind the teacher. Carlos was doing what he had been taught to do. He said the teacher doesn't seem to understand that he had no choice and meant no disrespect to her. What he does know, though, is that he is not wanted there, in the school, or at the rec center. Carlos, in the sixth grade, is already looking forward to being done with school and knows he is choosing a different path.

Late one evening outside the rec center, Carlos launches himself at Craig, a young man in his late teens who has been teasing Carlos, pressing him. The teasing has crossed some line into the unacceptable. Craig, the leader of a neighborhood crew, outweighs Carlos by a hundred pounds. Craig lifts Carlos off the ground and holds him at arm's length, upside down. Craig is playful, laughing. Tears of anger and shame are bright in Carlos's eyes, and he launches a kick at Craig's face, bites his hand so hard he is nearly dropped. Craig sets Carlos down and swears at him, shaking his hand. He looks at Carlos and says, "Whoa, little fucker, you got heart. My bad." He laughs.

Carlos hears only the roaring of anger and shame in his ears. Half an hour later, he is still trembling and breathing deep.

At the age of twelve, Carlos had already been through much of the process of violentization. He had learned to fight rather than allow himself or his friends to be bullied. He acted, and I believe was, unafraid, no matter the threat posed by his adversary. He was constantly coached by the most stable adult in his life, a person who loved him and was teaching him how to be an adult. He was no longer afraid of consequences from conventional institutions and their representatives. Getting suspended or expelled was met with sadness and a shrug. He could imagine how the teacher in his classroom saw the world, he understood her expectations—but he believed she was naive, "not from here," did not understand the reality in which he lived. Carlos wasn't concerned about finishing school, though he was smart, curious, articulate, and charismatic. Carlos thought he would likely follow in his uncle's footsteps. Carlos was not afraid to start a fight, but, more important, he did not see anything questionable about hitting a peer in the head with a chair or desk during the fight. His quizzical look when I asked him about this said it all: Why wouldn't you use what's available to win?

When I think about Carlos, whom I liked and continue to like a lot, I wonder about his future: he is clearly through the first three stages of violentization at a very young age. I wonder if he will embark on the final stage—internalizing a worldview and sense of identity defined by violence. Will his ability to turn his violence on and off—to be as sweet, kind, and insightful as he is occasionally violent—diminish over time and as he experiences cumulative traumas? Or will he weigh his situation at some critical point and decide—as Jose has done—to move in a less violent or nonviolent direction?

VIOLENTIZATION, PART 2: TRAUMA, COMMUNITY, AND SOCIAL CONTEXT

A danger in telling stories like those of Isaac's, Joey's, Anaya's, Jose's, Scott's, and Carlos's, and focusing on violentization as an individual experience, is that doing so masks or minimizes the amplifying effects of the larger social systems inside of which youth like Isaac, Joey, Anaya, Jose, Scott, and Carlos live. I have come to believe that there is nothing "wrong" with youth like them, even as I want to help them "undo" and heal from their experiences of violentization and violence. They are making choices that are understandable, reasonable, and often effective within a specific social and cultural context, but one of the biggest challenges the youth face as they get older is that many of the ways they have learned to think and act in this specific context are maladaptive in other, civil society, contexts. As psychiatrist Bessel Van Der Kolk concludes, "For abused children, the whole world is filled with triggers. . . . [I]n this light the bizarre behavior of the kids . . . made perfect sense" (2014, 108).

We assumed that most, if not all, of the youth who showed up at Rec Night had experienced a significant amount of violence, were often aggressive, and were somewhere in the process of violentization. We also assumed that external behavior could be different from internal meaning, especially in youth and young adults who are still experimenting their way into their adult identities. That is to say, while many of the youth in our program were victims of and perpetrators of serious violence, it was important to get an accurate read on how this was affecting them and shaping their current reality. Often, they were experimenting with violence, using violence to protect themselves, or were thinking about whether they would use violence under certain conditions. However defiant or aggressive their actions, they generally did not see themselves as being violent or disrespectful or oppositional, and they welcomed compassionate and empathetic responses, attention to their feelings, and serious discussion about the choices they were considering.

It is important to try to understand the personal, social, and cultural context in which the choice of violence makes sense and the ways in which that context contributes to the "production" or "social construction" of youth gangs and the violence with which they are associated. It is important to understand something of how personal trauma combines with social institutions and systems to shape the experience of violentization that predictably "produces" youth gangs. Thinking about violence in this complex, multilayered way allows us to begin to address the question of how and why some individuals become violent while others in seemingly similar social situations do not, it helps us recognize the divergent ways in which violence is interpreted across race and class, and it helps us to understand how race and class can combine with individual experience to produce youth gangs.

I'd like to open this argument with two additional stories, stories that suggest something of the range of ways youth experience, process, and respond to violence and trauma and how social context steers that response. The first is the story of William, a gang member shot and killed in 2013, and his brother Andre. The second is a story of Sam, a junior in a local gang who was left adrift by a friend's suicide.

WILLIAM AND ANDRE

In April 2013 I went to the visitation—wake—for William. He died of a gunshot wound to the head, at an intersection in South Providence, steps from two well-known community-serving organizations. He was twenty years old. I knew William a bit, from his irregular participation in Rec Night and occasional interactions spread over a four- or five-year period.

A *Providence Journal* article about William's death, published two days after his murder, notes that he was "troubled"; that he had been shot at, stabbed, and arrested on several charges in his short life; that he was a member of a local gang. The oddest sentence in the article, the third sentence in, says, "The center had closed early that evening, due to city budget constraints, so it was merely happenstance that none of the children who usually visit ended up witnessing the shooting."

I wish I knew how to parse this sentence: Is it sympathetic? Is it utterly cynical? Is it defining a communal standard of ethics? Is it a way of saying that the real victims when a gang member is shot and killed are the children who are endangered or witness it? If kids from the community center had witnessed William's death, should we blame William for having the nerve to get shot in front of them? Whatever else, it is a dehumanizing sentence without compassion and a sentence reflecting numbness. And it is representative, in my experience, of how youth like William are seen, and not seen, by the broader public. Why?

William was a courageous young man. He expressed his courage in fearlessness, recklessness with his physical well-being, and a near-absolute resistance to any form of what he perceived as disrespect. I'd like to know if it is an overstatement to say that one of the main reasons he was killed was because of his courage. And I'd like to know when and why and how he began to decide that this form of courage was the form for him. I'd like to know what this hard form contained—what it held in and hid from sight. What was its value to William, and what did he intend that his courage would protect him from? I don't believe he intended it to keep him safe—his goal was not security. I think he intended that his courage, expressed outwardly as a potential capacity for wild violence, would protect him from feeling some particular thing, that it was a response to some kind of pain. I'd like to know what that pain was.

A lot of people came to William's wake. He was loved by many people, and it's clear that his death traumatized many of them—family, friends, the crew he ran with. His brother Andre was not allowed to attend. I know Andre much better than I knew William. William's death found Andre finishing a six-month sentence at the

Adult Correctional Institution. According to a colleague helping to support Andre, the ACI indicated that they might let him out to attend the wake but said no at close to the last minute, citing concerns over the gang involvement of both brothers and the potential danger to the accompanying officer and the guests.

During the wake, I tried to imagine what Andre was feeling. To be more precise, I wondered if and how I could help carry part of the load I imagined he was carrying. Andre and William were arrested together in December 2012 on a robbery and gun charge. Andre took the gun charge, William was put on probation, and Andre got six months. As Andre was finding out about his brother's death, or just after he found out on the grapevine, he was put into segregation—solitary confinement. A volunteer with the Institute for the Study and Practice of Nonviolence, a former nun with long experience working in prisons, visited Andre that night and told him what had happened. An ISPN staff member visited Andre the next day. Without naming Andre, the staff member posted on his Facebook page shortly afterward:

> (Not a post for "likes" but about "a life") . . . today I went to console a young man who received dreadful news this last night . . . with tattoos blooming from his orange jumper, through the metal links that held his hands in forced prayer . . . his nose stuffed, veins on neck and hands throbbing from sobbing . . . words cannot explain . . . with both palms up, to show nothing up my sleeves, I asked the guard if could touch him. "See" . . . I gave him a hug, like I do my son; his cheek on my shoulder holding the back of his head with my hands, he yelped . . . a gush of purro dolor . . . and shook like a tree/ briefly/falling/leaves/to the ground.

SAM

In mid-March 2009 I attended the wake of Racha, a Laotian American man in his early twenties who had committed suicide several days earlier. The circumstances remain unclear, but he had taken his life, with a gun, during a tense interaction with two other people, one of them his girlfriend. I was sitting in Russell Boyle and Sons Funeral

Home, a place of historic significance in the Smith Hill neighbor-hood, one of a handful of white mourners in a crowd of 250 people. Sam, a sixteen-year-old man-boy I had gotten to know a bit, a junior in one of the local gangs, came and sat next to me. He leaned toward me, without making eye contact, and said quietly, "Racha was one of my heroes. He finished high school. He was working and going to college. He always had a smile for everyone. If he couldn't make it, how will I make it?" His despair opened me to a deep sense of loss.

I heard variations of this same question from other youth at the wake, and I could feel it in the eyes and comments of the adults who knew and cared for them: an ill-concealed mix of sorrow, despair, fear, and anger. I heard an important variation on Sam's question from several of ISPN's streetworkers—ex–gang members turned youth workers who knew this group of youth—who understood that the love and support they offered these young people were insuffi-cient to save them. The adults and streetworkers felt that young peo-ple like Racha and Sam were victims not only of their own demons but also of a society that had made them outcasts. Words and body language would tell two different stories: "That's just how it is here," one streetworker told me at the wake. Saying this, he broke eye con-tact, slumped his shoulders, adjusted his baseball cap, and walked away as though he had an errand to complete. There was no errand, and he walked through the crowd, saying hello here and there, but remaining, for the next hour, alone. This marked the end of talking openly about Racha's death. It was how things were, and externally everyone affected made an effort to move on.

I heard and believed the truth that was being communicated about the social construction of Racha's suicide. I could see, too, that Racha's death was another violent trauma to people who were already reeling—the youth of Sam's gang and their friends, but also the larger Laotian immigrant community and the Smith Hill neigh-borhood as a whole. The word spoken most often to summarize the feeling this trauma generated was "shame." I would say, "So sorry for your loss," and people would respond, "Yes, it's a shame." Shame that this promising life had ended in violence, shame that the adults failed the youth so regularly, shame that deep feelings were being repressed, shame as this event exposed to public scrutiny the struggles of a very private immigrant community. I heard over and over, with a growing awareness of the layers and paradoxes it contained, that Racha's death was "a shame."

I began to think of Racha's death as an indirect articulation of a much deeper, collective trauma, with roots in the experiences the parents and grandparents of this community had tried to escape in leaving war-torn Laos and Thai refugee camps, arriving in Smith Hill as refugees in the 1980s and 1990s.

VIOLENCE AND COMMUNITY

While Athens helps us to describe the violentization many of the youth at Rec Night were experiencing, and the role that traumatic experiences have in that process, a second major influence on our method was to consider the impact of individual and collective trauma and to think about particular experiences of trauma, the ways it was responded to, and the resulting patterns that shaped social interactions. The stories of William, Andre, and Sam describe some of this: trauma expressed as loss, isolation, guilt, shame, hopelessness, depression, and anger.

A multidisciplinary literature in psychiatry, psychology, social work, and youth development (Brohl 1996; Follette et al. 2014; Hardy and Laszloffy 2005; Monahan 1993; Perry and Szalavitz 2006; Tough 2012; Van Der Kolk 2014) describes a strong correlation between experiencing violent trauma and future violent behavior, to the point that it is captured in a truism: "Hurt people hurt others." As Paul Tough points out, the correlation between "adverse childhood experiences and negative adult outcomes" is linear and powerful (2012, 9–10).

Most often, this violent behavior is described as "reactive," or acting out, a spontaneous product of inner turmoil, something like a volcano erupting. Psychiatrist Bessel Van Der Kolk observes, "Long after a traumatic experience is over, it may be reactivated at the slightest hint of danger and mobilize disturbed brain circuits and secrete massive amounts of stress hormones. This precipitates unpleasant emotions, intense physical sensations, and impulsive and aggressive actions" (2014, 2). Poverty, racism, violence in the home, violence in the street or at school can all raise stress levels and combine to increase the intensity of traumatic experience, and for many street-involved youth their traumatic context is ongoing, even as their resistant behavior is punished and criminalized (Rios 2011a). As often as not, punishment and criminalization add to stress and become additional traumatic experiences, doing little or nothing to contribute to positive change.

While aggressive, violent behavior can theoretically be a spontaneous physical reaction to stress and trauma, most of the youth I have known who were involved in street and gang violence recognized, as Athens suggests they might, that they were choosing violence as a medium for engaging with the world around them. It wasn't reactive in the sense that it happened unconsciously but an "adaptation to circumstances" that made violence seem like the best path forward. They didn't necessarily like it, but it made sense to them because of the way they understood their lives and social context. They had given themselves permission to be violent when circumstances required it.

In other words, we can locate most of what seems to be violent, aggressive, and antisocial behavior as deliberate, meaningful choices that the actor has made, usually for what seem to her or him to be good reasons. Sometimes this violence is defensive. Sometimes it is provocative or calculated.

Most often, any and all of these violent choices grow out of a history of trauma and are intended to prevent further trauma and to get "respect": a recognition that the youth is expressing his dignity and power to the very authorities that contribute to his marginalization. The violent acts of youth are expressions of an emerging or held belief that violent force can be used to restore order and control, prevent further pain, and fulfill what they most desire. Failing to achieve these goals—an almost inevitable certainty as authorities exert their control up to and including criminalization and incarceration—is seen not as evidence that the analysis is wrong but as evidence that the threat is more powerful than was imagined and will require even greater resistance and violence if it is to be beaten. As Kenneth Hardy and Tracey Laszloffy point out, "The level of violence that exists within communities contributes to an atmosphere of fear and insecurity for young people. [They] learn that the world is not a safe place and the sense of threat makes them suspicious, untrusting, and prone to violence as a means of self-protection. . . . We have spoken to hundreds of young people who consistently report that they join gangs or carry guns not because they revel in violence, but as a form of protection" (2005, 17).

Very few individuals in our program, indeed few individuals involved in youth gang violence of the type found in Providence, ever become defined primarily by their capacity for violence, becoming what Athens calls "malignant." For nearly all of the youth I know, violence is a last resort, and choosing it was a damaging and difficult response to trauma. What they wanted was respect, security, and control: an environment that allowed them to de-stress and breathe and be themselves. They are aware of the paradox described by social movements scholar Pamela Oliver: resistance ends up reinforcing marginalization (cited in Rios 2011a, 123). Given better options, they would choose them, but healing from trauma, unlearning violence, and trusting in nonviolent alternatives take time, energy, and hope that they do not have.

My starting point for reflecting on the experience of trauma was the groundbreaking work of psychiatrist Jonathan Shay (1995) in the field of post-traumatic stress disorder. Shay's work on PTSD concentrates on the experiences of soldiers at war and the ways that trauma can cause psychological harm that is then manifest in somatic symptoms such as anger, irritability, anxiety, depression, trouble sleeping, trouble concentrating, and difficulty trusting or forming meaningful relationships with others. Dean Esserman, the police chief in Providence from 2001 to 2010 and a board member at ISPN, used to joke without humor that "nearly all the gang-involved youth in Providence have PTSD, only there's no P." Therapists today have a term for this: persistent traumatic stress.

Symptoms of PTSD (post- and persistent) were epidemic among the youth at Rec Night.

Shay argues that experiencing violence in itself rarely results in chronic PTSD. The additional necessary factor, he suggests, is that the trauma happens in a such a way that it violates the person's sense "of what is right." So, being affected by a violent event combined with a sense of ethical violation or betrayal—often by a leader or commanding officer or being forced to do something that violates core values and then act as if it is okay—is likely to result in PTSD or some of its symptoms. This is why it matters so much that youth who join gangs have most often reached the conclusion that the adults and civil institutions that should be caring for them are incapable of doing so: it is a petri dish for an ethical violation or betrayal.

The surest way back from PTSD, Shay argues convincingly, is "the communalization of grief," a process for rebuilding a shared ethical framework that helps the participants make sense of their lives. Communalizing grief means sharing your story of trauma with others, often beginning with a single person, who, instead of rejecting you as less than human, embraces you as a person struggling to be more fully human. The people listening respond with compassion. So trauma survivors often begin by telling their stories to other survivors, trusting that they will be heard honestly and with compassion. Expanding the circle is fraught and difficult. There is no one formula for it, and the path of every person healing from trauma is different from that of every other. Gang members, like soldiers, are often both perpetrator and victim. In addition, they are pariahs—outcasts—and often without people to talk to other than their immediate circle, people who are often implicated in the trauma itself. How then do we create space in which violentization can be undone, grief can be communalized, and hope becomes relevant?

VIOLENCE AND SOCIAL CONTEXT

Many analyses of street and gang violence suggest there is something inherent to experiences of poverty and racism that produce violence. They suggest this by correlating violence with particular social indicators associated with the perpetrators, and the correlation to poverty and racism is strong and consistent. These analyses rely on databases such as the FBI's Uniform Crime Reports (2012) or that of the Bureau of Justice Statistics, which find that "persons living in poor households at or below the Federal Poverty Line (39.8 percent) had more than double the rate of violent victimization as persons in high-income households (16.2 percent)" (2016). Violence—as actors and as victims—increases as poverty increases, and this correlation is often presented as evidence of a causal relationship, avoiding the confounding evidence that 60 percent of people in low-income households are not victims of violence, while 16 percent of people in wealthier households are victims.

A similar pattern emerges correlating violence and race: the FBI's 2012 Uniform Crime Report, for example, reported 402,470 arrests for violent crimes nationally. Whites, who make up 74 percent of the U.S. population, were arrested for 58 percent of the violent crimes, Asian Americans, roughly 5 percent of the population, for 1.4 percent. Blacks, who make up 14 percent of the population, accounted for 38 percent of the arrests (FBI 2012; U.S. Census Bureau 2016).

It is, of course, the case that poverty correlates with race in the United States (U.S. Census Bureau 2013). Twenty-six percent of African American citizens live at or below the poverty line and only 11 percent of whites. Among Hispanic residents, poverty varies by ethnicity, from a low of 16 percent for Cuban Americans to a high of 26 percent for Dominican Americans. Explanatory models vary, but the correlation of race and economic status is often seen as prima facie evidence of historical and continuing racism.

A common reading of all this data is that race and economic status have predictive value for violence: poor persons of color are more likely to be violent than their white counterparts and to be victims of violence. Just how deeply embedded this perspective is, as Michelle Alexander (2010) and others (Bobo and Thompson 2010; Hartney and Vuong 2009; Liberman and Fontaine 2015; Rosich 2007) point out, is evident in the disproportionate surveillance, policing, and incarceration of poor people of color, especially African Americans.

Based on my observations and experiences over twenty-five years working with high-risk youth in an economically poor, majority-minority community, I believe analyses correlating poverty and racism with violence profoundly misinterpret the data. My perspective begins by recognizing that poverty and racism are forms of structural violence and that experiencing them, especially in concert, has a profound influence on the ways individual people process other experiences of direct violence. In other words, poverty and racism do not produce violence but are a context in which the meaning of violence is constructed in powerful and consequential ways.

Living with poverty and racism, for example, creates ongoing dilemmas of identity and ethics that can be, over time, traumatic in themselves. How do you counter the structural violence of racism and poverty? How do you prevent it from hurting people you care about? How do you, as a parent, prepare your child for their first experience of public humiliation based on this aspect of their identity? How do you balance the benefits of cooperating with the institutions responsible for structural violence with the cost of knowing that collaboration perpetuates those institutions? Experiencing poverty and racism is much like experiencing bullying that has no end in sight. Shayla Reese Griffin, for example, sympathetically notes how black high school–aged youth come to experiment with and internalize "racial performance" (2015, 50). She observes that "otherwise well-off black students [at the school she studied] couldn't explain why they were fighting so much. . . . [This was] particularly disturbing because it suggests some middle-class, upwardly mobile black youth were struggling with identity to such a degree that they adopted behaviors that would be appalling to their parents, teachers and even their peers. They were engaging in and eagerly witnessing physical violence not because this behavior was sanctioned in their homes, but because being violent was at the core of their notion of what it was to be black" (79). Griffin concludes, after careful analysis, that this behavior is "not a harmless reflection of popular culture, but rather evidence of internalized racism" (80). Worse, she concludes that many educational institutions, such as this high-performing high school, unwittingly support this process of internalization. For a black student, attending this school is an ongoing, internal experience of structural violence.

While racism and poverty are forms of structural violence, they are not directly linked to violent individual behavior. When someone affected by poverty and racism also experiences direct violence—bullying, say—they are more likely to be traumatized, begin to undergo a process of violentization, and conclude that the world is a violent place and surviving will require developing a capacity for violence. The boundary between direct and structural violence blurs and thins. The only way to survive, physically, emotionally, and spiritually, is to construct an identity defined by resistance to the persons and institutions that are causing harm. Peace requires violence.

Victor Rios (2011a, 120) notes that this kind of resistance often becomes self-defeating, leading, for example, to suspensions and the misdiagnoses of learning and behavioral issues in schools. It is "the result of having tried and tried and being excluded nonetheless." A paradox of identity and social ethics emerges: resistance ends up reinforcing marginalization. "In other words," writes Philippe Bourgois, "although street culture emerges out of a personal search for dignity and a rejection of racism and subjugation, it ultimately becomes an active agent in personal degradation and community ruin" (1995, 9).

The sensible, predictable conclusion reached by youth experiencing structural and direct violence, and the attendant behaviors or resistance that emerge from this, is then interpreted by dominant social institutions as evidence that poor people, and especially poor people of color, are more likely to commit acts of violence—justifying ever-harsher institutional efforts to police and contain the violence. The only predictable outcomes of these renewed efforts are more poverty and racism and greater suffering, even as the dominant institutions assume they are doing the right thing under the circumstances.

A better way forward begins with understanding gang- and street-involved youth as young people doing the best they can in a context of persistent violent trauma. If we as a society don't want the violence of youth gangs, then we have to respond to the youth involved with compassion, help them heal, and support the emergence of nonviolent worldviews, especially in the larger public culture, that allow individuals fuller private and public lives. Simultaneously, we need to revise the values and practices on which the social institutions shaping the lives of the youth are based, so that they, too, are based on the nonviolent principles and practices of compassion, inclusion in civil society, and social equity. In short, we have to help individual youth heal, dismantle racism, and build a more equitable economy.

The next two chapters describe a way of working with youth entangled in street and gang violence, the potential (and challenges) of nonviolence as an alternative frame of reference, and some initial steps that can be taken in the longer process of cultural and social change.

CHAPTER FOUR

YOUTH POSITIVE

A PRACTICAL THEORY FOR ENGAGING AND
SUPPORTING GANG- AND STREET-INVOLVED YOUTH

These neighborhoods with gang problems don't have a lot of assets.
But there is a school, a park and a rec center. Those are public assets.
Let's use those to create social connections that replace gangs.

—Jeff Carr, director of gang reduction
and youth development in Los Angeles

This chapter focuses on working directly with youth who are involved in gang and street violence and describes the values and practices that emerged as the foundation for what we at Rec Night came to call "youth positive": safe space, compassion, contact, consistency, and community. The immediate goals of a "youth positive" approach are increasing the resilience of vulnerable youth, encouraging them as they pursue positive change, and reintegrating them into a broader, supportive community.

YOUTH ARE NOT THE PROBLEM: RESILIENCE AND SAFE SPACES

According to the International Resilience Project, "In the context of exposure to significant adversity, resilience is both the capacity of individuals to navigate their way to the psychological, social, cultural, and physical resources that sustain their well-being, and their capacity individually and collectively to negotiate for these resources to be provided in culturally meaningful ways" (Grotburg 1995). It is an understatement to observe that gang- and street-involved youth are facing adversity.

As Ann Masters notes, "Recent studies continue to corroborate the importance of a relatively small set of global factors associated with resilience. These include connections to competent, caring adults in the family and community, cognitive and self-regulation skills, positive views of self, and motivation to be effective in the environment" (Brooks and Goldstein 2003, x). The core idea of Rec Night and youth positive is built on this basic observation: giving youth who are stressed by ongoing trauma access to positive adults in a consistent, safe space is a simple, low-cost method for helping them begin to "overcome the damaging effects of adversity."

The goal is not saving, fixing, or changing the youth but trusting that they are "good enough as they are" and giving them access to an environment that affirms them as community members and values their gifts, talents, and interests. Over time, their experience of this kind of alternative space can disrupt a worldview based on the belief that the world is a violent place, in which a capacity for violence is necessary. This disruption, in turn, can open into a recognition that other, more life-affirming, worldviews and choices are possible.

Nonviolence, discussed at length in the following chapter, informs this safe space and acts as one powerful alternative to violence for engaging the world: it assumes that conflict is ongoing (incorporating a hard-won truth from the "old" worldview) and that personal and collective power can be organized to transform potentially destructive conflict into constructive energy (anchoring the emergence of a "new" worldview). In practice, this means that the alternative safe space must practice nonviolence in ways that make sense in the lived experiences of the youth.

Thinking about resilience in this way and having it as a goal for youth focuses attention on relationships, consistency, and safe space. This means meeting the youth on their terms, in their contexts, and "getting" how they perceive the world around them. Youth and community violence "cannot be solved from afar," writes Geoffrey Canada. "There is no way that government or social scientists, or philanthropy can solve this problem with a media campaign or operating from a safe distance. There is no safe way to deal with the violence that our children face. The only way we are going to make a difference is by placing well-trained and caring adults in the middle of what can only be called a free-fire zone in our poorest communities. Adults standing side by side with the children in the war zones of America is the only way to turn this thing around" (2010, 109). Rec Night operated in a space recognized and valued by the youth as safe. For the hours we ran the program, it was "their" space, on their terms, with only one rule: you can do anything except what hurts you or others around you. It was a space for adults to stand side by side with gang- and street-involved youth.

Youth positive's focus on relationships and safe space as keys to resilience is grounded in the basic insight that gang-involved youth have been profoundly affected and shaped by traumatic events they have experienced as victims and as perpetrators of violence. Bullying, domestic violence, street violence, racism, neglect, economic insecurity, expulsion from mainstream institutions such as schools, and social marginalization are common themes in the personal narratives of youth on the streets. Once they are labeled as gang members and as violent, they become cultural metaphors more than human persons, their options narrow significantly, and they are criminalized, surveilled, contained, and incarcerated. Youth positive, to adapt Paulo Freire's term, "rehumanizes" the youth, helping them "become persons for themselves." It does this not by changing the youth but by recognizing them as human persons and not cultural metaphors. The big shift called for by youth positive is in the perspective of adults around the youth: seeing the youth as fully human persons doing the best they can and what they believe makes sense given their experience.

This shift in perspective is the bridge between supporting individual youth and working toward changing the circumstances that shape their lives. Institutions express social values, and so the values on which institutions are built matter. As I argued in the first chapters of this book, seeing gang- and street-involved youth as fully human represents a huge shift in mainstream social values. For programs working with such youth, it leads to institutionalizing the companion values of compassion, contact, consistency, and community described below. These add up to a way of seeing youth more often labeled as dangerous, threatening, and "other" based on their strengths and potential rather than on their deficits and limitations, without denying the impact of what they are experiencing on a daily basis. This perspective doesn't excuse violence because it is a product of circumstances, and it does not see the youth as people who are "less than" and need fixing. It does argue that, with very rare exceptions, youth enmeshed in violence would prefer to live without it; that the youth want to thrive, as we all do; and that they need support, time, and space to heal and start a process of positive, life-affirming change. As I learned in the early 1980s from my mentor Jim Kielsmeier and his National Youth Leadership Council, "Youth are not a problem; they are the resource."

COMPASSION: "YOU FEEL ME?"

A healing process has to begin for people traumatized by violence before other positive changes in life or social circumstances can begin to take place. "Healing" is in itself a wildly complicated and only loosely defined objective. It can be approached as making peace with the past, healing a physical or emotional wound, coming to terms, making amends, reconciling, or developing a positive self-identity. That is, it can be viewed as an existential, medical, moral, social, or psychological and emotional process, or as something that entails all of these. As interesting as the problem of formally defining healing is, my primary interest here is not in defining the term but in recognizing and responding to the more general imperative offered by the possibility of healing and becoming whole: trusting that it can happen over time and take many forms.

Compassion is at the center of creating a relationship that contributes to the healing process. Efforts to fix youth or force change through controlled environments, behavioral modification, or punishment, while generally informed by a desire to help, are most often experienced by traumatized youth as additional sources of stress and further proof of their marginalization. When their failure to comply is met with punishment, it becomes one more hurtful experience in a long chain of violence, and youth respond with more resistance or by mentally or physically withdrawing from this new source of pain. People leading programs intended to help then blame—gently or harshly—the youth for their noncompliance: "If they would just get with the program . . . ," "If they would just do what they are told . . . ," "If they would just . . ." This pattern is so common and unproductive that it suggests we should look at the youth and youth-serving programs from another perspective. If the youth thought compliance made sense, they would comply. It is useful to assume, then, that their resistance makes sense. Recognizing this, we can begin to understand that the choice is between waiting for youth to change and changing the way we work with youth. The starting point for transformative change is changing the values on which institutions serving gang- and street-involved youth are built.

It is critical that youth workers, teachers, and police officers, as well as friends and family, realize that the ongoing experience of violent trauma means that interventions have to be built on strategies that help youth feel physically and emotionally safe and allow them to decompress, begin to trust, and accept hospitality. I believe that programs organized primarily around enforced structures, behavior modifications, or single or short-term interventions are more likely to result in greater stress, increased resistance, and a greater sense of marginalization and alienation and often result in an increase rather than a decrease in resistance and negative behaviors such as violence, disappearing, or self-medication with drugs and alcohol. Programs need structure to operate, but this structure can be organized around compassion rather than control.

"Compassion," as I use the term here, comes from the Latin roots of the word: literally, being with the suffering of another person. "Compassion" is distinguished from "sympathy" by the desire to help that accompanies it; it is about caring for and with. And "caring," in its turn, is rooted in the Gothic "kara," which means "lament: experiencing sorrow, grieving, and crying out with" (Nouwen 1974,

33–34). When I think of "compassion," I think also of the related word "anguish," which comes from the Norse and translates literally as "heart grief." It is this type of suffering, heart grief, that is felt by people who have experienced deep trauma. Compassion means feeling, at least partially, the pain of someone else as though it were our own, and showing compassion means communicating that you recognize it and are willing to carry some of that grief alongside them for a period of time.

This practice of compassion cannot be expressed as pity, as approval of counterproductive choices, or as excusing physically violent transgressions. It has to come in the form of genuine caring and empathy: it has to be relational and real and guided by an effort to help the young person name their own reality and identity and name their journey toward being their whole, best self. Compassion becomes empathy and care when we begin to connect it to our own life experiences and transfer what we are feeling into a willingness to help alleviate that suffering. More often than not, youth are finely attuned to the perspective and goals of people who want to help them. They resist control and respond to compassion.

A physician who helped define post-traumatic stress disorder and develop treatments for it, Jonathan Shay writes that PTSD results most predictably from the confluence of two experiences: a horrific emotional or physical trauma and the deep violation of "what is right," usually by someone in authority who could have taken better care and failed to do so. Very often, this combination of experience and ethical betrayal results in the symptoms associated with PTSD: hyperawareness, intrusive thoughts, anger, anxiety, depression, self-medication, numbing of emotions, difficulty sleeping. External behaviors evolve to protect the person with some or all of these symptoms—isolation, violence, getting high.

Shay argues that PTSD can be understood as a deep experience of grief—for what has happened, for the world, and for oneself. He suggests that a consistently effective process for healing from PTSD is "the communalization of grief." He means by this the experience of "being able to tell the story to someone who is listening and who can be trusted to retell it truthfully to others in the community." Shay notes how difficult it is for a person who cannot control their circumstances to grieve, as he "cannot assert choice over his own time to weep or the social and physical location of his own body when he mourn[s]" (1994, 65).

Safe space is compassionate and allows for the communalization of grief, often over time and in bits and pieces. Telling one's story about what has happened to another person or persons who can be trusted to listen with compassion is the path to healing. The simple act of listening—listening deeply and compassionately—is at the heart of working with gang-involved youth.

An enormous barrier in working with members of youth gangs is overcoming their sense that their feelings of love and grief do not matter. Writing about soldiers with PTSD, Shay notes, "If military practice tells soldiers that the emotions of love and grief—which are inseparable from their humanity—*do not matter* then the civilian society that sent them to fight on their behalf should not be shocked by their 'inhumanity' when they try to return to civilian life" (67). This is why showing compassion and encouraging it in the youth, particularly for themselves, is so critical. Like soldiers with PTSD, they are "returning" from the violent margins of our society, and from a reality that seems to operate under very different principles and assumptions about conflict, to their full humanity and participation in a larger civil community.

Talking about horrific events and violent transgression, about the ethical violations by leaders who should have taken better care, is often accompanied by feelings of shame and marginalization and by the intense feeling that telling your story puts you at further emotional risk: if people know what I have experienced and think, they won't want anything to do with me. Gang- and street-involved youth often sense that the adults in their lives have failed them, believe the adults don't care, and translate this into the idea that they, the youth, are not worth caring about. As a result, they view most efforts to "help" as hypocritical and simplistic extensions of the same feedback loop of control.

It doesn't make sense to stop fighting if you believe that fighting keeps you safe. It doesn't make sense to stay in school when you are already labeled a troublemaker (what Geoffrey Canada calls a "program buster") and constantly surveilled and policed. You have trouble hanging on to your own story and your sense of your self when so many others tell you who and what you are with such persistence. And if telling your story makes you vulnerable, it seems smarter to remain silent.

A characteristic of "genuine" compassion, then, is that it respects and supports the agency and autonomy of the other person. In other words, rather than saying, "What you are doing or did is wrong," you shift the perspective to say (even if as an internal dialogue), "I think I understand that you are doing what you are doing because it makes the most sense to you. But it looks likes it's hurting you and other people around you." Out loud, you ask, "Are you okay?"

More often than not, once physical integrity has been taken care of, the first helpful act is listening. It means paying attention from the right "focal length": close enough to keep things relational and in focus and distant enough to not lose sight of the larger context of the youth's life. The "right" focal length is a relative distance—sometimes closer and more intimate, other times more distant and abstract—calibrated and recalibrated to help the youth reflect, make more positive choices, and develop their capacity to have the meaningful life they want to have. Estimating and managing this focal length is a central craft for working with gang-involved and gang-affiliated youth—a learned skill informed by personal experience, perspective, local knowledge, and creativity (Magnuson 2007; Ross et al. 2016; Gebo and Bond 2012).

Listening is the fundamental practice in compassion, across the varied contexts that touch on working with gang-affiliated and gang-involved youth. It means something more than sitting down for "a talk": it means paying attention to what is being communicated verbally and nonverbally over time so that you begin to understand how someone else thinks, feels, and sees the world. Brenda Ueland and Nelle Morton describe the practice of listening as potentially transformative. "When we are listened to," Ueland writes, "it creates us, makes us unfold and expand. Ideas actually begin to grow within us and come to life" (1993). Morton suggests that listening can "break through political and social structures and image a new system" and that listening has the potential to "hear people into speech" (1985, 71). Listening figures centrally in the main theoretical influences on Rec Night, including the importance of voice in Paulo Freire's liberatory pedagogy, the creating of open space in Henri Nouwen's practice of hospitality, the use of oral testimony as a driver of community development in the work of Paul Thompson and Hugo Slim, Margaret Wheatley's recommendations for conversation as an engine of cultural change, and Jonathan Shay's emphasis on the "communalization of grief" as a way of healing from trauma.

The goal in this kind of deep listening over time, what educator Herman Blake (D. White 2012) calls "listening eloquently," is creating opportunities for someone to tell their own story and in the telling begin to reflect on what their life means to them and begin to imagine their future. It means recognizing the social and political context in which your identity and sense of self are embedded and claiming the right to resist or change that context. When we are listened to, we hear ourselves telling our stories and begin to ask if it is, in fact, our story—the one we want to tell about ourselves or a story that has been imposed on us from outside.

Athens's description of "violentization," for example, describes how a personal worldview and narrative—a story—can be developed about a violent world in which success is framed by one's capacity for violence. Undoing violentization is about unlearning this narrative—a process fraught with vulnerability and fear as an alternative slowly emerges. This fragile alternative is often buried deep—by our biases and limited perspectives, but also by the effects of trauma and violence. If the capacity for violence requires a numbing of emotion, then the truism, as Brené Brown (2012) points out, is that we do not get to choose which emotions are numb: they all are. Our stories of ourselves grow out of what we feel as well as what we think, and so feeling things and expressing those feelings, especially positive things like love or care for others, is to be vulnerable. How does a traumatized person practice vulnerability and begin to voice their own story? It can begin with access to one or more persons they trust, who can be trusted to listen with compassion.

In practice, compassion is about:

- recognizing that healing is done by, not to, survivors
- listening "eloquently"—hearing someone else into speech
- not judging—no person's suffering can be usefully measured against that of any other person
- constructing meaning and possibility from the ashes of suffering—something that is only genuinely possible as a member of a community; mentors and guides open up this possibility and do so in part by showing where bridges can be built to other communities of meaning
- encountering opportunities where you are offered and can claim membership in human community that helps you make meaning

CONTACT

Contact is about knowing what to say, and when to say it, but mostly it is about learning to listen deeply—a practice that expresses compassion and invites trust. Early in our program I learned from Tou how to effectively interrupt simmering conflicts and occasional fistfights outside the Rec by stepping into the conflict space and asking, "Everybody okay?" The question invited an answer; it was a question of concern, and the youth responding could choose to answer about their physical integrity (I'm hurt or I'm fine) or by responding emotionally and intellectually, usually by describing their feelings and the beef that had led to the conflict.

If a youth answers, "Yes, I'm fine," you say you are glad they are okay, and you wait, "keep contact" over the days and weeks ahead, listen, and gently and persistently introduce questions that cause some cognitive dissonance and prompt the youth to reflect on his or her life circumstances. Participation in a weekly program like Rec Night offers an opportunity to keep contact informally and organically.

When a youth answers with some form of, "No, I'm not okay," you begin by mediating the conflict—usually a process of helping the youth or the antagonists recognize that they are "justifying" their violence because of something someone else did and that they do have a choice about how to respond. You ask some form of "How is this way of responding working for you?" and you listen eloquently to their answers. Even for the person "winning," the answer is often mixed: they are not enjoying the violence, and they are not enjoying the consequences of being violent, such as coming under suspicion by the police or other authorities, being excluded from social spaces, or being isolated because others fear their violence. And they can recognize the opportunity cost of being violent: What is it costing you to make the choice of violence? Are you okay with that? Then, again over time and reframed variously depending on who is involved and the circumstances, you ask, "How can I or we help you do more of what is meaningful to you and less of what is destructive?"

All of this has to unfold over time, and there is no way of predicting how much time it will take for a youth to find his or her voice or become open to alternative ways of thinking about their situation. The goal is to create low-stress opportunities for paths to cross, in which the conversation can begin and continue. The youth have to be the ones to decide when this will happen, but they need recurring opportunities. ISPN's streetworkers describe much of their work as "keeping contact," a shorthand for this practice of knowing how to keep the opportunities available and open, without pressing too much or too little. And very often what they communicate is practical compassion: Let's get lunch. Do you have a place to stay? Do you need someone to go to court with you? Did you hear back on that job? Can you help me do this thing? Do you need a ride to or from school? Are you okay?

Contact is both simple and complicated. A big part of it is checking in—in person, by phone, or by text. It is being present and becoming a part of the everyday, relational world of the person you are trying to support. It is about knowing how to build and maintain relationships across lines of age, gender, economics, race, ethnicity, sexual identity, class, and life experience. And it is about representing an alternative that is available but not forced.

Rec Night was, by and large, a reliable space in which people could cross paths and check in with one another. It was a space in which people could expect to be heard with compassion and be welcomed even when they talked about things they expected would cause them to be excluded from the community.

CONSISTENCY AND SPACE

An image that came to mind early in Rec Night and has stayed with me is of a person, seen from above for some reason, holding their arms out in the shape of a loose half circle, in order to hold space for other persons to "be." It was how I pictured Rec Night: a space that held off, for a while, outside pressures and judgments. It left the space open for the youth to fill as they needed and wished. Mostly, they wished to relax, play, eat, and talk, loudly and quietly. And sometimes they vented, needed to be heard, or asked for support. Rec Night was just this simple: a place to just be for three hours a week, every week for eight years.

A great many things became possible because of this safe, free space: those of us "keeping contact" could do so repeatedly over time, and youth experienced the space as hospitable and not oppressive. Relationships had time to develop at their own pace, and over time people could learn enough about one another to have a sense of the complexity underlying all of our lives. We had time to listen eloquently. Consistency in the availability and quality of space meant that over time, it became possible to tell the truth about things that mattered. Because of this, it became a space in which community members could recognize when someone was beginning to "drift" into difficulty and use the relationships that had been developed to nudge them toward more deliberate and constructive decisions.

The chief characteristic of this space was hospitality. Henri Nouwen, a priest who worked with the L'Arche community for many years, describes hospitality as

> primarily the creation of a free space, where the stranger can enter and become a friend instead of an enemy. Hospitality is not to change people, but to offer them space where change can take place. It is not to bring men and women over to our side, but to offer freedom not disturbed by dividing lines. It is not to lead our neighbor into a corner where there are no alternatives left, but to open a wide spectrum of options for choice and commitment. It is not an educated intimidation with good books, good stories and good works, but the liberation of fearful hearts so that words can find roots and bear ample fruit. It is not a method of making our God and our way into the criteria of happiness, but the opening of an opportunity to others to find their God and their way. The paradox of hospitality is that it wants to create emptiness, not a fearful emptiness, but a friendly emptiness where strangers can enter and discover themselves as created free; free to sing their own songs, speak their own languages, dance their own dances; free also to leave and follow their own vocations. Hospitality is not a subtle invitation to adopt the lifestyle of the host, but the gift of a chance for the guest to find his own. (1975, 71)

This was the quality of hospitality we wanted to incorporate into Rec Night: a friendly emptiness in which all participants—youth and adults—could discover themselves, be encouraged, and be supported as they found their own way.

As Katy Radford points out, youth initially perceive "safe space" as "being 'with people that are like you,' 'with kids who are the same age and have the same sort of beliefs even if you are from a different religion,' 'where there is no alcohol and no one is going to talk about sex or drugs or that sort of thing,' 'with people who will understand what we can and cannot do.'" In other words, youth initially perceive safe space as a space of rules that excludes people who are different and, because of their difference, sources of threat and danger. In practice, however, this version of safe space doesn't do much to advance the sense of security and ends up artificially isolating youth in a temporary setting. "Safe space" in practice, Radford argues, is a space where, "after a period of working together the group spontaneously began to share intimacies that could be expected to leave them vulnerable and exposed. Revealing and poignant statements were punctuated with supportive silences. Participants appeared to instinctively allow for safe spaces to emerge and they enabled and allowed for one another's emotional openness to blossom rather than wither. . . . It was clear that intergenerational support was crucial to their [youth's] perceptions of safety" (2007, 146–47). Safe space is a space shaped by compassion, listening, and hospitality that allows people to speak their truth as they know it.

Craig was fourteen when he began coming to Rec Night. A little over three years later, he was arrested for armed robbery. He and a friend had robbed another youth of his phone and his pants and threatened him with a weapon. They meant it "as a joke," because this other youth had been disrespecting them to mutual acquaintances. Craig, charged as an adult, spent a month in intake at the ACI. He was found guilty but released with time served and put on probation with an order to pay restitution and court fees. In his few short weeks at the ACI he went from athletic, robust, and extroverted to ashy-skinned, hollow-eyed, and quiet. He continued coming to Rec Night every week and talked with a small group of longtime volunteers who kept encouraging him to tell parts of his life story and talk about what these stories meant to him. One of the Rec Night volunteers had started a music production group, called No Affiliation, that met on a separate evening. The older youth who participated wrote music, mostly rap, that they used to tell their stories. Craig wrote and performed.

In his songs and at Rec Night, Craig talked about being a young black man from the neighborhood. His words were laced with anger and bitterness, and he would get stuck as his thoughts looped back to the unjust and disproportionate violence he had experienced in prison. He talked about racism and how he thought he was treated and perceived. He talked about his older brother, who was on the streets and had been incarcerated, and about getting and keeping respect. He told stories of violence. He talked about having been a recognized high school athlete and losing that recognition. He was acutely aware of the gap between his sense of who he was and the generalized, diminishing narratives that were placed on him by the larger society. At one point, still struggling with his depression, he said, referring to Rec Night and No Affiliation, "This is the only place I can come where I'm seen as normal." He felt he was seen as a stereotype everywhere else he went, as a thug, a violent, unpredictable person to be "handled" or avoided or fixed. "Here" he could breathe, be himself, be a whole person, with a history and gifts and struggles and choices and agency.

It is worth saying something about how Craig was listened to. He was listened to informally, in fairly intimate settings, by people he knew who heard him with compassion, but who also shared their own reactions and questions to his stories. They pushed back when they thought his analysis was unfair, incomplete, or simply wrong on the facts. They offered alternative interpretations of what he was describing. They debated with him the meaning and ethics of the dozens of life questions and situations his stories surfaced: What would you do if . . . ?

As Craig talked over the weeks, he made a series of personal claims and resolutions: He would keep off the streets. He would do what he could to keep his friends safe and influence them to make positive choices. He would pursue his creative interests, especially photography and graphic design. He acknowledged that he was afraid to move on, to leave his neighborhood behind and go to college "somewhere else," even if that somewhere else was in Providence. He began mentoring, in his own rough way, younger participants at Rec Night. Over a period of eighteen months, he started a small business with a low cost of entry that drew on his interest in design.

It was, and continues to be, a long, winding road for Craig. It had begun three years before he was arrested, when he started coming to Rec Night and was selected for ISPN's summer jobs program. It continued through his arrest and long afterward. Resolving to keep off the streets, he started spending a lot of time at home in his bedroom, alone, which he found frustrating and depressing. He had a chance to sell some of his recorded songs to a producer but didn't want to "go commercial" and sell out—partly because he valued authenticity and didn't want to commodify his life story, but also because he didn't trust success. He felt isolated. He felt he was still vulnerable on the streets and had to accept it. But his generalized sense of the world shifted, and he began to trust the hope he had for a positive future. It is a truism, but change at this deep level is a process and not an event.

Rec Night, for all its attention to listening, was not organized as a therapeutic space. The goal was not to fix youth but to draw them into a community in which they could hear themselves. Being listened to was a gift that came with being in community—and being in a supportive community could also give them access to other "goods" that come with belonging.

COMMUNITY

While I will say more about Martin Luther King Jr.'s concept of the "Beloved Community" in the next chapter on nonviolence, I want to describe something of the way that community as a value and social experience fits into the concept of youth positive. Community is something more than "membership" or belonging to a social unit. Community (Morton and Bergbauer 2015) is a complex system with tangible value in our lives. Its absence or presence has consequences for the long-term success of children and youth.

Inspired in part by Wendell Berry's essay "Does Community Have a Value?" (1983), I would argue that thriving communities—located in people and place—do four things that are useful and are hard to replace if the community weakens: they pass general and local knowledge and wisdom on from one generation to the next; they help people make meaning, celebrate, and exercise creativity; they help people grieve and get through suffering and loss; and they help people make a meaningful livelihood, work that pays enough to live well and is respected by other members of the community.

Primarily as a consequence of economic and policy changes instituted by federal, state, and local governments that gained momentum in the 1950s (Rothstein 2017), the economic dimension became increasingly detached from the rest of communal life. This was particularly true for people of color living in cities. Financial institutions and factories fled to the suburbs, and local businesses declined; absentee home ownership became the norm in the "inner city" that grew out of this change. This trend was compounded by additional policies and practices (Halpern 1995; Hilfiker 2002; K. Jackson 1985; Rothstein 2017) that left lower-income black, Hispanic, and Asian citizens in inner cities that were being stripped of their economic infrastructure, producing the modern "ghetto." Access to capital and ownership of real property became increasingly difficult for inner-city residents, and a new form of poverty began to take shape. Since that time, social policies contributing to the "school-to-prison pipeline" and mass incarceration (Alexander 2010) have further amplified the systems effects of institutionalized poverty and racism on inner-city communities.

Several dynamics contributed to the new shape of inner-city poverty. The deep and relatively sudden separation of economic life from the rest of communal life simultaneously erased financial prosperity and weakened the capacity of the those left behind to provide one another with what was needed outside of the money economy. In the new economy, if you were fortunate to have enough money, you could buy resources that had previously been offered by your community. Informal sharing of child care, as one example, was increasingly replaced by formal, paid day care. The meaning and experience of poverty began to change, as financial and social capital became harder to access.

The field of community development (Zautra, Hall, and Murray 2009) assesses "community resilience," as well as individual resilience, and uses these criteria to do so:

- Neighbors trust one another.
- Neighbors interact on a regular basis.
- Residents own their houses and stay for a while.

- Residents have a sense of community and cohesion.
- Residents work together for the common good and are involved in community events and affairs.
- Formal and informal civic places are available for gathering.

Over time, communities generally, and inner-city communities particularly, have become less resilient.

As inner-city communities became economically weaker and more isolated over time, their capacity to provide residents with opportunities to organically educate, celebrate, and grieve was diminished. In Smith Hill, the Providence neighborhood that was home to Rec Night, the result by the middle 1970s was that residents increasingly found themselves living in a community under siege, with traditional practices of mutual support significantly weakened and with limited access to the wealth of the new economy. It is no accident (Kendi 2016; Rothstein 2017) that gang and street violence are concentrated in poor urban neighborhoods or that these places are disproportionately home to people of color.

Community is a systems effect: when it is working well, the feedback loops of its various elements reinforce one another, producing an effect that is greater than the sum of its parts. Youth thrive in a strong, healthy community, and strengthening community is one of the best ways to prevent youth from becoming involved in street and gang violence. In a healthy community, adults invite youth into experiences of learning, celebrating, grieving, and making a livelihood. Youth know they matter to the community because they benefit from and contribute to it. The goal is not rebuilding community by returning to a false ideal of a golden past, but building community by supporting the development of complex, interconnected social systems that result in lived experiences of community.

This argument is an invitation to take seriously the concept of community as both process and product: talking across our personal and social differences to figure out how to strengthen what we think is working and build a new version of community that supports our collective thriving. The goal is a community in which everyone has access to a meaningful livelihood, has opportunities for learning and creativity, and gives and gets support when they are struggling and grieving.

As a practical matter, this concept of community informed Rec Night in two major ways. First, we worked to establish networks of opportunities for youth that would provide experiences of all four dimensions of community, including creativity, learning, grieving, and meaningful work. We wanted them to experience Rec Night as a "hub" that was committed to helping them access the experiences that would ordinarily be provided by an intact, thriving community.

Second, our analysis of the history of community provided an additional layer to our argument that youth are not the problem; the problem is their circumstances and the choices they are given. Further, we argued that the circumstances producing the choices that led to gang and street violence were not random or accidental, fate or luck, but a direct outgrowth of historical policies and institutional practices. In the short term, Rec Night was about helping youth connect to opportunities to learn, create, grieve, and experience meaningful work. Learning about the history of their neighborhood, they could recognize that they were not solely and privately responsible for their situations and experiment with ways to more successfully navigate their context. It also allowed us to suggest that they had a role to play in the long-term social objective of building community.

There is, I believe, a "community ethic" similar to Aldo Leopold's "land ethic" (1949), which provides a foundational value for ecology. This "community ethic" became a foundational value in Rec Night: respect for the integrity of the community and all that it contains—including one another. Violence gets in the way of this and is a symptom of a community under siege.

REC NIGHT

Rec Night, as described in the introduction to this book, was a deceptively simple program. At the outset, I had imagined I would be joining Tou in organizing fairly conventional youth development programming at a neighborhood recreation center I had visited often over the years. We would use college student volunteers in a weekly program to organize interest and activity groups around sports, arts, music, community service, board games, education, and work; let participants sign up for four- to six-week rotations through the evolving set of programs; steer participants toward personal and leadership development; and organize a youth leadership team of participants over time. We'd also have open basketball, but I saw the slow development of program structure as the important objective. This initial approach worked in small ways: it gave college student volunteers a formal role, increasing their sense of comfort when they joined Rec Night; it satisfied the interests of some youth; and it created a structure that fitted the expectations of other stakeholders, such as the Recreation Department.

The problem was that the youth we were interested in weren't very interested in these program activities. They liked the hard physical exercise and energy of basketball and the status that went with holding the court as long as your team kept winning. They liked to sit and talk and joke around. They liked to decompress and act like the kids they were. They didn't want to be "developed." They were surprisingly polite about it. And Tou, while not blocking the way to something more structured, argued from the beginning that all Rec Night needed to be was a safe, hospitable space that, in systems theory terms, was self-organizing. We scrounged up some money and added food to the program—a slice of pizza and something to drink for everyone. We kept the structure simple, while emphasizing relationships, hospitality, and connectivity.

As we adjusted our expectations to the reality in front of us, Rec Night and "youth positive" emerged into view. Each week, for three hours, staff and volunteers from the Institute for the Study and Practice of Nonviolence, Providence College's Feinstein Institute for Public Service, and local community members created a "safe space" for gang-involved, gang-affiliated, and high-risk youth from Providence's Smith Hill neighborhood and Chad Brown housing project.

An average of seventy-five to ninety youth participated each week. While the number of ISPN staff and volunteers varied, we averaged fifteen volunteers a week.

The youth walked into the rec center and signed in using any name they wanted—often just first names or nicknames. Usually, they would head into the gym—a big box of a space with room for two short full courts across its width or one regulation-size full court running its length. One of the two short courts would be used by older participants and serious ballers: they would play four-on-four elimination games all night. The other court was more fluid in its use: younger kids usually organized into half-court games, while others shot at the extra basket in between. Sometimes break-dancers set up a soccer goal in one corner for protection, blasted a little music, and practiced. Others sat on the bleachers and talked.

There were also a few activities the youth liked a great deal: the younger ones liked board and table games, especially Jenga, checkers, and chess. Everyone liked foosball (table soccer) when it was available. And the older youth—fifteen or so and up—liked being invited on other days of the week to hike or bike in new places. They liked being connected with part-time and summer job opportunities and programs. They liked getting together for food at different times. Word got out, and Rec Night became a "hub" where people could drop in and hang out and connect. It developed the vibe of a relaxed, no-alcohol party.

We were also joined every Monday for most of the first three years by two or three additional streetworkers and local police officers who would stop by as we were starting and closing down. If we knew things were stressed on the streets, we might invite a specific streetworker because she or he knew the people we were worried about or ask the police to maintain a low-key presence for a longer period.

The youth ran, bounced balls in the hall, swore, sometimes teased one another to the point of bullying, rode trick bicycles through the front door, showed off new tattoos and cuts and bruises. Kids with street beefs would "mean mug" and give each other the "stink eye" and stiffen their spines. Disputed fouls on the basketball court would turn into loud shouting with chests nearly touching. But everyone respected the basic rule: do not hurt yourself or others in this space.

If enough trusted adults were around, there would occasionally be a slow-speed confrontation between youth that brewed through very predictable stages—predictable enough, once I learned what to look for, that it was clear the youth wanted someone to step in and mediate: a face-saving way to de-escalate a beef that could blow up on the street. Very occasionally, people engaged in a serious conflict on the street would show up at the same time, and things would simmer and begin to look scary. We, or someone in their crew, would say, "Remember—not here," and the enemies would either ignore one another for the rest of the night or leave. But things did not escalate. As word got around that things were cool during Rec Night, other neighborhood youth began participating. Within the first year the program had grown from thirty to ninety or so youth most Monday evenings.

If youth didn't want to go into the gym, they could stay in the entry area and talk with other people. Snacks were usually laid out—fruit, chips, candy—that people brought. Much of the talk was about what was happening locally, who was doing what, or something that had happened to upset people; much of the talk was teasing or challenging—often about race and ethnicity and gender and looks and smarts. This is also where people gave updates as they walked in, about something good or bad that had been going on. Often this was just a sentence or two that wouldn't make sense if it weren't embedded in a longer series of similar updates. The first few years, there was a foosball table in the entry, and people often paused to play or watch or offer commentary. We set up board and card games in the reception area and hallway and occasionally turned this into a tournament.

Tou or I always greeted people at the door. We didn't insist on daps or handshakes or even eye contact, but we always said, "Hi, how you doing?" And we generally said something positive, intended to communicate that we were noticing the person: like your kicks, new T-shirt, missed you last week, glad you're here. While the youth were generally polite, it could take weeks for some of them to decide to shake my hand, make eye contact, or acknowledge something I said. It generally went faster for Tou, unless it was someone who had a beef with one of the gangs he had been connected to or worked with.

A third option for the youth was to drift into a "game room"—a beat-up twenty-by-fifteen room with one window, two cabinets of board games missing pieces, a couch, and a slowly changing menu of games like table tennis or pool. This room was a favorite of the younger teens—boys and girls who were into the middle-school relationship scene. Most often, people would sit and talk, but someone's feelings usually got hurt, most often when they made their affections known and this was used as a weapon to humiliate them. The girls and young women ran this space when they were around. It was all about establishing—very loudly—a pecking order.

The adults helping with Rec Night simply joined in what was going on, playing games or ball, watching from the bleachers, joining in conversations. If we were worried about a conflict bubbling up, we made an extra effort to engage the youth about whom we were concerned. The goal was to listen to the youth—to help the youth get to the point that they could talk about things that were or could be meaningful in their lives—their interests, values, dreams; to share some of our own; and to look for ways to help the youth pursue more of what was meaningful in their lives and experience less of what diminished that meaning.

Each week, around 6:45 p.m., I would leave the rec center and drive a few minutes to a local pizza place that gave us a break on the price of fifteen pizzas and eight bottles of soda and tea. Three or four youth would accompany me. They helped me carry the food and helped serve it on our return. The owners of the pizza place were appreciative of them and gave them a free order of "cheesy sticks"— pizza dough sprinkled with parmesan cheese and garlic powder—to eat on the ride back to the rec center. Youth competed to ride with me every week—first come, first served—for several reasons. Some just because they liked it. More because they could get some cheesy sticks. But most wanted to go because they turned it into a status chip: I got to do this, and you didn't. They liked to crank some music, introduce me to new rap songs, slouch in the front seat of the pickup truck. It was a safe and positive way to be seen.

In the summers that we remained at the rec center, rather than moving to Davis Park, about a mile away on the border of the neighborhood, many of the youth would relax outside—tossing a ball, playing tag, playing "psyche" (an Asian version of hacky sack), or standing around talking.

Every so often someone would bring in a dessert—a birthday cake, usually—or we would break the monotony of pizza with sticky chicken and fried rice from a nearby Asian restaurant or with a cookout of hamburgers and hot dogs.

Every so often, visitors from other organizations would drop by: offering information on sexual violence, on nutrition, recruiting for charter schools or sports leagues or youth programs.

At 8:30 we would flash the lights to let people know we'd be wrapping up soon, and people would begin drifting out. A small number of youth would wait so they could get rides to wherever they were going next; this was usually done to help them keep safe.

We used the contact at Rec Night, and the more robust relationships developed by ISPN's streetworkers and our longer-term volunteers, to help steer the youth toward other options: we organized field trips, hikes, bike rides, a couple of times camping trips. We introduced and helped youth apply for jobs programs, part-time work, health care, counseling. We talked with them about their lives. If they expressed interest, we steered them toward high school "credit recovery" and GED programs or toward arts programs such as those run by New Urban Arts and AS220, local programs that we knew would make them welcome. We invited them to sit in on college classes, to meet for lunch. As the streetworkers say, we used Rec Night to "keep contact" and as a hub for relationship building and communication. That's it.

When we were starting Rec Night, we adopted the long list of rules published by the rec center; one year in we had whittled this down to our one rule, reminiscent of A. S. Neill's (1960) Summerhill school: you can do whatever you like here, as long as you're not hurting yourself or someone else.

This single rule of *ahimsa*—Gandhi's nonviolent principle of "do no harm"—was always open to debate and redefinition. I want to describe a situation that unfolded in Rec Night's first year of operation, one I hesitate to write about because it is such a charged example and very vulnerable to misinterpretation. When the program was only several months old, a youth brought a pistol to Rec Night, concealed in a backpack. Worried (with good reason) that this could mean the end of Rec Night if it were found out, two other youth distracted the person who had brought the gun, while a third stole it and took it somewhere else, well away from the rec center. Then, three others—leaders in two crews—invited the gun's owner outside, just off the rec property, and started a "small" beating. Tou and I stopped the pummeling almost before it started and slowly teased out the story. Short version: they wanted to make it clear that Rec Night was a safe and valued space. We affirmed their goal and commitment and had some serious conversations about methods. Importantly, we found a way to honor their deep sense that they were trying to do the right thing, even as we talked about alternative ways to handle the situation. The larger point is that the youth valued their safe space so much that in Rec Night's eight years of operation, the only violence that happened was a brief fight that lasted two punches.

LEARNING FROM EXPERIENCE

I was inspired to start committing our "practical theory" of youth development to paper shortly after I sent an email to Beth Charlebois, then director of the Recreation Centers in Providence, Rhode Island, that included the excerpt below. I sent this to her when Rec Night was a little over four years old, because of a small friction that surfaced over and over again between the staff of the rec center we used and the staff and volunteers of our program, who used the center once a week:

> One of the youth we are spending a lot of time with is kicked out (of the rec center on another night) for fighting. He's told he can't come back in until his family comes and "works it out." I understand the goal, here: educate about "good behavior," get the parents involved. But we look at the situation somewhat differently. This is a young boy—about 12—who has gang-involved family members, an often abusive home situation, and is being tossed from school as well as the rec center. He started out a year ago thinking the solution to any dispute was to launch himself and fight. He comes to get the pizza with me. Tou, two of the Streetworkers and a couple of the volunteers are spending a lot of time with him, and he's learning not to fight, and alternative ways to have self-respect. He used to get into four or five minor confrontations every Monday—now it's once every four or five Mondays. We're keeping track of him outside Rec Night. He is the inspiration for our planning a "parents' night" one of the Mondays in the next month—we want to establish contact with his family, but not in a way that will get him punished at home or otherwise reinforce what a bad kid he is. I'm not describing this because I think our approach is the right one, but to ask for some help figuring out how to negotiate this with the Rec staff. Kids like the one I describe here wear them out and seem pretty unwelcome. We get that, but these are explicitly the youth we want to work with—that means our boundaries are a little different and are maintained a little differently. We understand excluding him from other Rec opportunities, but would rather not have him kicked out of Rec Night, especially without our knowledge.

A few obvious things became clear to us: respect and trust were essential for building effective relationships with the youth. This trust was developed in an unexpected way: by relaxing judgment and structure; by beginning with the assumption that individuals had reasons for making the choices they were making, especially choices that looked ridiculous to many observers; and by creating dialogue about the ethics of situations they were in: How does the situation look to you? How have you felt in the past, and how are you feeling now? What is at stake? What are your options and why? Why does one path look better to you than the others? Can we imagine any alternatives that would be more effective? Would you handle it the same way again? We did this all while taking care to affirm the agency, courage, and values of the actors, even as their choices were dissected.

"Youth positive" emphasizes the importance of paying attention to the youth and what they are "saying" in their words and their behaviors. It is about observing, not in order to judge or correct but to learn from the youth. As Margaret Wheatley suggests, "We have to be willing to let go of our certainty and expect ourselves to be confused for a time. . . . We need to acknowledge that their way of interpreting the world might be essential to our survival" (2009, 34–35). It is not that we should come to see the world as the youth do, or that we should use what we learn to bring them over to our way of seeing things, but rather that in observing and listening closely, we can begin to understand why the youth perceive and act as they do. Through them, we can begin to discern the systems that "produce" the patterns of their lives. Simultaneously and reflexively, we will begin to discern our own perspectives and the limits of our understanding. "My shock at your position," Wheatley writes, "exposes my own position. When I hear myself saying, 'How could anyone believe something like that?' a light comes on for me to see my own beliefs" (36). This is an important step toward beginning to recognize that gang-involved youth (and in fact each of us) think and act in ways that make sense to us. Understanding—and grieving—how and why youth can become violent to themselves and others is a first giant step toward being able to help them construct alternative paths.

A startling insight comes from this perspective: the violence and self-defeating behavior of these youth, however it looks to the outside, express what they believe to be their best options under the circumstances. This is not to say that the gang-involved youth are happy with their situations or their options. They know they are living dangerously, that they are backing into a corner with little room for escape. Even more startling, and what they welcome over and over, is any effort to really understand why they are doing what they are doing.

Seeing the world from the point of view of any one of these youth is a complicated exercise in compassion, communication, grief, pride, and fear. In short, the youth invite us to see the world as they do before we judge them—not to condone what is messed up in their lives but to understand it and in understanding it begin to help them figure out how things could get better. This is what I mean by a "practical theory." When we open opportunities for dialogue in which we try to explain the truth as each of us sees it, we begin to describe our experiences of the world, explain why things are the way they are, and imagine how they could be changed for the better. Safe space, compassion, contact, constancy, and community.

CHAPTER FIVE

NONVIOLENCE AS A MEANINGFUL ALTERNATIVE

We think that by protecting ourselves from suffering we are being kind to ourselves. The truth is, we only become more fearful, more hardened, and more alienated. We experience ourselves as being separate from the whole. This separateness becomes like a prison for us, a prison that restricts us to our personal hope and fears.

—Pema Chodron, *When Things Fall Apart*

THE STUDY AND PRACTICE OF NONVIOLENCE

One winter evening in 2013, Danny came to Rec Night, walked onto the basketball court, and began shooting baskets with the younger participants. Danny was a big, powerful twenty-year-old Asian American man and a member of a local gang. He had been shot in the leg the night before when two members of another local gang drove by the place his crew hung out. Members of both gangs came regularly to Rec Night, though the shooters stayed away for several weeks following the attack. I asked him why he chose to come to Rec Night and play with the younger participants. "I'm not going to retaliate," Danny said. He wanted people to see him in public, to know he was not afraid, and to see him doing something positive. He believed, rightly as it turned out, that showing up and shooting some baskets with younger kids communicated his intentions. Danny did not quit his gang, did not get off the streets, and did not become a consistent advocate for nonviolence. He did recognize that he had a choice in this instance, he chose a nonviolent response, and he was courageous and creative in communicating it. With Tou's help as a mediator, the beef was squashed, and members of both gangs stopped viewing the other as a threat for an extended period of time.

More often than not, when people hear the word "nonviolence," they locate it in a binary with "violence" and move rapidly to a debate about the extremes. It's all or nothing, one or the other. Even Barack Obama, accepting the Nobel Prize for Peace in 2009, felt moved to caution the prize committee, "Nonviolence could not have stopped the Holocaust." What interests me here is not the accuracy of Obama's statement, but his need, as president of the United States in a setting celebrating peace, to name violence as the underlying social and political reality.

I have introduced the concept of nonviolence to literally hundreds of people, and arguing to the extreme—posing a world of Mad Max levels of apocalyptic violence against the passive torpor of "kumbaya" harmony—is the most common initial response. Violence is perceived as the natural state of the world and nonviolence as a passive, idealistic, unrealistic, and potentially dangerous counterconcept to be used in a limited number of specific circumstances, if at all. The great majority of people I have talked with, taught, and trained insist that peace ultimately requires violence. They reject as fanciful A. J. Muste's succinct observation: "There is no way to peace; peace is the way" (1967). For all this skepticism, I also find that most people are open to reconsidering the way they think about violence and working for less violence. Nearly everyone is in favor of less violence.

Arguing from the extremes diminishes the value of positive choices like Danny's and seems to me a way of skirting the central questions posed by the concept of nonviolence: Would you (and we) rather live in a world in which deliberate violence is the normative value or a world in which deliberate violence is the exception to the rule? Would you prefer we individually and collectively operate out of values of fear, security, and order or out of values of relationship, community, and creativity? If your answers are less violence, relationships, community, and creativity, then the next question is how do we move in this new direction, making these our personal, cultural, and institutional values? We always have a choice, even if we don't get to choose the circumstances framing our choices.

Choosing nonviolence isn't a single step or a sudden transformation or a final destination. In her useful book *When Things Fall Apart,* Buddhist nun Pema Chodron (2000) tells the story of the guru Milarepa. In his youth he participated in thirty-five vengeance killings of people who had stolen his family's inheritance. Then he started on the path to enlightenment, faced twelve-plus years of trials, and achieved it when he was forty-five. We don't have to be seeking enlightenment, but we can choose to study and practice nonviolence regardless of our personal histories—and embark on a journey of change that is simultaneously slow, incremental, full of detours and dead ends, and life affirming, creative, meaningful, and satisfying. Danny was exercising this choice when he showed up at Rec Night the day after he was shot. As poet Anthony Machado (1978) observes in his poem of the same title, "We make the road by walking." My focus in this chapter is the challenge of introducing nonviolence to young people whose lives have been shaped by violence and walking with them as they make their way.

STARTING THE CONVERSATION

Rather than introducing nonviolence to people as a fully articulated concept, I think it is more effective to start a conversation about violence and nonviolence that emerges from their lived experiences and to practice nonviolence in your relationships with them. When a youth tells a story about a fight, for example, I can respond by passing judgment on it, or I can respond by asking if she or he is okay and ask what they think of the proposition that "there will always be conflict, and we always have choices about what to do with it." I can ask them to tell more about the context of this fight and share related stories from their own experiences. Can they imagine the same context with different outcomes? Where does the violent version lead? Where might a nonviolent version go? Would approaching conflict with values of nonviolence rather than violence generate more positive options on a more consistent basis with less likelihood of catastrophe? Or not?

Most often, the youth believe their exercise of violence was a way of taking control of a situation, that someone else's choices "made" them do this, a thought pattern people who study conflict call "justification": we respond emotionally and psychologically to the actions of someone else, assume that our emotional response indicates a "truth," and react based on this perceived truth. We then argue for the truth of our justification, the error of the opponent, and the righteousness of our position. As Terry Warner points out, "One of our dominant, almost unexamined fictions is that we are not responsible for our emotions. They are caused in us, we believe, by events outside of our control. Recently this dogma has been undergoing reexamination and it is becoming increasingly clear that it is false. Accusing emotions are performances in which we engage. . . . [B]ecause we're angry with someone, we cannot fail to believe that this person is making us angry" (1986, 44–45).

Most often, each side digs into their position, justified by their feelings, ratcheting up mutual resistance and animosity, and creating perfect conditions for ongoing conflict. The alternative is to recognize that we have a choice in how we respond: our feelings of fear or anger or frustration are our feelings. They lead us toward particular interpretations of the world around us, but they are not the world, and it is in our power to decide whether our feelings are telling us the truth and whether and how we are going to act on them.

Recognizing and being able to interrupt the reactive violence that flows from unchecked justification is, I believe, a fundamental insight of nonviolence. It is widely and deeply supported by evidence from histories of spiritual practice, psychology, communication, and conflict resolution. It is also perceived initially by people who have experienced violent trauma as naive and dangerous.

Becoming aware that we are justifying our decisions offers an interesting new way to look at the choice of violence: you thought you were taking control, but really you were giving away your control to the other person who "made" you react. Real control lies in making deliberate, rather than reactive, choices. Presented with humor, this argument nearly always leads to a passionate discussion of power, respect, free will, and violent and nonviolent alternatives. The incident that precipitated this discussion becomes the context for evaluating claims and alternatives: Would they work in practice?

Beginning with stories and reflections that grow out of personal experience rather than abstract principles of nonviolence creates space in which we can begin to recognize what we have in common with other people and simultaneously discover how we are unique as persons: while we can recognize patterns of experience across multiple stories, your experiences and your stories ultimately belong to no one but yourself. Unlike declarative statements, stories postpone judgment and invite reflection. Telling stories helps people who are not used to being heard find their voices. Everyone, as oral historians Hugo Slim and Paul Thompson (1994) note, has a story. Everyone. Stories allow us to suspend judgment, to reflect on complexity, and to play with alternative versions. They allow us to imagine multiple points of view and the intersecting trajectories of values, emotions, ideas, and actions. They give us an opportunity to talk about meaning. And telling our own stories—finding our own voices—is a first big step toward personal and social change.

The goal, in other words, is not converting anyone to an already defined belief system called nonviolence or debating to a conclusion the ultimate power of violence and nonviolence as abstract ideas, but opening a discussion about the core values on which we want to base our personal and social ethics. Nonviolence offers an exercise in imagination: a startling vantage point from which we can gain perspective on our personal beliefs and behaviors, our communal values, and our public culture. It opens the door to imagining and experimenting with alternative ways of being that hold out the promise of being more life affirming and meaningful than violence.

Nonviolence is based not on a moralized vision of people becoming better than they are—revolutionizing human nature—but on changing our institutions and "making it easier," as peace activist Peter Maurin often said, "for people to be good" (n.d.). At its core, nonviolence is not a method for eliminating conflict. Nonviolence asks that we change the values and assumptions framing our interpersonal and social interactions, and defining our institutions, and so change our relationship to conflict. The goal is not the elimination of conflict but the transformation of potentially destructive conflict into something creative and life affirming.

Put a little differently, nonviolence is to human conflict what composting is to waste: a method for transforming a problem into a source of energy. Each of them begins with the recognition that there is no problem but only a system that fails to recognize and value the resource. This is the connection between practicing nonviolence as a person and moving person by person and institution by institution toward a nonviolent world. Gang- and street-involved youth are products of a cultural system that views them as problems. Recognizing their potential to be fully realized human beings and helping them get there begins with an act of imagination, moves on to supporting individual youth, expands into changing the collective story we tell about youth and violence as parts of our community, and changing our institutions to reflect our changed values. At the core of nonviolence, I believe, is the belief in the equal worth and potential of every person and a corollary belief that all of our lives will be enriched as we become better at realizing this.

The first, and hardest, step on the road to nonviolence, then, is being willing to imagine that an alternative to violence is even possible. Paradoxically, I find that many of the youth and young adults involved in gangs or on the streets are very conscious of the costs of violence and are willing to stretch their imaginations, however cautiously. The greatest resistance I encounter comes from people who benefit the most from current economic and social inequality; live in safe, often predominantly white neighborhoods; and have little experience of personal or structural violence. They believe their continued safety and prosperity depend on the maintenance of the current social order and on institutions such as the police, the military, or security forces who create an impassable barrier protecting an amorphous "us" from an imagined and threatening "them."

Discussing violence and nonviolence across this divide is where the debate becomes political and embedded in processes of social and cultural change. Recent public arguments about the interwoven histories of racism, policing, and violence surfaced by the Black Lives Matter movement, and captured in the persons-become-symbols of Trayvon Martin and Michael Brown, suggest something of the emotional resonance and divergent worldviews that inform the debate. The divide is evident, as well, in growing calls by African American, Latinx, and Asian American high school students for incorporating multicultural and ethnic studies into K–12 education. They are making the claim that stories out of these unacknowledged histories and experiences matter as part of our collective public identity. A dynamic at the heart of all of these examples is that the activists are challenging the fundamental assumption that there is an "us" and a "them," and advocating for a plural "we," and so undermining the justifications of unequal treatment.

Nonviolence is about getting to and living in this physical, emotional, and ethical space: everyone's story matters, and everyone is included and heard with compassion and respect. And when you inevitably discover differences and conflicts, you have to find a way to live together that maintains the integrity of the community.

Once you become open to exploring the world through the lens of violence and nonviolence, you begin to see personal and social experiments with it all around, across a wide range of scale. Jonathan Schell (2003), for example, makes the argument that democracy is in itself a nonviolent institution: it is the cultural agreement to use political organizing, public debate, voting, and laws to make collective decisions rather than accepting that force will impose a decision or status or way of being. At a minimum, democracy requires that minority interests accede to those of the majority, expects the majority to honor and protect the rights of minorities, and requires the orderly transfer of power.

In another, more localized, example, criminologist David Kennedy points out that policing is most effective when police officers are trained and supported in choosing tactics that prevent and de-escalate conflict with suspects or with entire communities, embracing values of service, relationship, and community. Describing his experience working with Boston police officers in a successful community-oriented violence reduction program during the 1990s, he writes, "And people were changing. We had cops acting like social workers and trying to get gang members jobs, outreach workers acting like cops and bringing law enforcement to bear, street ministers acting like prosecutors and fingering impact players, prosecutors organizing jobs programs, gang members turning in other gang members, neighborhood people reinforcing the law enforcement message" (2011, 73). This is community policing, and it begins, in Kennedy's estimation, when "the cops and the neighborhoods and the streets . . . really see each other, hear each other, trust each other." The biggest barriers? Learning to see street violence as a systems effect that everyone wants out of, including gang members, and facing the truth that "where we are now is infused with racial history, racial understanding, racial misunderstandings" (125). Nonviolence offers a way of facing this truth that strengthens relationships, builds community, and, along the way, reduces violence. It offers something everyone—neighborhood residents, gang members, and police—wants.

Another powerful example of nonviolence at the grassroots level in the past thirty years is hip-hop (Chang 2005) and its disciplines of emceeing, deejaying, b-boying, and graffiti. While "gangsta rap" commodifies and commercializes inner-city violence and dominates public perceptions about the inner city with its confrontational, violent, and dystopic worldview, most of the hip-hop aesthetic is about deliberately creating an alternative to violence: rap battles are not street fights. Break dancing—done informally or in highly produced competitions—is about testing one's athleticism, integrity, creativity, and aesthetic sensibility head-to-head against someone else without resorting to physical violence. Graffiti is a way of marking territory and claiming presence; it processes conflict through public sharing of aesthetic sensibility, symbols, imagery, ink, and paint, but it is not armed combat. B-boy Facce Maldonado, a longtime ally of ISPN and Rec Night, and an "old head" in the Providence hip-hop scene, makes it clear:

Nonviolence is a way of life for courageous people. Hip Hop serves the same purpose through our own principles and elements, upliftment and most of all the Knowledge, Wisdom and Understanding of our Culture in order to figure out the full Empowerment aspect. We started in the "Ghetto." . . . Understand, Hip Hop before we coined the term, it was a Nonviolent Escape from the Streets and Gang Violence. . . . This is where we was able to battle and add violent gestures to your face and feel like a fight but never get "Touched." Hip Hop is something we live not what we do, Graff Murals are like the visual excitement and way of empowering a collection of different Writers, Dancers. We don't just prance around or Clean floors. Like a Emcee we use our voices to clean our neighborhoods with Dance, Art, Music and Cultures of all different Races. (2017)

One of the most effective and powerful projects to come out of Rec Night was No Affiliation, a tiny, nonviolent music production experiment. Chris Horn, a Providence College student who had studied nonviolence and helped coordinate volunteers at Rec Night, got to know a number of the participants very well. He shared their interest in music, recognized that being identified as a rapper (especially one who had been recorded) increased social status, and believed that creating music was a powerful vehicle for very tough young people to express their feelings and ideas. He and a couple of other volunteers started No Affiliation to provide an additional space for a subset of Rec Night youth to gather weekly, develop their skills as rappers, and record some music. Not surprisingly, talent varied greatly, and much of the music started out driven by feelings of anger, grief, and frustration; described violent situations; and articulated a deep desire to be so powerful as to be immune to threat. Over time, though, relationships were built around deeper feelings and new values, and much of the music moved on to social analysis, love, future dreams, and strategies for achieving the lives the musicians envisioned for themselves. In an interview with the campus newspaper (O'Brien 2013), Chris said, "Many of the kids had disagreements, but one theme that concurrently ran through each individual was their love for music. I saw this connection as an opportunity to amplify a noticeable touch point between youth in hopes of both allowing them to express their emotions through musical and lyrical recording sessions and to build relationships with youth from other sides of town or opposite sides of feuds." Chris's insight reflects that of historian Jeff Chang, author of *Can't Stop, Won't Stop: A History of the Hip-Hop Generation* (2005), who asks, "What if cultural change actually preceded political change?" (2014).

Violence and nonviolence remain in tension with one another across all of these experiments (democracy, community policing, hip-hop), even as they suggest that we can choose our relationship to conflict—that violence is not an inevitable reality. Discussing nonviolence with gang- and street-involved youth, then, begins with helping them see that they have a choice, that they are in fact already familiar with many of the ideas of nonviolence, and grounding the conversation in their day-to-day lives.

We kept the principles and steps of Kingian nonviolence posted at Rec Night and encouraged many program participants to also join in one of ISPN's thirty-hour nonviolence trainings. For several years that Rec Night operated, ISPN ran a six-week summer jobs program, with every Friday reserved for nonviolence training, and we would have as many as thirteen Rec Night youth enrolled. In all of these settings, the principles and steps of Kingian nonviolence were tools we could turn to as ways of framing conversations that helped people reflect on their life experiences, imagine alternative interpretations of their experiences, talk about steps they could take, and identify where they could find support.

It is also the case that much of ISPN's formal and informal training is done by people whose life experiences mirror those of the youth in Rec Night: for example, the head of ISPN's Training Department for most of the time Rec Night ran was Sal Monteiro (2013), who grew up in Providence and was introduced to nonviolence while he was "inside" the state prison. Streetworkers and other community members with experience in gangs or on the streets also offered their stories and played an active role in ongoing discussions. At Rec Night we rarely did anything didactic with the principles and steps—but we would refer to them as a values statement and framework for maintaining our "safe space" and shaping informal discussions about large-scale issues such as racism and immediate issues such as whether to respond to a threat or follow up on a beef.

Streetworkers regularly spent time at Rec Night, dropping by for visits and staying around if we had any concerns or when the conversation was especially rich. For the first three years, police officers from the local district committed to community policing would drop by, and Lieutenant Dan Gannon, the district commander, made himself a consistent and valuable presence. Neighborhood residents would come by to hang out and talk, and much of Rec Night's impact was the rich, organic conversation taking place in the lobby of the rec center each week. College student volunteers were instructed that they weren't there "to help" but to simply join in conversations with participants, and when these relationships flourished, the conversations would regularly turn to "big" questions like racism, inequality, and violence but also to daily life and what people found meaningful and wanted to do with their lives. We usually had one to three offenders sentenced to "community service" attending, and they played the same role as the college volunteers. The principles and steps of nonviolence helped us organize the activities and interpersonal relationships at Rec Night as a physically and emotionally safe space that youth could use to address their conflicts and talk about their lives. It wasn't a space without conflict but a space in which it was safe to name, talk about, and reflect on conflict.

As I've mentioned in earlier chapters, Rec Night had only one rule: you are welcome here as long as you don't act in ways that hurt you or the people around you. "Hurt" was often a matter of debate: it clearly meant no fighting, but questions about aggressive behavior, swearing, the boundary between teasing and bullying, calling fouls on the basketball court, coming in high, or leaving trash around called for a perpetual conversation about the meaning of "hurt." What were the boundaries of behavior we wanted for our community, and how would we discover and maintain them without resorting to force, while keeping the space hospitable to everyone? Rather than naming a hard line, we wanted the conversation to continue, because the debate itself was a powerful learning tool. This was the fundamental way we studied and practiced nonviolence as a community. Rec Night's "safe space" was created not by establishing a set of rules and enforcing them, but by introducing the nonviolent concept of *ahimsa,* which translates from Sanskrit as "do no harm"; reflecting together on our experiences of being with each other; and arriving over and over again at a collective interpretation of what *ahimsa* meant in our community.

Over eight years, we asked only two people to stop coming to Rec Night. We had only one physical fight, and it lasted all of two punches. New participants, especially middle school–age boys, would begin attending and test the system: they would act out in various ways and be deliberately disrespectful, and we—coordinators, volunteers, other participants—would reiterate our one rule. We would always ask, "You doing okay? Everything all right? We want you to be here, but it's on all of us to make this space good for everyone, including you. Can you help out? What can we do?" We would ask a streetworker or more experienced volunteer to engage the youth: play a board game, shoot some baskets, set aside a piece of pizza, simply check in at the start of the evening. Almost without exception, within six weeks or so, the "hurtful" behaviors would begin to disappear. Relationship, hospitality, being seen and heard, respect, a voice in making the community: this is a way of practicing nonviolence.

SO WHAT IS NONVIOLENCE, ANYWAY?

The philosophy and practice of nonviolence have deep and far-flung roots. Gandhi famously described it as a relentless experiment with "truth," pursued through cultivation of our inner lives, constructive social programs, and political change. Buddhism approaches nonviolence through the spiritual practice of "nonattachment," and the Dalai Lama says the practice and goals are simple: more kindness, less suffering, and more happiness. Nonviolent political activists such as Lech Waesa, Václav Havel, Aung San Suu Kyi, and

Nelson Mandela have helped organize successful nonviolent social and political movements in Poland, Czechoslovakia, Myanmar, and South Africa, respectively. As I write this paragraph, the nonviolent "water protectors" of Standing Rock, North Dakota, have just won a temporary victory, announcing a decision from the Army Corps of Engineers that they will request an environmental impact study and reroute the North Dakota Access Pipeline. The water protectors locate their nonviolent campaign as the most recent conflict in a four-hundred-year history of conflicts Native Americans have had with the colonial and expansionist agendas of European and U.S. institutions.

Of course, many nonviolent efforts falter along the way, notably the recent Arab Spring movements that could not prevent or replace civil war in countries such as Egypt, Libya, and Syria. And as I edit my earlier draft of this chapter, the North Dakota Access Pipeline is being completed; the water resistors "lost" but plan to continue their resistance. The predictable outcome of these violent failures is a dramatic and tragic increase in human and ecological suffering.

KINGIAN NONVIOLENCE: PRINCIPLES AND STEPS

The work of the Institute for the Study and Practice of Nonviolence and Rec Night is grounded in the principles and steps of Kingian nonviolence. These are based on the ideas and experiences of Martin Luther King Jr. in the civil rights movement of the United States. Father Ray Malm, a priest at Saint Michael's Parish in Providence, one of the cofounders of ISPN, and the driving force behind its training program, argues that the principles and steps are as applicable to individuals, schools, and gang violence as they are to people's movements for social change.

King was introduced to nonviolence (Kapur 1992) in 1944 when he read Thoreau's *Civil Disobedience* as a freshman at Morehouse College. His awareness of it was reinforced when he heard a lecture on Gandhi by Mordecai Wyatt Johnson, president of Howard University, while at seminary in 1948. King learned of Gandhi's long correspondence with W. E. B. Du Bois, a highly regarded scholar and opponent of "the color line."

In 1955, propelled by his role in the Montgomery Bus Boycott, King began to emerge on the national stage as a civil rights leader, a role he fulfilled until his assassination in 1968. Influenced by theologian Reinhold Niebuhr's *Moral Man and Immoral Society* (1932), which he had read in seminary, King recognized that nonviolence must have some basis in power—in political force—in order to achieve the larger vision of the "Beloved Community." The exercise of power, even revolutionary power, was moral, King argued, as long as it aimed at the Beloved Community and as long as it remained strictly nonviolent (Chernus 2004, 169).

The King Center (n.d.), based in Atlanta, Georgia, combed King's speeches, articles, and archives to articulate the six principles and six steps of Kingian nonviolence, drawing heavily on his 1967 book, *Community or Chaos: Where Do We Go from Here?* These principles and steps provide the values base for ISPN's mission and for its Streetworker, Victim's Services, Youth Development, Jobs, and Nonviolence Training programs. They are what led Tou Pathoummahong, who was working as an ISPN streetworker at the time, to start Rec Night. The principles and steps are not so much a formal theory of nonviolence—King never produced one—as they are a framework that comes out of his reflections on his experiences as a leader of a nonviolent movement. ISPN and Rec Night use the philosophy and principles in a similarly reflective way, inviting people to draw on them as they reflect on their own situations and the potential for positive change.

There is an enormous literature on Kingian nonviolence, and it has been rigorously examined by political philosophers, social scientists, peace advocates, and a wide range of critics (Sharp 1970; T. F. Jackson 2007; Moses 1997; Kurlansky 2006; Lafayette and Jensen 1995a, 1995b). My interest here is not to review that literature but to acknowledge that nonviolence is complex and contested and turn more directly to using the principles and steps of nonviolence to reduce gang and street violence. Over the years, I have annotated the principles and steps based on my experience using them at Rec Night and in teaching, training, and reflection. I offer them first as a list (with a brief notation I have added in parentheses), followed by more expansive descriptions of each.

PRINCIPLES

- moral courage (requiring a community of interpretation and support)
- Beloved Community (offering a vision of humanity as a whole)
- attack evil, not persons (learn to name the sources of conflict)
- accept suffering without retaliation (practice charity and compassion)
- avoid inner violence (self-love, forgiveness, consistency of values and actions)
- universe is on the side of justice (hope, justice)

STEPS

- gather information (with whom am I in relationship, and what are our interests?)
- share information (self-educate, build team, ground action)
- strengthen your own commitment to nonviolence (examine own strengths, weaknesses, and practice)
- negotiate with dignity for all (are the various interests fairly balanced?)
- direct action (use it as a way to increase creative tension in a search for resolution)
- reconcile (celebrate what is meaningful and binds the community together)

Principles of Nonviolence

Moral Courage

One of the first points to make in advocating nonviolence as a realistic and meaningful alternative for youth who are involved in street and gang violence, and who are affected by racism and poverty, is that it is a way of having more, and more sustainable, power; that it is a way to a life that will be more meaningful; and that it requires more courage than violence. In short, the odds of living a good life are better with nonviolence than they are with violence, where the knowable outcome is perpetual war. Novelist Tan Twan Eng translates the Cantonese phrase "Toi chut kong wu" as "Warriors who have voluntarily left their violent world to seek peace" (2008, 12). ISPN and Rec Night invite youth who are contemplating leaving street violence behind to think of themselves in this way. Nonviolence is "not for cowards" and requires moral courage.

Youth often respond to nonviolent trainings by saying something like, "I like this stuff, I get it, but if I practice it on the streets, it will get me killed." When they say this, they are saying three things: They want a way out of their current situation. They calculate that performing violence will keep them safer than nonviolence in the short term. And they are naming the risks inherent in adopting nonviolence as an individual strategy rather than as part of a larger social group. It is as though they are standing on one shore of a wide river and can see the other shore, the place they'd like to be, but don't know how to get there. The first act of moral courage is deciding to cross this river.

For most youth, the hardest part of making this decision is the prospect of doing it alone, leaving a community that doesn't share your new values, and knowing that you will continue to be seen as a threat for some time. The hard answer: you have to help change your community. This means taking care of yourself, but it also means organizing and educating other people: the more people committed to nonviolence there are, the more power you will have and the stronger your voices will be. If you are the only person in your circle committed to nonviolence, you will be at greater risk when violence happens. If you are one of a hundred people, your odds of making it work are a lot better. It is one thing to train and support individual youth; it is another to help them find like-minded peers and adults, get connected, and find mutual support. This is the long-term goal.

In short, our responses to these challenges are quite practical: nonviolence may get you killed, but the odds of getting killed or badly hurt are much higher if you keep choosing violence. And it's the transition that is dangerous—that period where people around you still fear your "old" self and don't trust your new "nonviolent" self. It will be easier if you don't do it alone: Who in your circle is also ready to step up? And, if you think violence takes courage, think about what it takes to not respond to violence with violence: this is called "vulnerability," and vulnerability is one of the major paths to personal growth. You can't grow or make change without taking some risks. Vulnerability is hard, especially for people who have spent years trying to make themselves invulnerable. It takes practice.

Finally, think about how people in your circle and community will look at you if you become positive: some will just be waiting for you to fail, but you'll have a lot of people support you and come to depend on you. Can you imagine using your energy and strength and courage and willingness to commit to improving your community? What kind of power comes with that? Is it equal to the power you have now? Less? More? Do you think you can carry this kind of weight on your shoulders?

Beloved Community

The longer-term goal of nonviolence is the "Beloved Community." While grounded in the work of early-twentieth-century philosopher Josiah Royce (Herstein 2009), the concept of the Beloved Community is not intended to be abstract and teleological. Royce's basic insight was that one of the main benefits of community is "interpretation," the dialogical process in which people discuss their different points of view until they reach a provisional consensus about what is "true" and use that consensus to direct their social decisions and relations. King's Beloved Community reflects Royce's emphasis on interpretation: it argues that arriving at a shared truth across differences is a goal of nonviolence, that conflict is necessary for this truth to be realized, that it is important for persons to speak their truths in public, and that the product of civil conflict will be something socially useful.

The Beloved Community isn't intended to be utopian but something concrete and practical. It is not something you join but something you help make with your participation. Rec Night aspired to be, on a very limited scale, an experience of the "Beloved Community": a place where people felt secure, knew they would be welcomed as their whole self, and as a result could argue and disagree about their interpretations of what was happening around them and the best way forward. Everyone involved could find positive challenges and affirmation, and opportunities to help out, with a goal of moving forward as a community. It was a space that organically provided access to positive people and connections to new opportunities. It was also a space for grieving and healing, having fun, and celebrating.

One of the more important gifts of community is that we discover how we are unique by recognizing how we are different from one another and the others around us. This is an understanding of difference that is the opposite of being excluded on the basis of stereotypes, which see only a group defined by limited and selective characteristics, with the intent or result of excluding the "other" from membership in community.

The concept of the Beloved Community is also an invitation to think practically about how you would like to live your life. What kinds of support and opportunities do you need to live the good life you imagine for yourself? What would enable you to give back to the community that supports you? It is a vision of community as a relational and geographic space for living that provides tangible benefits. It is also a "civil" community that makes dialogue the normative process for resolving conflict, a process that Royce called a "community of interpretation."

Attack Evil, Not Persons

As I noted above, one of King's significant theological influences was Reinhold Niebuhr. Niebuhr considered himself a progressive liberal but took issue with what he saw as the naive pacifism of most social justice advocates of his day. He argued in his *Moral Man and Immoral Society* that corporations, governments, and all social institutions inevitably operated based on self-interests that were always immoral by the standard of individual ethics and that it was unrealistic to expect them to do otherwise. Getting institutions to do the right thing required conflict, and engaging successfully in conflict required power. Attacking evil, not persons, then, is a framework for changing institutions—stopping them from producing suffering and pressuring them to do what is right for persons and communities.

Youth involved in street violence can understand Niebuhr's point from their own experiences and connect it to the concept of "justification": How does it feel to be seen and treated as evil by the larger community? Why are you beefing with people who are fundamentally like you? Why are young men like you from this community shooting other young men like you from this community? Why is this kind of violence in your community and not in other communities? What would it mean to step back from attacking persons and consider "why" your situation is what it is? What becomes possible when you don't use your anger to "justify" attacking another person but redirect it toward asking about and changing the systems that make this violence seem normal?

How do you begin to recognize that attacking other persons does nothing to solve the underlying problem and often has the reverse effect of amplifying the problem as each side uses the other's violence to justify its position? How do you practice compassion and see that your enemy thinks and feels much like you? How do you confront violence and injustice without backing the other side(s) into a corner? How do you open up space for dialogue, humanization, creative resolution? How do you tell your truth and hear the truths of others?

How do you and we recognize the need for structural and systemic change rather than locating our suffering in individual enemies? How can you help give others the same opportunities for growth and development that you would want for yourself?

How do you learn that your emotional response to a situation is not a reflection of what is "true" but is simply how you feel? Learning this can give you some breathing room and is the first step to recognizing that how you respond to any situation is a choice and that you always have a choice.

Accept Suffering without Retaliation

In my experience, people find this principle to be the most difficult in theory and in practice, and it is this principle that creates the perception that nonviolence is passive or weak. An initial response to this critique would be that nonviolence is intended not to promote passivity but rather to force the moral and ethical violation of the other side out into the open and to hold space in which it is possible to reframe the relationship on other, more just, terms. But this is an abstract response to questions that are motivated by fear and suffering.

In practice, even advocates of nonviolence recognize the quandary of self-defense. Gandhi, for example, said, "Though violence is not lawful, when it is offered in self-defence or for the defence of the defenceless, it is an act of bravery far better than cowardly submission. The latter befits neither man nor woman. Under violence, there are many stages and varieties of bravery. Every man must judge this for himself. No other person can or has the right" (1966, 146). King agreed.

For youth involved in street violence, the qualifier "without retaliation" is enormously significant: it is both permission and challenge to not retaliate when you have been harmed. It is what Dan did when he came into the gym the night after being shot and played ball with the younger kids. You do it because someone has to if the cycle of retaliation is going to be broken. Breaking that cycle is an act of moral courage that has meaning for the person making the decision and for the larger community. Accepting suffering without retaliation is not passivity but a way of communicating an alternative interpretation of reality, and an alternative way forward, to everyone watching.

King and Gandhi recognized that suffering is not inherently valuable or redemptive, though as a Christian King reflected deeply on the symbol of the cross and the meaning of crucifixion. Both recognized that suffering gained meaning only when it was exercised as a deliberate choice. Suffering that is chosen has the potential to be transformative; in choosing to accept it, you paradoxically gain some control over it and ethically differentiate yourself from the perpetrator. We ask youth to note how much they are already doing this—living with suffering that they don't or didn't choose. It helps them begin to recognize the moral truth of the violence being done to or by them and to realize that they have, at a minimum, a choice in how they respond.

Avoid Inner Violence

Avoiding inner violence is very complicated for people who are suffering the effects of trauma and who may have internalized a sense of themselves as "less than" or unlovable. If a youth is anxious or depressed, they see the world through that lens and easily find evidence to validate their perspective, often deepening their depression. Experiences of exclusion and marginalization increase sensitivity to rejection, sometimes to hair-trigger levels. Self-harm, violence against others, self-medication with drugs or alcohol or sex, and risking physical safety for the rush it produces are common reactions.

Inner violence is also a way of describing what it is like when we are divided against ourselves—acting in ways that go against the values that ground our best and true selves. Avoiding inner violence begins with being true to yourself and learning to trust that you are good enough just as you are. It invites you to practice living an undivided life because it will be a better way to live over time. It often begins with taking care of yourself—physically, emotionally, spiritually. It is an invitation to practice happiness and forgiveness. When you are deep in some lonely place built by trauma, it can be hard to believe that you can ever be happy or that happiness is anything but a sign that you aren't paying attention to the suffering around you. It takes practice. This principle invites you to forgive yourself and love yourself. It invites you to discover and pursue what gives your life meaning. Don't numb yourself with drink and drugs. Avoid doing things that you are ashamed of doing. Value your personal integrity. Be kind. Let others love you. Trust and believe that you are enough, just as you are (Brown 2012).

Above all, this principle argues that our individual choices matter and that the path to social transformation begins with the decisions of individual persons.

Universe Is on the Side of Justice

This has always seemed to me the most abstract and speculative principle of the six. A friend of mine who oversaw the citywide youth programs run through the mayor's office of a big midwestern city told me that he had been inspired by King's vision of the "mountaintop" as the place we are trying to get to. "I think of myself climbing this mountain every day: 363 days of the year I just keep my eyes on what's in front of me, trying to make it up the trail and not fall off. It's only one or two days a year that I pause and take a look backwards and towards the top. Then I put my head down and start taking steps again."

This principle does not say that progress is inevitable. Instead, it supports three somewhat different interpretations. The first can be found in the declaration of the nonviolent activist and priest Daniel Berrigan, who argued that "hope is out of time." He meant that there is a potential spiritual wholeness or truth to the universe and that we will not recognize or realize it in chronological or human time. Instead, we will get there in "sacred time." We have to trust that doing the right thing contributes to this journey and let go of the idea that we will find evidence of our success in real time. Like my friend in the mayor's office, we take more steps on the journey, because the journey is important, and we stop judging our success by the fruits of our labor. Berrigan and my friend argue that staying hopeful and doing the work is important and meaningful in itself: be hopeful even when you are not optimistic. Trust that the universe will meet you more than halfway.

The second way I interpret this principle is quite outside the larger spiritual framework that King and Berrigan shared. Rather, it is a more existential perspective: How do you want to live your life? Pick your rock and push it up your hill. This is the method for seeking happiness. Being a force for goodwill embeds you in community, gives meaning to your existence, and supports your happiness. It makes sense to choose happiness over fear, alienation, and suffering.

A third way to interpret this principle is to find ways to measure progress in both the short and the long terms. Progress, from this perspective, is not inevitable but is a possible consequence of people learning over time and coming together to "do the right thing" and act in ways that are more life affirming, inclusive, and civil. Steven Pinker, for example, notes that the human past was much more violent than the present and makes the case that "it makes no sense to test for historical changes in violence by plotting deaths against a time line from the calendar. If we discover that violence has declined in a given people, it is because their mode of social organization has changed" (2012, 42). The biggest factor in the decline of human violence? The rise of the centralized state and the emergence of civil society. "So holding many factors constant," he writes, "we find that living in a civilization reduces one's chances of being a victim of violence fivefold" (51). How might we measure this?

In the United States, violent crime has been in a steady decline, even through economic changes: in 1994 there were 714 violent crimes per 100,000 inhabitants; in 2013 there were 368. A slight uptick in 2016—the first in twenty years—still leaves levels below the 2011 rate of 387 per 100,000 (FBI 2012). And in Providence, deaths caused by gang violence are at an all-time low (Milkovitz 2017), with *no gang-related deaths in 2016!* While it is difficult to account for this pattern with any causal explanation, the available evidence does suggest that the collective efforts of persons and civil society institutions to reduce violence and choose peace are having an impact.

Any of these interpretations requires a belief that things can get better and argues that the alternative is staying stuck with violence and injustice, another name for violence. All of them argue that our individual choices and commitments matter. What do you choose?

Steps of Nonviolence

The steps of nonviolence are intended to put the principles into practice and integrate them as a system for addressing conflict: I am experiencing or witnessing suffering that seems unjust; what can I do about it? The steps ask that you make sure you understand what is happening from as many perspectives as possible, that you have a good grasp of the situation and any relevant history or facts or interests. They require you to analyze your strengths and weaknesses—how much or how little power you have and how you can have enough to enter into balanced and productive negotiations with the source of the injustice. The steps point toward expanding membership in shared community and offer a straightforward, if challenging, process for putting the principles into action.

Gather Information

Gathering information is important for resolving street conflicts as well as untangling systemic violence. It is the antidote for the process of justification: What is the history, what are the immediate causes, who is involved, what do they have at stake, what could bring them to or keep them from coming to the table? What solutions are possible? Gathering information ties into Gandhi's sense of nonviolence as a pursuit of truth: understanding how diverse viewpoints generate explanatory models and emphasize or de-emphasize certain facts along the way. It is a first step in describing your own interests, perspective, and goals and recognizing the interests, perspectives, and goals of the "other" with whom you are in conflict.

This kind of perspective taking helps to separate "facts" that are objectively indisputable from "truths" that are contingent on perspective. It assumes that most conflicts are a result of divergent truths and that reconciliation—the final step—will happen when the conflicting parties can agree on a shared truth. Gathering information is, in the deepest sense, a process of discovering and articulating self-interest—not selfishness, but literally "self among others."

Share Information

This principle asks that you share information—what you are learning—with a larger circle of people: get it heard, understood, affirmed, clarified, amplified, challenged, and revised. This is the stage when you begin testing what you think you know about a situation, comparing it publicly against what others know. It is when your interpretation, your story, your truth is most likely to undergo significant revision. It is when you find allies and begin to build a base for organizing among people interested in your information, people asking similar questions for similar reasons, people willing to act based on a shared interpretation of the social reality. It is the stage in which you and your growing circle begin to name your own reality and describe what can be done to change it for the better.

Organizers argue that power comes from combining any two of money, information, and people. Sharing information is the pivotal step in organizing information and people into potential "people's power."

Strengthen Your Own Commitment to Nonviolence

Terry Warner of the Arbinger Institute argues that every act of violence is also an act of self-betrayal and that we justify it to ourselves as a way of affirming our feelings of anger, accusation, and blaming. Self-betrayal indicates that we are acting in ways that divide us against ourselves and against other people and elements of existence, when the alternative is to act in ways that recognize and advance interconnectedness. "Since in blaming the other person we actually feel offended," Warner writes, ". . . we can convince ourselves that we are justified WHATEVER we do—justified if we give in to the provocation and justified if we rise 'nobly above it'" (1986, 8–9). Self-betrayal creates a "virtual reality" in which "others are resented and we ourselves are freed from responsibility" (10).

We end up "divided against ourselves," as Parker Palmer points out, when we justify to ourselves actions that are betrayals of what we know is right, in which we blame others for our anger, inaction, or irresponsibility. When we blame, act irresponsibly, or justify our anger, we are betraying ourselves. The positive alternative is to act on what we know is right—the path opened up to us when we have brushed away our blaming, anger, and self-justification. Thomas Merton, in his *Nonviolent Alternative,* offers a simple "test of our sincerity in the practice of nonviolence . . . : are we willing to learn something from the adversary?" (1981, 214). Strengthening my commitment to nonviolence means reflecting honestly on Merton's question.

It is also the case, as Michelle Alexander and others remind us, that gains made through the personal sacrifices of nonviolent action are always at risk, sometimes rolled back, and sometimes replaced by alternatives only marginally better than the original. Slavery gave way to Jim Crow gave way to civil rights gave way to the New Jim Crow. What are our expectations of success and progress? Are they realistic? What personal costs are we willing to carry and for how long?

Strengthening our commitment to nonviolence invites us to ask, what am I contributing to the conflict? How can I be more honest with myself, as well as with others? Can I understand the perspectives of my adversaries and learn from them? Am I open to being changed by my practice of nonviolence? Are my reasons for practicing nonviolence genuine or a way of being "noble" and seeking social affirmation? What choices can I make that will increase the potential for positive outcomes? What am I willing to risk in order to grow?

Negotiate with Dignity for All

Chuck Matthei, a lifelong nonviolent activist and friend, argues that we exist in a web of relationships and that there are two questions that matter most: With whom are you entering into relationship? Are the interests fairly balanced?

Practicing nonviolence means stepping into a relationship with the persons you see as adversaries, problems, enemies. Where violence exaggerates difference—how we are unlike our opponent and so justified in imposing our values and interests—nonviolence argues that stepping into conflict with someone is establishing a relationship and that resolving the conflict will require a solution that is recognized by all sides as the best possible under the circumstances.

Gandhi (Erikson 1993) approached his negotiations for workers' rights, national independence, and antiracism by holding in mind a concept of "the moral minimum." Rather than starting high and negotiating for a middle ground or compromise, he advised being clear about the minimum you would accept, making sure it was ethically valid, taking into account the reality of the other sides, and asking for no more than the minimum necessary to achieve a just relationship.

The goal in negotiating with dignity for all is not beating your opponent but entering into a relationship with the other side(s) in order to remedy an injustice and arrive at an equitable way to live together. Negotiate fairly, continue learning about the interests of the other side, and seek solutions that do not diminish the humanity of anyone involved or affected. Keep open the possibility that a remedy may be something that you didn't expect, as likely to transform you as the people with whom you are negotiating.

While a truce may be the best you can do for the moment, the longer-term goal is restoring relationships so that we can each live without fear of traumatic violence—a characteristic of individual and communal resilience. One simple tool for envisioning this type of negotiation, and tied deeply into the dynamics of justification, is distinguishing between needs and wants: what I need is not negotiable, because it is tied into my existence and my core identity; what I want is always negotiable. As fraught as it can be, a careful process of negotiation can help all parties distinguish the difference and use this insight to figure out a way forward.

Direct Action

Direct action is the most visible element of nonviolence, nearly the archetypal symbol that is taken for the whole. Gene Sharp (1973), a scholar of nonviolent direct action, describes 198 different forms of direct action, each of them specific to a relational context. Noncompliance, boycotts, marches, sit-ins, protests, and strikes are not intended as ends in themselves, however, but as methods of bringing the other to the table for negotiation and creating momentum for the truth of the activists. In practice, direct action is a kind of witness: speaking truth to power in a social context that opens space for relationship, conversation, and negotiation. Direct action can be an expression of deep anger, but that anger and the action it inspires have to be tempered with the recognition that the goal is getting to a common truth and that the dignity of the persons on the "other" side(s) matters over the long haul.

The goal in direct action is bringing to the surface the moral and social contradictions that result from the behavior of the adversary and bringing the adversary to the table to resolve these contradictions. Direct action is an organizing tool, it is an expression of power, and it is a way of bringing counternarratives into public view.

Direct action is also about learning to "step into fear," by going directly to the source of what we believe is the root of the violence we are trying to end. Stepping into fear can be a part of healing from traumatic violence and a step toward learning to live in ways that are not based on fear.

Reconcile

Practicing nonviolent dissent is a way of humanizing the opposition on all sides of a conflict. "The basic challenge of pluralistic politics," writes Chantal Mouffe, is ". . . converting antagonistic into agonistic relations" (Ivie 2007, 4). Reconciliation is based on the value of cultural and political pluralism: recognizing that people with competing truths can live together and thrive. It is not the simple pluralism of each interest group keeping to itself but recognizing that our foundational truths are ultimately provisional and exist in tension with one another.

We each believe in our foundational truth deeply enough that we try to organize our lives around it: living out the story of who I believe I am is the essence of culture. Pluralism argues for valuing our coexistence as much as our own truth. Its social expression is the ongoing dialogue we must have with one another to keep our community intact, diverse, and resilient. "The importance of cultivating a humanizing discourse of dissent" in a pluralistic community "would be difficult to overstate," writes Robert Ivie (5).

Reconciliation is what happens when relationships that have become sources of conflict are restored and transformed into a source of positive energy. Genuine diversity—and the ongoing public conversation needed to agree on the meaning of this dynamic, perennially contested value—is a hallmark of reconciliation.

Reconciliation is often expressed in the form of celebration: honoring the history that has led to the new place, affirming the restored relationships, embracing diversity, and, to paraphrase Margaret Wheatley, "restor[ing] hope to the future" (2009).

GETTING REAL: CRITIQUES OF NONVIOLENCE

While the principles and steps add up to a useful and inspiring whole, you don't have to spend much time talking with people about nonviolence—including the youth at Rec Night—to realize that they have strong, mostly critical, opinions about it. Once you get past the initial rush to the extremes, the question that comes up most often has to do with limits: How far would you go with nonviolence before turning to violence to protect the people or places you care about? When the youth ask this question, the unstated subtext is, "Can I depend on you to keep me safe?"

I know one ex-gang member, now quite dedicated to practicing nonviolence, who went to prison for killing a person who had harshly assaulted a family member. He is not sorry to have done so and thinks he did the right thing. He also talks regularly with gang-involved youth about the circumstances and consequences of their choices, consistently helps them de-escalate violent situations, and introduces them to nonviolent alternatives for settling conflicts. Like many nonviolence advocates I know, he approaches it with something akin to his own "just war theory": while nonviolence is preferable, choosing violence is regrettable but allowed under certain narrow conditions. He thinks violence should be reserved to the state, usually in the institutions of the police or military, also under very narrow conditions, but believes there are exceptions to this rule. He takes nonviolence seriously and uses it as a first and second line of response, but he doesn't believe it can work in all circumstances. Over time, the circumstances in which he does believe it can work are expanding.

Growing out of the debate about limits, the second most common challenge has to do with nonviolence as a way of life or as a strategy or tactic that can be employed for social change under certain conditions. Is nonviolence something you are or something you do? King himself initially adopted nonviolence as a strategy in the Montgomery Bus Boycott and only gradually came to embrace it as a way of life. The main focus of ISPN and Rec Night is on working with individual people impacted by violence and suggesting to them that studying and practicing nonviolence can help them construct an alternative, more positive way of being in the world. It is about "praxis"—helping people learn to move back and forth between action and reflection in order to achieve positive change. Praxis focuses not on the binary of strategy or way of life but on the "cash value" of practicing nonviolence: if it is valuable and meaningful, people will do more of it over time and begin to internalize it as a way of being.

Tou and I debated these questions about limits and ways of being many times over our eight years of working together on Rec Night and regularly drew program participants and volunteers into the conversations. Tou also believes in a street version of just war theory. He understands and practices nonviolence and has a deep and complex commitment to fairness. He understands structural violence but believes that the most important thing to focus on is being an honorable person and helping "your people," members of your geographic, identity, and experiential communities. At the end of the day, he believes that nonviolence works only when it can be backed up by legitimate force. He understands "legitimate" not so much in legal terms as in terms of honor and respect: using force only in ways that the larger community would recognize and affirm as necessary and just. Tou grounds his perspective in his family's experiences in Laos during the Vietnam War, his and their time in refugee camps, his parents' subsequent struggles with the effects of trauma, his experiences of racism and poverty as a new immigrant in California and Providence, and what he believes his time in a gang taught him about the inevitability of violence. He says nonviolence is a good idea, and something he believes in and practices, but he believes it has limits. Who's to say he is wrong?

I, on the other hand, have come to believe that there are no circumstances in which violence is a good option. I can imagine resorting to it in self-defense, and wanting to resort to it if someone close to me were deliberately harmed, but I would expect to experience my action as a self-betrayal in which I would have failed myself and initiated a ripple effect that would undoubtedly shape my life and the lives of many others for months or years to come. I believe that one value of being in a nonviolent community is that other members can intervene and help search for more productive responses. My reasoning is that if I allow myself to keep violence on the table as an option, then it is all too easy to justify using it when conflicts reach what I believe are a critical stage. This can be a real barrier to forcing myself to stretch, live with discomfort and ambiguity, learn, and think of creative, nonviolent alternatives. We can be sure that a guaranteed consequence of violence, no matter how much we believe it is justified, will be more suffering, while nonviolence holds out the possibility of less suffering. So, my colleagues and the youth from Rec Night know I am moving toward pacifism; they know, too, that I believe we are all on the journey together and no person alone has the right answer. Who is to say I am right?

A third concern that comes up frequently has to do with forgiveness: the soul-deep fear that forgiving yourself or someone else for harm done is undeserved or will be somehow disrespectful of the suffering that was caused. How can I be nonviolent if I have to face the person who injured or killed my friend or brother? How can I be nonviolent if I have not been forgiven for serious harm I have caused? How can I forgive myself, or hope for forgiveness from others, when I have deliberately damaged or killed someone else? Isn't reconciling with my enemy a betrayal of everyone who has suffered at their hands and been sacrificed in battle?

The short answer, I think, is that forgiving does not mean forgetting (Doblmeier 2008). It does not mean pretending nothing happened or that everything is okay. It is, rather, about not holding on to anger or the wish to retaliate. It is about practicing compassion—literally, being with suffering—because it is a more life-affirming way forward. Forgiveness cannot be forced, and is not a straightforward option, but pursuing it, as victim or perpetrator or both, is a choice, and it is possible to establish conditions in which it is more possible, as with "restorative justice" practices in schools or "truth and reconciliation" processes following civil wars or institutional oppression such as apartheid.

Two of the most challenging conversations about forgiveness I have experienced have taken place during nonviolence trainings that I was helping ISPN facilitate. Both were prompted by the group's viewing of the documentary *The Power of Forgiveness* (ibid.). In one instance, a mother whose son had recently been murdered talked about how she had felt since learning of her son's death. He had been in a street crew, but she did not think of him as a violent person. She was exhausted from bouncing between anger and grief and wanted to forgive the young man she had heard was responsible for her son's death. She imagined he was a lot like her son. She didn't believe she could forgive him. During the next day of training she said she had stayed up all night thinking about it and wanted to practice forgiveness for her own well-being; she didn't think she could continue as she was. The vehicle for "practice" that she chose was talking to classes at local schools, meeting with youth programs, and speaking at ISPN events: telling her story and trying to communicate her pain so that others would think before they acted. Over the next months it worked and it didn't work. She said she had to continue to practice forgiveness but was getting there. She was finding a way to incorporate her new reality into her thinking and way of being in the world, to feel what she was feeling. She was slowly finding ways of using her son's death to do something that was life affirming and, in the process of helping her community, healing herself.

The second instance was with a brilliant, sensitive African American man in his early twenties who had been involved with a gang and drugs. He was a new father and in the process of changing his life. He had recently struggled with a deep depression and had considered suicide, something that had surfaced several times in his life. He told his story, first privately to one of the facilitators and then to the group. He wanted to forgive his father, who had emotionally and physically abused him and his siblings. He wanted to do this because he was now a father, and he thought that forgiving his father was a way of ensuring he would never behave as his father had behaved. He traced his participation in street violence and drugs, and much of his depression, to the abuse. He was moved by the documentary *The Power of Forgiveness* and by its presentation of Thich Nhat Hanh's meditation on imagining the person who hurt you as a five-year-old child and finding compassion for what must have happened to them along the way. I saw this man, his girlfriend, and their new child a few months later at a local restaurant. He was working part-time and pursuing a bachelor's degree in education. He believed he had forgiven his father but had decided to not introduce him to his grandchild.

These stories are complex, unfinished, moving, and terribly sad, and they are all too common. Michael Brown's mother writes, in her memoir about his killing by a police officer in Ferguson, Missouri, that she is reaching for forgiveness and nonviolence because it is the right thing to do, but she isn't there, yet. Tou Pathoummahong and Ray Duggan both ended up as streetworkers at ISPN, working together on the streets. Tou's best friend, a fellow gang member, had died in his arms of a gunshot wound several years earlier. Even now, almost two decades later, Tou is transported emotionally and deeply into that moment whenever he tells the story. Ray, a member of a rival gang, was shot in the spine during a drive-by and paralyzed from the waist down. It is likely—neither shooter was ever named or charged—that someone from Ray's gang shot Tou's friend. And someone from Tou's side shot Ray. In order to work together, to be effective and trust one another, they had to achieve some kind of forgiveness for what had happened. They did so separately and together over a long stretch of time, exceptionally careful and honest with their words and actions. Forgiveness can happen instantly and fully, but more often it is a process and has to be revisited. As Everett

Worthington says in *The Power of Forgiveness,* there is no way to make it happen. You just have to start by opening yourself up to the possibility and hope for the best. It helps to have a community of support.

A fifth objection people raise regarding nonviolence has to do with the relationship between individual and social change: Doesn't being "kind" or practicing positive psychology deny the violence that is happening? Was A. J. Muste (1967) correct in arguing that "there is no way to peace, peace is the way"? Rec Night's bridge from individual to social change took place at the neighborhood level, a scale identified as promising by criminologist David Kennedy in *Don't Shoot* (2011), sociologist Elijah Anderson in *Code of the Street* (2000), and educator Geoffrey Canada in his *Fist, Stick, Knife, Gun* (2010).

This scale makes sense because it is where normative practices for addressing conflict are established. Sociologist Lonnie Athens (2003; Rhodes 2000, 228) makes the case that "the norms that people use for settling dominance disputes [are] the major source of a community's organization." He goes on to distinguish among "civil," "virulent," and "turbulent" social contexts: In the first, people expect laws, procedures, dialogue, or mediation will be used to resolve conflict and as an alternative to violence. In "virulent" contexts—a neighborhood, a street, a particular school, a family, a gang—violence will be used to resolve conflict, distribute resources, or solve social questions. In turbulent communities the method of resolution is inconsistent and unpredictable and very unsettling as a result. Athens cites sociologist Robert Park, who recognized this type of context in 1890s Chicago: "Everything is loose and free but everything is problematic."

Many inner-city neighborhoods are turbulent, as the great majority of residents value and act out of civil society values, but individuals or groups in that place—often related in kinship networks to the first group of residents—use violence. The need to continually assess what potential threats mean and how you should respond adds to stress and creates a sense of insecurity. Turbulent contexts are, Athens argues, the most dangerous because it can be hard to know how to behave in a given situation. Rec Night began as a "turbulent" space and became a "safe space" only when participants believed they could count on it to be civil. You cannot create safe space by denying or abolishing conflict or violence; you create safe space by making it a space in which conflict will be resolved nonviolently.

A final critique I sometimes encounter is that nonviolence is not only naive but racist. Kingian nonviolence and its symbolic alignment with civil rights are greeted with some skepticism by community members who continue to experience the daily and systemic effects of racism. Ta-Nehisi Coates captures this skepticism in his memoir, *Between the World and Me*. Writing as an African American father passing on to his son hard-earned wisdom about surviving racism, Coates recalls celebrations of Martin Luther King Day during his public school years and asks, "Why were our only heroes nonviolent? . . . How could they [educators] send us out into the streets of Baltimore, knowing all that they were, and then speak of nonviolence?" (2015, 32).

Nonviolence, as Coates understands it, is about willingly giving one's body over to the violence of the oppressor, and Coates coaches his son to do otherwise: "You preserved your life because your life, your body, was as good as anyone's. . . . You do not give your precious body to the billy clubs of Birmingham sheriffs nor to the insidious gravity of the streets" (35). Coates believes his schools lied to their students—to him—when they promoted nonviolence rather than the right to personal integrity and self-defense.

Coates's preferred alternative was voiced by Malcolm X, who asserted the right of self-protection: "Malcolm never lied, unlike the schools and their façade of morality, unlike the streets and their bravado, unlike the world of dreamers. . . . [H]e spoke like a man who was free" (36). Rather than nonviolence or violence, Malcolm X offered "self-defense," the right to protect the integrity of your body and your community when it is threatened, "by any means neces-sary." "Concerning nonviolence," Malcolm X said, "it is criminal to teach a man not to defend himself when he is the constant victim of brutal attacks" (1964, 22).

Why, Coates asks, do we celebrate King's nonviolence in our schools and not Malcolm X's right to self-defense and self-determination? He answers his own question: watered down, sentimentalized nonviolence is offered by white America for the unspoken purpose of keeping African Americans in their place. Otherwise, white America would have to admit its fear, acknowledge racism and its effects, listen to the truths of black America, and change its core values and institutions.

This critique seems logical and compelling and offers some deep truths about power and what it is to grow up in a context of racially determined violence. Coates, like Malcolm X, offers not a theoretical perspective but one grounded in lived experience that asks, how will you respond when you are threatened—directly and institutionally—for being black?

At the same time, Coates's perspective minimizes the subtlety and complexity of the ongoing debate that King and Malcolm X had about nonviolence and violence. When asked about his differences with King, Malcolm X noted, "We both want the same thing: freedom." Historian and theologian James Cone observes, "Though their views on nonviolence and violence were different, they complemented and corrected each other, showing us that an abstract, absolutist, and uncritical commitment to violence or nonviolence, to Malcolm or Martin is wrongheaded. We do not need to choose between Martin and Malcolm but rather to acknowledge the value in both" (2001, 182).

My response, and what we tried to practice at Rec Night, is similar to Cone's: we are studying and practicing nonviolence because we all want freedom. Nonviolence is a debate and a practice. Nonviolence does not offer a utopian vision of a world without conflict, or of a world without fundamental and deep disagreements between persons and between states. While Malcolm X and King differed somewhat about self-defense, and had very different perspectives on "accepting suffering without retaliation," they came to share a broad social analysis of the intertwined histories of what King called the "triple evils" of racism, poverty, and militarism. Both men grounded their resistance and activism in their searches for spiritual truth. Each of them combined his politics with life practices aimed at becoming a full and authentic human being while living inside the contradictions forced on him by racism and other forms of structural violence. And, in the months before each of them was assassinated, their views on social change were slowly converging around understandings of human development, social transformation, conflict, and authentic power.

Ethics ultimately is about the way your choices and actions affect my choices and actions, and conflict happens when our choices and actions infringe on one another in small or large ways. As Parker Palmer says, "Real community is that place where the person you least like always is, and when they leave somebody worse takes their place" (2014). Nonviolence is a way of thinking about ethics—about our choices and actions, our relationships to others, and the values and interests that lie behind these. Our interests are always negotiable. Our core values are not. How do we learn to distinguish between interests and core values, to negotiate, and to live in community with people who hold different values than ours?

Nonviolence is intended to be practical and oriented toward stepping into and through conflict in the belief that transformative solutions can be found. In practice, it confronts suffering and injustice directly: the problem Coates encountered, from this point of view, was not being taught nonviolence but being taught that racism had been ended by King's movement and that nonviolence had nothing to do with having and exercising power. The version of nonviolence offered by his school failed to tell the truth and did nothing to keep him safe and for these reasons was hypocritical. Nonviolence assumes that conflict will always exist and that what we choose to do with it is what matters most—but we have to learn to use it. As Jonathan Larson put it in the musical *Rent* (2008), "The opposite of war isn't peace, it's creation."

The goal in introducing nonviolence to youth deeply affected by racism, poverty, and violence is helping them describe and interpret their own situations in their own voices, helping them study their situations deeply and continuously on their own and with others, and supporting them as they figure out their own answers to these hard questions. It is about supporting them as they organize for personal and collective change and about inviting them into efforts that are already under way. Rather than making an abstract case for nonviolence, it is more productive to dive into this basic question: Given your understanding of the reality in which you live, and your knowledge of who you are and want to be, how will you live your life?

PRACTICING NONVIOLENCE

In the spring of 2011, one of the youth I know was arrested for participating in a drive-by shooting. A few days later I went to visit him at the intake center of Rhode Island's Adult Correctional Institution. Visitors pass through a series of checkpoints and walk for several minutes down stairs and hallways to a windowless cafeteria. You check in at another desk and take a seat at a cafeteria table. The prisoner you are visiting enters through a door at the opposite end of the room and joins you. "You're disappointed in me, huh?" Jamal asked as he gave me a hug. After checking in a bit on other people, he told me a version of what had happened that night: His friend Peter had wanted to drive by some people from a gang in another neighborhood of Providence and shoot at them. It was part of a conflict that went back years and had heated up recently. Peter asked Jamal to support him. Jamal said no, then yes. He told me, "I was thinking of you, thinking how to be nonviolent. I went along and offered to be the shooter. I fired one shot into the ground and then pretended the gun had jammed. It was the best I could think of to make sure no one got hurt. Then the police flashed on us, we tried to run, and they caught us." I told him I believed him but doubted anyone else would. He said Peter would back up his story. Was Jamal practicing nonviolence? Violence? Both?

On another occasion, I was driving with five thirteen- to fourteen-year-old boys to pick up pizza for Rec Night. They were talking about a fight that had happened just after school that day. A kid they knew had been confronted by three other youth and threatened with physical violence in front of a gathering crowd. Three other youth, all juniors in a local gang, stepped in with the youth who was on his own and faced down the aggressors, who swore a little and then left. The youth in my truck were excited. "He must be a junior in [this crew]!" "Did you see how they got his back? I'd like somebody to have my back like that." They told stories of times it would have been useful.

I asked them, do you like to fight? A lot? No, of course not, they said. They explained that it was a way of being safe, of not fighting. I asked, how many people in that crew, do you think? Maybe twenty? So, every time one of them has a beef, everyone in the crew has to get his back. And part of being in a gang is that someone always has a beef. So, you join for security but you end up always fighting. You have to like fighting to be successful in a gang. They considered this and thought they could fight if they had to. You willing to use weapons? I asked next. Because you are small and not very strong yet, if you have to go up against people older than you. And the other side might have weapons. You'll need something to even it up, in either case. Before you sign up, you might want to think: You want to fight a lot? You willing to use weapons and hurt other people? You see any alternatives? The conversation ended as we arrived at the pizza place. On the way back to the rec center they cranked a rap station and sang along. While the details varied, this kind of conversation was a pretty regular occurrence. Was it about violence? Nonviolence? Both?

These examples—unique in their particulars but not their logic—capture something of the cognitive, ethical, spiritual, and strategic space in which youth involved with gang and street violence pursue the study and practice of nonviolence. What is our relationship to violence? What do we believe about it, and what do we learn when we start to pay attention to the evidence it offers? What are the alternatives? The answers, if they are to be meaningful, have to be that choosing nonviolence will give you more power, more choices, and more opportunities to do more of what is meaningful to you.

CONCLUSION

You can't understand most of the important things from a distance.... You have to get close.

—Bryan Stevenson, *Just Mercy*

SUCCESS?

I haven't talked directly about "success" in the preceding chapters. This is mostly because I have ceased thinking in those terms. I agree with activist Rebecca Solnit: "Hope is an embrace of the unknown and the unknowable, an alternative to the certainty of both optimists and pessimists. Optimists think it will all be fine without our involvement; pessimists take the opposite position; both excuse themselves from acting. It's the belief that what we do matters even though how and when it may matter, who and what it may impact, are not things we can know beforehand" (2016, xiv). Hope is needed to sustain the long haul and is different from optimism. Constructive programs such as Rec Night and practical interventions such as youth positive do make a difference in the lives of individual youth, but by themselves they do little to change the structural and social causes of the problem at hand.

Instead, constructive programs motivate and help us to discover and understand the root causes of social problems—the underlying institutional systems that result in a consistent, problematic outcome. The more I learn about the systems that produce street violence by and on youth, the more hopeful I am that things will change and the less optimistic I am that they will change anytime soon.

The problem of youth gangs can be solved by a simple, common-sense shift in the shared cultural values that shape our public institutions. I am realistic enough to appreciate that I have no idea if and when our current faith in the efficacy of violence will begin to give way to values of compassion, community, and nonviolence, especially with respect to youth who are routinely positioned as "other."

It also seems just a little ridiculous to argue that a few hours of safe space and support per week can counter a lifetime of experience and an ongoing reality. I start from the perspective that the youth are not the problem—but are doing what any of us would likely do under similar circumstances. So, I don't think that Rec Night fixed anyone or saved anyone. This was never the goal. It did help many youth become more resilient; it did help them describe and analyze their situations, it did help them name some options, and it supported many of them in pursuing those options. To borrow Walker Percy's apt phrase, it "hand[ed] them along a ways on their dark journey" (1961, 233). Youth, police, and community members told us they noticed things calming down over time. Now that the program has been shut down for a while, several of the past participants and community supporters have approached Tou and me, saying they would like to bring it back—saying simply that "it is needed."

I think of Franklin, a gang member with juvenile charges for possession of a handgun, who decided to get out of Providence and took a job with a migratory environmental remediation company and then hooked up a number of his friends, so that they can stay safe, travel, and save up some money. He is smart, funny, and a philosopher. He got neck tattoos to remind him of where he came from and to ensure that he never gets a "straight" job. I think of Kham, who suffered from some serious mental health problems and had people in his crew close around and support him until he got back on an even keel. There were nights at the rec center when Kham would stand against the wall for all three hours, staring into space, saying nothing to anyone. We went to court with him as he faced charges that grew out of his illness and helped keep him out of prison. I think of Fabio, who did become a rapper and manager and successful young adult. The second month of Rec Night, Fabio was pointed out to me as one of the most dangerous youth in the neighborhood and one of the most likely to be killed. I think of Keo, a gang member who became a prep cook and then a chef at a local restaurant. He recalibrated his relationship with his family and his gang and keeps off the streets. I think of Craig, arrested for armed robbery, who subsequently started a small-scale graphic design and clothing line while working part-time in a restaurant. I think of Will, who got an athletic scholarship to a small local college and managed to hang in until he finished. He has no record and would like to be a state trooper. I think of Jason, the first in his family to finish high school, the only one of several siblings to not join a gang, who is now working as an assistant manager at a gas station. I think of Vong, who was sent into deep depression by street violence and a chaotic home life but used Rec Night and related supports to disconnect from his crew, find hourly work, and pursue his interests in video games and anime. I think of Isaac, connected to several crews at a local housing project, who joined a series of service and education corps and just got his first job as an assistant high school basketball coach. I think of Anaya, who is dedicated to raising her daughter and continues to pursue her own personal healing and development. I think of Chan, who left street violence behind, struggles to stay enrolled in community college, works part-time, and remains in his family's violent household in order to protect and care for his younger siblings.

I also think of all the youth on the bubble—the handful I worry will end up on the streets or in prison. I think of the ones who are struggling emotionally and psychologically and will have a hard time hanging on. I think of the ones who are staying around to raise younger siblings and take care of needy parents, giving up much of their own dreams. I think of the challenges many will have bridging their aspirations and potential, on the one hand, and the limits of responsibility and meaning they may face in the paid work and stunted opportunities that are available, on the other. I think of the many who still love the adrenaline rush that comes with high-stakes experiences, from boxing to gambling to extreme sports. I think of the two young men I knew personally who were killed and the dozen who were shot. I think of a couple of young men whose immigration status is problematic and who may face deportation to countries of "origin" they have never visited, because they are identified as "gang members." Rec Night made a difference, but it solved nothing. This is the paradox; it is the difference between optimism and hope.

RESISTANCE

For the eight years Rec Night ran, it was one of the largest weekly programs happening in Providence rec centers. We had "big" numbers—averaging eighty-plus youth each week, along with fifteen or more volunteers—and the program stayed safe. One thing I have not discussed, though, was the resistance Rec Night encountered throughout the eight years it ran, especially in the first couple of years. In many ways it is this opposition that inspired me to write this book and makes it necessary to describe what I see as the commonsense "method" of youth positive.

The director of the rec center where we ran the program had an active distaste for many of the youth we invited in. He had two lists of rules: the fourteen rules posted on the door and a second list that he kept in his head. All fourteen of the posted rules were prohibitions, followed by consequences for violating them. While he was, in many ways, a kindhearted and community-minded person, the director believed access to "his" rec was a reward for the "good kids" in the neighborhood, and he actively worked to exclude youth who were in gangs or ran the streets. He was an African American man in his late thirties who had grown up in the neighborhood and was deeply involved in a socially conservative Protestant church. He was, to use Elijah Anderson's loaded and accurate phrase, "decent." "Decent" community members, Anderson writes, "tend to be strict in their child-rearing practices, encouraging children to respect authority and walk a straight moral line. They have an almost obsessive concern about trouble of any kind" (1994, 3). Our program was an affront to all he stood for. In his view, our program "rewarded bad behavior." We were always on the verge of "losing control." We "didn't understand how bad" the kids were. He had no trust for, and constantly baited, Tou, who knew him from his younger days.

Most of the youth didn't trust the rec director and several disliked him. He said that some of our older youth and some of the adults in the community who remained involved in the streets had threatened him; he felt threatened, and they were not allowed in. For months he kept the police on speed dial, calling them every time youth exchanged heated words or argued too loudly about something on the basketball court. He wrote his supervisor an email every week after our program ended, "documenting" the ways our participants had broken his rules and describing a scene of chaos perpetually on the brink of violence. We had meeting after meeting "mediated" by his supervisor, until we finally just asked her to attend our program and judge for herself. She decided to trust us, blunting the complaints of the director and creating a politically complex dynamic.

For a while in the early months, the police and the director wanted us to either collect or outlaw backpacks, because they knew the youth carried weapons. The director also wanted to insist that no one could play basketball unless they changed into proper athletic clothes. In combination, these demands would have profoundly altered our program: collecting and storing backpacks would have been very difficult in the space offered by this rec center, and most of the youth we were interested in showed up and played in street clothes: they had limited access to athletic wear. The youth also recognized the conundrum: I need a backpack to bring a change of clothes, but I'm being discouraged from bringing a backpack because it could conceal a weapon.

The director also wanted the youth to sign in with their full names—a practice we ended the first time a police officer from the gang unit came by unannounced and demanded to see our sign-in sheet. We did ask youth to sign in so we could keep a head count; we greeted people at the door so we knew who was in attendance, but the youth could put any name they wanted on the sheet, typically just a first name or nickname. If a cell phone was stolen, as it was on three occasions, we were reminded that many of our youth were "criminals" and that we shouldn't trust them.

The rec director wanted to punish all infractions and suspend anyone who broke a rule "until they came in with a parent." This was an impossible demand for many of the youth: their parents often worked swing shifts or two jobs, or they had a single parent with other children at home, or their parents were not "decent," not the kind of people who would ever sit down with the director. The director would shake his head. He believed parental neglect was the source of street violence and social disorder, and he was willing to visit the moral failure of parents on the youth. For him, it was just the way it was. For our part, we kicked no one out and suspended no one in eight years; over the life of the program we asked only two people to voluntarily stop attending: a volunteer and an older participant whose behavior we found inappropriate. Even they left with no hard feelings.

Residents regularly showed up at our program needing to do "community service" as a condition of parole or probation, and we invited them in. Many of ISPN's streetworkers had criminal records. We did not do background checks on our volunteers—since we were welcoming in participants and volunteers with criminal records, the information would not have influenced our decisions. Instead, we told youth how to let us know if they ever felt uncomfortable, we watched new volunteers and participants carefully, and we never allowed conditions in which a single volunteer could be alone with a youth. Youth did tell us they felt uncomfortable a couple of times, and we followed up accordingly. In neither instance was their discomfort with a person under court supervision.

Still, our critics charged that we allowed "good" youth to interact with criminals and gang members. This seems like a reasonable concern until you recognize that the criminals and gang members were relatives and neighbors, from the community, and already known to most of the youth. It meant something to the youth to see them helping out, serving pizza, being positive, talking about work or relationships or their encounters with the justice system. And it meant something to the community volunteers as well.

The first summer we ran the program, we had to move from the rec center to a nearby park for a couple of months. This park was in a different police district, and our first evening at the new site, three police cruisers roared into the parking lot next to the basketball court. An irate district commander asked us, "What the fuck do you think you are doing in my park?" He hollered at a Laotian American teenager to turn off his music because it was illegally loud (it wasn't). We asked him what we needed to do to continue using the park—we knew we were there legally and had notified the proper city authorities. He said he would keep a close eye on us and we'd better not do one thing wrong. He stormed out as aggressively as he'd stormed in. The following week—and for the next six or seven weeks—two young officers dressed in tactical SWAT gear stood at parade rest on a small rise about a hundred feet away from our group. Their visors were down, arms crossed in the summer heat. The youth didn't know if they should be intimidated or amused. I was sent by Tou and the community volunteers to ask the officers what they were guarding us from, to thank them for preventing drive-bys, and to ask if there was anything we could do to support them. I offered them pizza and cold drinks in the sweltering heat. By the fourth week they made eye contact; by the fifth they accepted a cold drink. They stopped coming shortly after that. This was my value as a white, male, middle-aged college professor.

On a regular basis over all eight years, someone in a leadership role in park and recreation, the police, or a community organization would come by and tell us that it was great our "numbers were so high," but that "we should do something since we had so much influence on the youth" and not just let them hang out. There was little or no recognition that we were informally, if deliberately, connecting youth to other opportunities and resources and using the program as a "hub," building a sense of community. There was no recognition that, despite tense moments, it remained a safe space. Some police and some community members periodically spread a story that Tou was still a gang member and was using Rec Night to recruit. Their evidence? They had seen him driving around with youth from Rec Night. As part of his job, Tou transported youth to field trips, jobs programs, court dates, school, meetings with parents, mediations, out to lunch, even shopping for clothes on occasion. But once a gangster, always a gangster.

By "do something," our well-meaning observers meant we should create structured programs with more rules and institute a behavioral modification strategy that would "inculcate good values." Instead of open-play basketball—self-organized four-on-four for the serious basketball players at one end of the gym, younger kids trying a lot of different approaches at the other end, board games in the lobby—they wanted the basketball game played "right," with proper dress and a referee. Perhaps a league. They didn't seem to make the connection that the absence of their formula and the "hidden" structure of hospitality, openness, relationship, and self-organization were major reasons for the popularity and effectiveness of Rec Night.

The youth knew how unwelcome they generally were and that many of our observers were, in fact, looking for a reason to shut down the program. They self-monitored, and word spread that Rec Night was a "safe space." As I described in an earlier chapter, their self-monitoring was serious, direct, sometimes paradoxical, and provided its own teachable moments. The youth knew how closely the program was being watched and self-monitored because they valued the safe space of Rec Night and did not want to lose it. This was also an ongoing opportunity to practice nonviolence.

The second summer of the program we were again at the park, this time with a new district commander: he sent a horse-patrol team with instructions to let the kids pet the horse. The mounted officer spent most of her time on the ground talking to the youth, especially the girls. A second officer would visit for an hour or so—throw a football around, eat some pizza, chat. And periodically the new commander would drop by for a social visit. A world of difference. The youth understood the difference, and the difference was a source of much conversation.

Over time, the rec director dropped back as his supervisor came to trust, appreciate, and advocate for Rec Night. He left his position about five years into our program, and the new center director, aware of the prior history, stayed mostly neutral: supporting us but carefully distancing himself in case anything went wrong.

MOVING TOWARD "YOUTH POSITIVE"

It is the basic premise of this book that youth become involved in gang and street violence because it makes sense given what their lives have taught them about their options: the world is a threatening place, and they can't count on the adults around them to care for them. Joining a gang or hanging out with a crew promises a way of keeping safe, of being cared for, and of being a part of something. It seems to offer opportunities to pursue what is meaningful and valuable. It also results in being exposed to more violence, becoming socially marginalized, and discovering over time that choosing violence as an "adaptation to circumstances" is maladaptive in nearly all other contexts—home, school, work, and public life.

The paradox is that youth joining gangs are simultaneously victims and perpetrators of traumatic violence—against themselves, against other persons, and against their communities. The ongoing, persistent presence of youth gangs is in itself evidence that our social systems are organized in such a way that they consistently produce a small but significant number of youth who will experience this kind of trauma, resulting in this paradox.

The preferred public response to youth involved in gangs and street violence has been to see them as "other"—and to increasingly surveille, police, and incarcerate them. At worst, street- and gang-involved youth (and youth believed by authorities to be "associated" with gangs) are positioned as enemies of society, at best as tragic casualties of racism and poverty. Paying attention to their real lives, however, suggests that neither of these caricatures is accurate enough to be helpful. More often than not, the youth have experienced direct and structural violence, precipitating and reinforcing a process of violentization. In the short term, change happens when youth can heal and develop alternatives ways of being and change their relationship to their immediate social context and institutions. Over the long haul, change happens as we collectively learn to look at and respond effectively to angry, violent youth with compassion: new values cause social context and institutions to change.

The "youth positive" approach we developed at Rec Night grew out of this fundamental insight: youth are a resource, not a problem. They are good enough just as they are, but they need communal support to heal from trauma, develop a worldview that is not based on violence, and become reengaged with mainstream institutions of belonging and meaning. Rec Night helped them begin this process by offering access to safe spaces characterized by consistent experiences of hospitality, compassion, and community.

As Paulo Freire says more generally about people who are oppressed, these youth "are not 'marginals,' are not living 'outside' society. They have always been 'inside' the structure which made them 'beings for others.' The solution is not to 'integrate' them into the structures of oppression, but to transform that structure so that they can become 'beings for themselves'" (1970). If we want different outcomes, gang- and street-involved youth need to be seen and treated as youth, as whole human beings, as people who are experiencing trauma, and as people who want lives that are meaningful. No matter how damaging their behavior, they are not "others" defined by a simple label. They are members of our communities, and it is up to our communities to hold space in which they can no longer harm themselves or others and become "whole" and their "best selves."

Change processes are a kind of praxis—a cycle of action and reflection, of behaving in new ways and clarifying values and developing new systems that reflect those values. Individuals change because they decide it is in their interest to do so; institutions change when the values on which they are built change and practices have to be brought into alignment with the new values. Ending street and gang violence means changing the values by which mainstream individuals and institutions operate—and particularly replacing the broad cultural belief that violence works with the desire to study and practice nonviolence. Youth don't need lectures on nonviolence: they need to experience nonviolence and have opportunities to reflect on their lives and what they want. Their practice of nonviolence has to result in lives that are more meaningful, more powerful, and more sustainable than the alternative.

It matters how the institutions of which youth are a part respond to their anger and belligerence and aggression. The tendency is to want to contain and control that energy—to believe that the best response is to be as firm as necessary to interrupt it. But if a youth is processing the trauma of brutalization, or is somewhere further along in the process of violentization, then efforts to contain and control violent behavior with force are only going to be met with more resistance and increased alienation—the things traumatized people do to protect themselves that seem perfectly reasonable to them and problematic to nearly everyone else.

The alternative is to start with the assumption that people are doing the best they can and doing what makes sense to them. They want meaningful lives: to love and be loved, do meaningful work, and be happy. Ask what is in the way of this, and help to remove the obstacles. Help to find alternative paths forward. Help people learn to tell their stories, deal with their fears, differentiate between their emotional reactions and objective reality, gain the skills needed to have the life they want to have. Learn to deal with conflict constructively.

We can also work to change the systems that make violence seem like such a good option for so many. This begins by looking in the mirror and asking what I can begin to do now, where I am, with what I have. We have to be honest about systems effects, allow public policy to embrace what is complex and messy, and realign our social values so that the institutions and systems of racism and inequality do not exist to produce violence.

SOME BIG IDEAS

I believe that one of the biggest challenges of working with street- and gang-involved youth is that it has to be done in such a way that it makes clear that their circumstances, and not they, are the problem. As Greg Boyle, S.J., founder of Homeboy Industries, points out, if you want to be effective, "you work with gang members and not with gangs" (2017). The stakes in getting this right are high. As David Brotherton argues:

> In the United States our solutions still primarily lie within law enforcement and a range of half-baked programs aimed at belatedly changing perspectives of individual youth by offering them some mediocre opportunities so they can change themselves, ie. we are not the problem; they are. We do this rather than mobilizing them to change the world, convincing them that we are in this together, affirming with them that this brutally irrational societal condition cannot be tolerated for generation after generation but that they must become the subjects and not the objects of this history. (2015, 180)

As challenging as Brotherton's standard is, it is an idea with a solid grounding in reality and a solid base of support. Moving it forward in the current political climate, with its resurgent commitment to suppression, militarization, and criminalization of the youth I have described in this book, will be difficult. Nonetheless, a growing number of colleagues, allies, activists, and reformers are trying to move things in this direction. Here is an initial list of goals and practices that I think align with Brotherton's challenge and have the potential to leverage systems change. This is followed by descriptions of some representative organizations that offer places to get connected, find allies, and add your shoulder to the wheel.

- We can insist that our public institutions treat youth as youth first and as gang-affiliated or street-involved second, and we can make sure the financial and people resources necessary for doing this well are available.
- We can work toward policies in schools and education more generally that do not criminalize, marginalize, or exclude youth who

behave in problematic ways. This is one powerful way to work toward ending mass incarceration and its harsh effect on low-income communities of color.

- We can change school and community center policies so that we are *not* kicking out, suspending, or expelling youth.

- We can acknowledge the consistent research finding that zero-tolerance, scared-straight, authoritarian interventions, while well intentioned, do not work.

- We can think through, talk about, and clarify our personal and public assumptions about child rearing and "discipline," informed by what we know about violence, nonviolence, and human development.

- We can recognize the structural violence of racism and poverty as two powerful, often intertwined, sources of physical and emotional stress that directly and negatively impact young people, even resilient young people.

- We can build into public education and public policy knowledge about the immediate and long-term effects of chronic stress on youth and adapt policies and practices accordingly.

- We can continue to educate schools, parents, and the public about the effects of bullying and ways to intervene in and prevent bullying that are effective on the streets and in the lived experiences of the youth involved.

- We can educate schools and the public about the relatively low threshold for traumatic experiences that can produce symptoms of PTSD and the effects of this on education, health, and human development.

- We can recognize how widespread trauma is; become more knowledgeable about its physical, emotional, and social effects; and weave what we learn into the ways our institutions engage children, youth, and adults.

- We can build nonviolence into schools' practices and curricula as a way to make them "safe spaces" and as a way to link education to changing the systems that produce structural violence.

- We can recognize that we need to keep youth close and cared for and use our care to allow them time and space for decompression and healing when it is needed.
- We can take seriously the "communalization of grief" as a practice woven into institutions that serve youth, especially youth organizations and schools. Grief is a normal part of everyday life, and learning to share and process it in a community of support can help reduce its traumatic effects and transform it into a source of energy for positive social change.
- We can recognize that conflict is a normal and healthy fact of life—and learn and teach how to "do" conflict well, so that it is a source of energy and creativity rather than fear and destruction.
- We can look carefully at restorative justice practices across social institutions—for both victims and perpetrators of violence, but especially for victims of crime, victims of bullying, victims of abuse of all kinds.
- We can develop and fund prevention and intervention programs in the spirit of ISPN/Rec Night that are "youth positive." Funds for this can be directly transferred from incarceration to "prevention" with a net decrease in both street violence and incarceration.

All in all, we can use what we have where we are to build a beloved community that we all consider good enough for our own children and grandchildren.

SOME ORGANIZATIONS

Implementing any, never mind all, of these ideas is incredibly daunting until you begin to look at the number and diversity of efforts to move them forward that are under way (Web addresses for the organizations named below can be found in the Works Cited.)

In Providence, Rhode Island, STEP UP (Standing Together to End Profiling and Undo Poverty) is sponsoring passage of the Providence Community Safety Act. While getting it passed is politically complicated, the goals of the legislation are straightforward and ambitious: stop racial profiling in the justice system, resist using local police departments to enforce Immigration and Customs Enforcement holds and deportation orders, and bring the list of gang members kept by law enforcement into the daylight. Similar efforts are happening in many communities across the United States.

The Providence mayor's office has established a Children and Youth Cabinet, a "coalition of 150 organizations and individuals who work together to ensure *all* Providence children thrive—from cradle to career." The cabinet focuses on social and emotional well-being, chronic absences, school climate, and health equity. It is concerned with impacts of racism, poverty, and violence and acts as an "honest" forum for all kinds of difficult discussions and ideas. One key ally in the cabinet's work is Rhode Island Kids Count—the local chapter of a national data-analytics project supported by the Annie E. Casey Foundation. Kids Count is dedicated to collecting and using data to improve the lives of all children and youth, but especially those most at risk.

At the national level, the Youth Sentencing and Reentry Project and the Equal Justice Initiative are working to roll back laws and practices that allow juvenile offenders as young as twelve or thirteen to be treated as adults in the criminal justice system. YSRP "is a Philadelphia-based nonprofit organization that provides comprehensive support to kids prosecuted in the adult criminal justice system, including individuals who were sentenced to life without parole as children ('juvenile lifers')." Key among their four priorities is "advancing policy reform that is rooted in the experiences of young people, juvenile lifers and their families." This effective organization challenges negative social constructions of "child" and "youth" and invites us to be a compassionate society.

The Equal Justice Initiative has become well known because of director Bryan Stevenson's public advocacy and the wide circulation of his 2015 book, *Just Mercy.* In addition to advocating for treating youth as youth, EJI also defends convicts on death row, documenting the consistent and racialized fact that for every nine convicts executed, one is exonerated. EJI is also a good resource for learning about and helping to undo mass incarceration.

The Children's Defense Fund is a powerful national advocacy, policy, and programmatic leader with a long-standing interest in reducing gun and community violence, specifically in contexts of racial and economic inequality. Gun violence, they note, is the leading cause of death for black children ages one to nineteen. Their research, recommendations, and examples are powerful and useful. Like most of the resources listed here, they make a compelling case for seeing youth as youth and all youth as members of our communities for whom we are all responsible.

The National Child Traumatic Stress Network is a source of knowledge, best practice, and policy about the effects of trauma on children and youth. A significant part of their mission is educating the public about the pervasiveness and effects of trauma and supporting institutional change strategies that incorporate this new knowledge.

Michelle Alexander's 2010 book, *The New Jim Crow*, has spawned large-scale study and organizing work aimed at ending mass incarceration, addressing the institutional racism on which it is built, and creating positive social change. A companion website of the same name is dedicated to engaging in this work. Working with Alexander's organization, Daniel Hunter has written a follow-up organizing guide, *Building a Movement to End the New Jim Crow: An Organizing Guide* (2015).

Harvard University's Center on the Developing Child and the American Psychological Association are developing and disseminating effective research on increasing resilience in children. Resilience can be taught, it can be learned, and it can be practiced.

The National Network for Safe Communities was launched in 2008 by scholar-activist David Kennedy and the John Jay College of Criminal Justice. It "supports communities implementing strategic interventions to reduce violence and community disorder, minimize arrests and incarceration, enhance police legitimacy, and rebuild relationships between law enforcement and distressed communities." Kennedy's work was the inspiration for Providence's Institute for the Study and Practice of Nonviolence and, indirectly, Rec Night. It is a good introduction to a different way of thinking about ending community violence, and he describes it superbly in his *Don't Shoot: One Man, a Street Fellowship, and the End of Violence in Inner-City America* (2012).

These examples are, of course, suggestive rather than comprehensive. They indicate something of the range of knowledge and institutions engaged in ending violence by and on youth and point toward ways of getting more involved. Collectively, they suggest that we already know most of what we need to know if we are serious about ending youth violence and that the path forward will be made by coming together locally and nationally and figuring out the long-term politics of what to do with what we know to be true.

ONWARD

My thinking often drifts back to the stories of William and Andre, shared in the chapter on violentization: how William was murdered on the street and his incarcerated brother, Andre, was locked into solitary confinement as he learned of his brother's death. I wrote this book in large part to process my experiences of moments like this, and in closing I want to return to this reflection and say a bit more about what it means to me.

I wish I could make sense of a system that deliberately responds to elemental grief such as Andre's with isolation. I so appreciate the words of ISPN's staff member when he went to visit Andre in solitary and his compassionate description of Andre's "gush of *puro dolor*." Pure sadness. Anguish. These words connect. They tell me how Andre is feeling, and they indicate, with indirect precision, how the staff member is feeling. It is a human moment. They connect and create the potential for connection. I wish I knew how to communicate the bedrock, existential abyss that Andre was experiencing to people who would view him and William as somehow less than fully human. Another friend told me that Andre didn't want his mother to come visit him after his brother's death. It just seemed too overwhelmingly painful and threatened to unleash feelings that he believed he would have to bottle up if he was to get through to his release.

There are so many things I wish I knew about William's death: How the shooter is feeling now and how he imagines his future. The moments to come when Andre will tip the bubble one way or another, toward or away from retaliation or forgiveness. How William's mother and father and other brothers and sisters will be affected—how this singular event will show up in their lives and the lives of their children and grandchildren. I wish I knew how to tease apart the embedded narratives of race and poverty and violence and personal identity—and recast them as narratives of equity, value, connection, belonging, and being.

I wish we knew how to transform all of this pain, simply, into compassion, and compassion into rec centers and other spaces that were safe spaces and open all the time, and from this into a mind-set that looked at incarceration and punishment of our youth with revulsion and dismay and did everything in its power to prevent its use.

I do know that it costs $40,000 or more per year to incarcerate an inmate like Andre at Rhode Island's state prison and roughly $100,000 per year at the Training School for youth offenders. It's such a cliché—or truism—but the money is there to turn this whole thing around. Where we spend our money reflects our values, not an objective reality. We are getting what we pay for. It seems we choose to believe this scale of expenditure for criminalization and incarceration is inevitable and necessary. It suggests that we—the larger public "we"—must find some value in demonizing youth like William, in blaming people like Andre, in seeking to deport people like Tony and Isaac, in allowing Carlos and Joey to begin "falling through the cracks" as they enter middle school. I think this because it is the system we have created and where we put our money, whether that is our intention or not.

I wish I understood this. Actually, I don't mean that. It can be explained, but it passes understanding. I really mean to say, I wish I knew how to get all of us to understand that when an angry, proud young man like William is injured or killed by another angry, proud young man, it isn't the natural course of things; it isn't simply a bad decision by two misguided individuals who think it makes sense. What would we do differently if, instead, we kept our heads up and considered this death the terrible result of our collective failure to care for our young?

WORKS CITED

Adler, Leonore Loeb, and Florence K. Denmark. 2005. *International Perspectives on Violence.* Westport, CT: Praeger.

Alexander, Michelle. 2010. *The New Jim Crow: Mass Incarceration in the Age of Colorblindness.* New York: New Press.

American Psychological Association. "Resilience Guide for Parents and Teachers." http://www.apa.org/helpcenter/resilience.aspx.

Anderson, Elijah. 1994. "Code of the Streets." *Atlantic,* May. https://www.theatlantic.com/magazine/archive/1994/05/the-code-of-the-streets/306601/.

———. 2000. *Code of the Street: Decency, Violence and the Moral Life of the Inner City.* New York: W. W. Norton.

Armstrong, Karen. 2014. *Fields of Blood: Religion and the History of Violence.* New York: Anchor Books.

Athens, Lonnie. 2003. "Violentization in Larger Social Context." In *Violent Acts and Violentization: Assessing, Applying and Developing Lonnie Athens' Theories,* edited by Lonnie Athens and Jeffrey T. Ulmer, 1–41. Boston: JAI.

———. 2007. "Radical Interactionism: Going beyond Mead." *Journal of the Theory of Social Behavior* 37 (2): 137–65.

Bailie, Gil. 1994. *Violence Unveiled: Humanity at the Crossroads.* New York: Crossroad.

Berry, Wendell. 1983. "Does Community Have a Value?" In *Home Economics,* 179–92. New York: North Point Press.

Black Lives Matter. N.d. "About Black Lives Matter Network." http://blacklivesmatter.com/about/.

Bobo, Lawrence D., and Victor Thompson. 2010. "Racialized Mass Incarceration: Poverty, Prejudice, and Punishment." In *Doing Race: 21 Essays for the 21st Century,* edited by Hazel R. Markus and Paula Moya, 322–55. New York: W. W. Norton.

Bochco, Steven, and Michael Kozoll, producers. 1981–87. *Hill Street Blues.* National Broadcasting Company.

Bonilla-Silva, Eduardo. 2003. *Racism without Racists: Color-Blind Racism and the Persistence of Racial Inequality in the United States.* New York: Rowman and Littlefield.

Bourgois, Philippe. 1995. *In Search of Respect: Selling Crack in El Barrio.* New York: Cambridge University Press.

Boyle, Father Greg. 2010. *Tattoos on the Heart: The Power of Boundless Compassion.* New York: Free Press.

———. 2017. "I Thought I Could 'Save' Gang Members. I Was Wrong." *America: The Jesuit Review.* https://www.americamagazine.org/faith/2017/03/28/father-greg-boyle-i-thought-i-could-save-gang-members-i-was-wrong.

Brillat-Savarin, Jean Anthelme. 1825 [2009]. *The Physiology of Taste.* New York: Merchant Books.

Brohl, Kathryn. 1996. *Working with Traumatized Children.* Washington, DC: CWLA Press.

Brooks, Robert, and Sam Goldstein. 2003. *Nurturing Resilience in Our Children.* Chicago: Contemporary Books.

Brotherton, David. 2015. *Youth Street Gangs: A Critical Appraisal.* New York: Routledge Press.

Brown, Brené. 2012. *Daring Greatly: How the Courage to Be Vulnerable Transforms the Way We Live, Love, Parent and Lead.* New York: Avery.

Buber, Martin. 1971. *I and Thou.* Translated by Walter Kaufmann. New York: Touchstone.

Bureau of Justice Statistics. 2016. "Household Poverty and Nonfatal Violent Victimization, 2008–2012." http://www.bjs.gov/content/pub/pdf/hpnvv0812.pdf.

Canada, Geoffrey. 2010. *Fist, Stick, Knife, Gun: A Personal History of Violence.* Boston: Beacon Press.

Carter, Stephen. 2011. *The Violence of Peace: America's Wars in the Age of Obama.* New York: Beast Books.

Center on the Developing Child. https://developingchild.harvard.edu/science/key-concepts/resilience/.

Centers for Disease Control and Prevention. 2012. "Gang Homicides—Five US Cities." *Morbidity and Mortality Weekly Report.* http://www.cdc.gov/mmwr/preview/mmwrhtml/mm6103a2.htm.

———. 2015. CDC WONDER Search: "10 Leading Causes of Death, United States 1999–2014, All Races, Both Sexes." https://wonder.cdc.gov/ucd-icd10.html.

Chang, Jeff. 2005. *Can't Stop, Won't Stop: A History of the Hip-Hop Generation.* New York: Picador.

———. 2014. "Jeff Chang on Hip Hop, Street Art and Racial Justice in America." *NBC News.* http://www.nbcnews.com/news/asian-america/jeff-chang-hip-hop-street-art-racial-justice-america-n239936.

Chernus, Ira. 2004. *American Nonviolence: The History of an Idea.* Maryknoll, NY: Orbis Books.

Children and Youth Cabinet, City of Providence. http://www.cycprovidence.org.

Children's Defense Fund. http://www.childrensdefense.org/library/misc/violence.html?page=1.

Chodron, Pema. 2000. *When Things Fall Apart: Heart Advice for Difficult Times.* Boston: Shambhala Press.

Coates, Ta-Nehisi. 2015. *Between the World and Me.* New York: Spiegel and Grau.

Cone, J. H. 2001. "Martin and Malcolm on Nonviolence and Violence." *Phylon* 49 (3–4): 173–83.

Conquergood, Dwight. 1995. "The Power of Symbols." http://gangresearch.net/GangResearch/Media/Power.htm.

Crane, Stephen. 1895 [2009]. *The Red Badge of Courage.* Edited by Paul Sorrentino. Cambridge, MA: Belknap Press.

Department of Justice. 2015. "Federal Officials Close Investigation into Death of Trayvon Martin: Press Release, February 24, 2015." https://www.justice.gov/opa/pr/federal-officials-close-investigation-death-trayvon-martin.

Doblmeier, Martin, director. 2008. *The Power of Forgiveness.* Journey Films.

Douglas, Mary. 1966 [2002]. *Purity and Danger: An Analysis of Concepts of Pollution and Taboo.* New York: Routledge Classics.

Drinnon, Richard. 1980. *Facing West: The Metaphysics of Indian Hating and Empire Building.* Minneapolis: University of Minnesota Press.

Eastwood, Clint, director. 1985. *Pale Rider.* Malpaso.

———. 2008. *Gran Torino.* Matten Productions.

Eng, Tan Twan. 2008. *Gift of Rain.* New York: Weinstein Books.

Equal Justice Initiative. http://eji.org.

Erikson, Erik. 1993. *Gandhi's Truth: On the Origins of Militant Nonviolence.* New York: W. W. Norton.

Farmer, Paul. 1997. "On Suffering and Structural Violence: A View from Below." In *Social Suffering,* edited by Arthur Kleinman, Veena Das, and Margaret Lock, 261–84. Berkeley: University of California Press.

FBI. 2012. "Arrests by Race Table 43A." https://ucr.fbi.gov/crime-in-the-u.s/2012/crime-in-the-u.s.-2012/tables/43tabledatadecoverviewpdf.

Follette, Victoria M., John Briere, Deborah Rozelle, James W. Hopper, and David I. Rome. 2014. *Mindfulness Oriented Interventions for Trauma: Integrating Contemplative Practices.* New York: Guilford Press.

Freire, Paul. 1970 [2007]. *Pedagogy of the Oppressed.* New York: Continuum.

Gandhi, Mohandas K. 1966. *The Mind of Mahatma Gandhi: Encyclopedia of Gandhi's Thoughts.* Edited by R. K. Prabhu and R. R. Rao. Ahmedabad: Jitandra Desai and Navajivan Mudranalaya. http://www.mkgandhi.org/ebks/mindofmahatmagandhi.pdf.

Garland, Sarah. 2009. *Gangs in Garden City: How Immigration, Segregation and Youth Violence Are Changing America's Suburbs.* New York: Nation Books.

Gebo, Erika, and Brenda J. Bond, eds. 2012. *Looking beyond Suppression: Community Strategies to Reduce Gang Violence.* Lanham, MD: Lexington Books.

Giroux, Henry. 2010. *Youth in a Suspect Society: Democracy or Disposability?* New York: Palgrave Macmillan.

Griffin, Shayla Reese. 2015. *These Kids, Our Schools: Race and Reform in an American High School.* Cambridge, MA: Harvard Education Press.

Grossman, Dave. 2009. *On Killing: The Psychological Cost of Learning to Kill in War and Society.* New York: Back Bay Books.

Grotburg, Edith. 1995. *A Guide to Promoting Resilience in Children: Strengthening the Human Spirit.* Netherlands: Bernard Van Leer Foundation. https://bibalex.org/baifa/Attachment/Documents/115519.pdf.

Hagedorn, John. 2008. *World of Gangs: Armed Young Men and Gangsta Culture.* Minneapolis: University of Minnesota Press.

Halpern, Robert. 1995. *Rebuilding the Inner City: A History of Neighborhood Initiatives to Address Poverty in the United States.* New York: Columbia University Press.

Hardy, Kenneth, and Tracey Laszloffy. 2005. *Teens Who Hurt: Clinical Interventions to Break the Cycle of Adolescent Violence.* New York: Guilford Press.

Harland, Ken. 2007. "The Legacy of Conflict in Northern Ireland: Paramilitarism, Violence and Youthwork in Contested Spaces." In *Work with Youth in Divided and Contested Societies,* edited by Doug Magnuson and Michael Baizerman, 177–90. Rotterdam: Sense.

Hartney, Christopher, and Linh Vuong. 2009. *Created Equal: Racial and Ethnic Disparities in the US Criminal Justice System.* Oakland, CA: National Council on Crime and Delinquency. http://www.nccdglobal.org/sites/default/files/publication_pdf/created-equal.pdf.

Herstein, G. 2009. "Roycean Roots of the Beloved Community." *Pluralist* 4 (2): 91–107.

Hilfiker, David. 2002. *Urban Injustice: How Ghettos Happen.* New York: Seven Stories Press.

Hinojosa, Maria. 1995. *Crews: Gang Members Talk to Maria Hinojosa.* New York: Harcourt Paperbacks.

Hopper, Dennis, director. 1988. *Colors.* Orion Pictures.

Hughes, Albert, and Allen Hughes, directors. 1993. *Menace II Society.* New Line Cinema.

Hunter, David. 2015. *Building a Movement to End the New Jim Crow: An Organizing Guide.* N.p.: Hyrax. https://wordery.com/hyrax-publishing -publisher.

Ivie, Robert. 2007. *Dissent from War.* West Hartford, CT: Kumarian Press.

Jackson, Eldra, III. 2017. "How Men at New Folsom Prison Reckon with Toxic Masculinity." *Los Angeles Times,* November 30. http://www.latimes .com/opinion/op-ed/la-oe-jackson-men-group-therapy-folsom -prison-the-work-toxic-masculinity-20171130-story.html.

Jackson, Kenneth T. 1985. *Crabgrass Frontier: The Suburbanization of the United States.* New York: Oxford University Press.

Jackson, Thomas F. 2007. *From Civil Rights to Human Rights: Martin Luther King, Jr. and the Struggle for Economic Justice.* Philadelphia: University of Pennsylvania Press.

Jervis, Robert. 1976. *Perception and Misperception in Foreign Relations.* Princeton, NJ: Princeton University Press.

Kapur, Sudarshan. 1992. *Raising Up a Prophet: The African-American Encounter with Gandhi.* Boston: Beacon Press. 1992.

Keiser, R. Lincoln. 1969. *Vice Lords: Warriors of the Streets.* New York: Holt, Rinehart, and Winston.

Kelly, Thomas. 1941 [1984]. "The Eternal Promise." In *Quaker Spirituality: Selected Readings,* edited by Douglas Steere, 306–11. New York: HarperCollins.

Kemper, Yvonne. 2007. "The Socio-political Approach: Youth—a Peace Constituency?" In *Work with Youth in Divided and Contested Societies,* edited by Doug Magnuson and Michael Baizerman, 43–45. Rotterdam: Sense.

Kendi, Ibram. 2016. *Stamped from the Beginning: The Definitive History of Racist Ideas in America.* New York: Nation Books.

Kennedy, David M. 2011. *Don't Shoot: One Man, a Street Fellowship, and the End of Violence in Inner-City America.* New York: Bloomsbury USA.

Kidder, Tracy. 2009. *Strength in What Remains.* New York: Random House.

King, Martin Luther, Jr. 1967 [2010]. *Where Do We Go from Here: Community or Chaos?* Boston: Beacon Press.

King Center. "The King Philosophy." http://www.thekingcenter.org/king -philosophy.

Kivel, Paul. 1999. *Boys Will Be Men: Raising Our Sons for Courage, Caring and Community.* Gabriola Island, BC: New Society.

Kleinman, Arthur, Veena Das, and Margaret Lock, eds. 1997. *Social Suffering.* Berkeley: University of California Press.

Kouf, Jim, producer. 1997. *Gang Related.* Orion Pictures.

Kozol, Jonathan. 1991. *Savage Inequalities: Children in America's Schools.* New York: Harper Perennial.

Kretzmann, John, and John McKnight. 1993. *Building Communities from the Inside Out: A Path toward Finding and Mobilizing a Community's Assets.* Chicago: ACTA.

Kurlansky, Mark. 2006. *Nonviolence: The History of a Dangerous Idea.* New York: Modern Library.

Lafayette, Bernard, and David C. Jensen. 1995a. *The Briefing Booklet: An Orientation to Kingian Nonviolent Conflict Reconciliation.* Galena, OH: Institute for Human Rights and Responsibilities.

———. 1995b. *Leaders Manual: A Structured Guide and Introduction to Kingian Nonviolence.* Galena, OH: Institute for Human Rights and Responsibilities.

Lancaster, Phil. 2007. "Categories and Illusions: Child Soldiers in Burundi." In *Work with Youth in Divided and Contested Societies,* edited by Doug Magnuson and Michael Baizerman, 15–26. Rotterdam: Sense.

Larson, Jonathan. 2008. *Rent: The Complete Book and Lyrics of the Broadway Musical.* Milwaukee: Applause Theatre and Cinema Books.

Liberman, Akiva M., and Jocelyn Fontaine. 2015. *Reducing Harm to Boys and Young Men of Color from Criminal Justice System Involvement.* Washington, DC: Urban Institute. http://www.urban.org/sites/default/files/publication/39551/2000095-Reducing-Harms-to-Boys-and-Young-Men-of-Color-from-Criminal-Justice-System-Involvement.pdf.

Leopold, Aldo. 1949 [1986]. *A Sand County Almanac.* New York: Random House.

———. 1993. *Round River: From the Journals of Aldo Leopold.* New York: Oxford University Press.

Machado, Anthony. 1978. "We Make the Road by Walking." In *Selected Poems of Antonio Machado,* edited by Betty Jean Craig. Baton Rouge: Louisiana State University Press.

Magnuson, Doug. 2007. "The Perils, Promise and Practice of Youthwork in Conflict Societies." In *Work with Youth in Divided and Contested Societies,* edited by Doug Magnuson and Michael Baizerman, 3–12. Rotterdam: Sense.

Magnuson, Doug, and Michael Baizerman, eds. 2007. *Work with Youth in Divided and Contested Societies.* Rotterdam: Sense.

Malcolm X. 1964 [1965]. "A Declaration of Independence." In *Malcolm X Speaks,* 18–22. New York: Grove Press.

Maldonado, B-boy Facce. 2017. Personal communication with the author, June 13.

Malinowski, W. Z. 2008. "Gangs of Providence." *Providence Journal.* http:
//app.providencejournal.com/hercules/extra/2008/gangs/stories
/main_story.html.

Malinowski, W. Z., and Amanda Milkovitz. 2014. "Deadly Mix of Feuds, Job-
lessness and Guns on Providence's Mean Streets." *Providence Journal,*
July 26. http://www.providencejournal.com/article/20140726/NEWS
/307269993.

Mankell, Henning. 2009. *Italian Shoes.* New York: Vintage.

Matthei, Chuck. 1993–94. "Economics as If Values Mattered." *Sojourners.*
http://equitytrust.org/category/resources/matthei-values/.

Maurin, Peter. N.d. *Easy Essays.* http://www.easyessays.org/foreword/.

McEvoy-Levy, Siobhan. 2007. "Youth Narratives in Contested Spaces and
Their Implications for Youthwork." In *Work with Youth in Divided
and Contested Societies,* edited by Doug Magnuson and Michael Baizerman, 87–108. Rotterdam: Sense.

McKinney, Mike. 2008. "Update: Sidewalk Bump Spurs Latest Killing." ProJo
.com.

Merton, Thomas. 1981. *The Nonviolent Alternative.* New York: Farrar, Straus
and Giroux.

Messner, Michael A., Max A. Greenberg, and Tal Peretz. 2015. *Some Men:
Feminist Allies and the Movement to End Violence against Women.*
New York: Oxford University Press.

Metcalf, Josephine. 2012. *The Culture and Politics of Contemporary Street
Gang Memoirs.* Jackson: University Press of Mississippi.

Milkovitz, Amanda. 2017. "In 2016 There Were No Gang-Related Deaths Recorded." *Providence Journal,* February 1, A5.

Miller, Ted. 2012. "The Cost of Gun Violence." http://www.childrenssafety
network.org/sites/childrenssafetynetwork.org/files/TheCostofGun
Violence.pdf.

Monahan, Cynthia. 1993. *Children and Trauma: A Parent's Guide for Helping
Children Heal.* New York: Lexington Books.

Monteiro, Sal. 2013. *The Complicated Simplicity of Nonviolence.* TED Talk,
Moses Brown School, November 17. https://www.youtube.com/watch
?v=AiZL_U9tpYA.

Morgan, Chris, director. 2014. *Gang Related.* Imagine Television.

Morton, Keith, and Samantha Bergbauer. 2015. "A Case for Community:
Starting with Relationships and Prioritizing Community as Method
in Service-Learning." *Michigan Journal of Community Service Learning* 22 (1): 18–31.

Morton, Nelle. 1985. "Beloved Image." In *The Journey Is Home,* 122–46. Boston: Beacon Press.

Moses, Greg. 1997. *Revolution of Conscience: Martin Luther King, Jr. and the
Philosophy of Nonviolence.* New York: Guilford Press.

Muste, A. J. 1967. "Debasing Dissent." *New York Times,* November 16, 46.

National Child Traumatic Stress Network. http://www.nctsn.org/about-us/mission-and-vision.

National Drug Intelligence Center. 2009. *National Gang Threat Assessment.* Technical Report 200909. https://ntrl.ntis.gov/NTRL/dashboard/searchResults/titleDetail/PB2009105649.xhtml.

National Gang Center. 2008. "Guidelines for Establishing and Operating Gang Intelligence Units and Task Forces." https://it.ojp.gov/documents/d/guidelines%20for%20establishing%20Gang%20Intelligence%20units.pdf.

———. 2016. "Measuring the Extent of Gang Problems." https://www.nationalgangcenter.gov/Survey-Analysis/Measuring-the-Extent-of-Gang-Problems#estimatedgangmembers.

National Network for Safe Communities. https://nnscommunities.org/who-we-are/mission.

Neill, A. S. 1960. *Summerhill: A Radical Approach to Childrearing.* New York: Hart.

New Jim Crow. http://newjimcrow.com.

Nhat Hanh, Thich. 1987. *Being Peace.* Berkeley, CA: Parallax Press.

Niebhur, Reinhold. 1932. *Moral Man and Immoral Society: A Study in Ethics and Politics.* New York: Charles Scribner's Sons.

Nouwen, Henri. 1974. *Out of Solitude.* Notre Dame, IN: Ave Maria Press.

———. 1975. *Reaching Out: The Three Movements of the Spiritual Life.* New York: Image Books.

Obama, Barack. 2009. "A Just and Lasting Peace." Nobel Lecture, Oslo City Hall, Oslo, Norway, December 10. https://www.nobelprize.org/nobel_prizes/peace/laureates/2009/obama-lecture_en.html.

O'Brien, Sarah. 2013. "No Affiliation: Music with a Message." *Cowl,* January 31. http://digitalcommons.providence.edu/cgi/viewcontent.cgi?article=2895&context=cowl.

Ortony, Andrew, ed. 1993. *Metaphor and Thought.* Cambridge: Cambridge University Press.

Oxford English Dictionary. "Gang." http://www.oed.com.providence.idm.oclc.org/search?searchType=dictionary&q=gang&_searchBtn=Search.

Palmer, Parker. 2014. "Parker Palmer's 13 Ways of Looking at Community." http://www.couragerenewal.org/13-ways-of-looking-at-community_parker-palmer/.

Percy, Walker. 1961. *The Moviegoer.* New York: Vintage.

Perry, Bruce D., and Maia Szalavitz. 2006. *The Boy Who Was Raised as a Dog.* New York: Basic Books.

Petrie, Daniel, director. 1981. *Fort Apache, the Bronx.* Producer Circle.

Pinker, Steven. 2012. *The Better Angels of Our Nature: Why Violence Has Declined.* New York: Penguin Books.

Pollan, Michael. 2002. *The Botany of Desire: A Plant's Eye View of the World.* New York: Random House.

Providence Community Safety Act. https://providencecommunitysafetyact .wordpress.com.

Pyrooz, David C., and Gary Sweeten. 2015. "Gang Membership between Ages 5 and 17 Years in the United States." *Journal of Adolescent Health* 54 (4): 414–19. doi:10.1016/j.jadohealth.2014.11.018.

Radford, Katy. 2007. "'It's Not Just Bagels and *Bhajis*': Reflections on a Research Revolt, Youth Participation and Minority Ethnicity in Northern Ireland." In *Work with Youth in Divided and Contested Societies,* edited by Doug Magnuson and Michael Baizerman, 141–51. Rotterdam: Sense.

Reynolds, Mark. 2015. "Murder in Providence Is Up, but Violent Crime Overall Is Down." *Providence Journal,* January 2. http://www.providence journal.com/article/20150102/NEWS/301029970.

Rhodes, Richard. 2000. *Why They Kill: The Discoveries of a Maverick Sociologist.* New York: Vintage Books.

Rich, Adrienne. 1991. *An Atlas of the Difficult World: Poems, 1981–1991.* New York: W. W. Norton.

Richard, Alain. 1999. *Roots of Violence in the US Culture: A Diagnosis toward Healing.* Nevada City, CA: Blue Dolphin.

RI Kids Count. N.d. "Community Snapshots." http://www.rikidscount.org /Portals/0/Uploads/Documents/Factbook%202015/Community%20 Snapshots/Providence-2015.pdf.

Rios, Victor. 2011a. *Punished: Policing the Lives of Black and Latino Boys.* New York: New York University Press.

———. 2011b. *Street Life: Poverty, Gangs and a Ph.D.* N.p.: CreateSpace.

Robbins, Jerome, and Robert Wise, producers. 1961. *West Side Story.* Mirisch.

Rodriguez, Jose. 2016. *I Won't Love You If.* Written, produced, and performed by Jose Rodriguez. MS shared privately with the author.

Rodriguez, Luis. 1993. *Always Running: La Vida Loca: Gang Days in LA.* New York: Touchstone.

Rosich, Katherine J. 2007. *Race, Ethnicity, and the Criminal Justice System.* Washington, DC: American Sociological Association.

Ross, Laurie, Shane Capra, Lindsay Carpenter, Julia Hubbell, and Kathrin Walker. 2016. *Dilemmas in Youth Work and Youth Development Practice.* New York: Routledge.

Rothstein, Richard. 2017. *The Color of Law: A Forgotten History of How Our Government Segregated America.* New York: Liveright.

Schell, Jonathan. 2003. *Unconquerable World: Power, Nonviolence and the Will of the People.* New York: Henry Holt.

Shakur, Sanyika. 1993. *Monster: The Autobiography of an L.A. Gang Member.* New York: Grove Press.

Sharp, Gene. 1973. *The Politics of Nonviolent Action.* Vols. 1–3. Boston: Porter Sargent.

———. 1990. *The Power and Potential of Nonviolent Struggle.* Lecture at the National Conference on Nonviolent Sanctions and Defense, Boston. https://www.youtube.com/watch?v=QQV_4-rXXrE.

Shay, Jonathan. 1995. *Achilles in Vietnam: Combat Trauma and the Undoing of Character.* New York: Scribner.

Shore, Bradd. 1996. *Culture in Mind: Culture, Cognition and the Problem of Meaning.* New York: Oxford University Press.

Simon, David, director. 2002–8. *The Wire.* Blown Deadline Productions.

Singleton, John, director. 1991. *Boyz n the Hood.* Columbia Pictures.

Slim, Hugo, and Paul Thompson. 1994. *Listening for a Change: Oral Testimony and Community Development.* Gabriola Island, BC: New Society.

Sloan, Cle. 2005. *Bastards of the Party: The History of L.A.'s Notorious Bloods and Crips as Told from the Inside.* Fuqua Films, Home Box Office.

Slotkin, Richard. 1973. *Regeneration through Violence: The Mythology of the American Frontier.* Norman: University of Oklahoma Press.

Solnit, Rebecca. 2016. *Hope in the Dark: Untold Histories, Wild Possibilities.* Chicago: Haymarket Press.

State Police Uniform Crime Report. 2014. http://www.risp.ri.gov/documents/UCR/2014.pdf.

Stevenson, Bryan. 2015. *Just Mercy: A Story of Justice and Redemption.* New York: Penguin.

Sue, Derald Wing. 2010. *Microaggressions and Marginality: Manifestations, Dynamics and Impact.* New York: Wiley.

Supreme Court of Rhode Island. 2003. *Grieco Doe v. Napolitano, No. 2000–299-Appeal.* https://caselaw.findlaw.com/ri-supreme-court/1132574.html.

Sutter, Kurt, director. 2008–14. *Sons of Anarchy.* SutterInk.

Swaner, Rachel, and Elise White. 2010. *Drifting between Worlds: Delinquency and Positive Engagement among Red Hook Youth.* New York: Center for Court Innovation, a Project of the Fund for the City of New York. http://www.courtinnovation.org/sites/default/files/Youth_ECHO.pdf.

Thomas, Piri. 1967 [1997]. *Down These Mean Streets.* New York: Vintage Books.

Thrasher, Frederic. 1929 [2009]. *The Gang: A Study of 1,313 Gangs in Chicago.* Chicago: University of Chicago Press.

Tolstoy, Leo. 1894 [2006]. *The Kingdom of God Is Within You.* Translated by Constance Garnett. www.nonresistance.org.

Tough, Paul. 2012. *How Children Succeed.* New York: Houghton, Mifflin, Harcourt.

Tull, Jim. 2016. *Positive Thinking in a Dark Age: Essays on the Global Transition.* New Orleans: Puma Negra.

Ueland, Brenda. 1993. "The Art of Listening." In *Strength to Your Sword Arm!* Duluth, MN: Holy Cow Press. http://traubman.igc.org/listenof.htm.

U.S. Census Bureau. 2013. "Poverty Rates for Selected Detailed Race and Hispanic Groups by State and Place." https://www.census.gov/prod /2013pubs/acsbr11–17.pdf.

———. 2016. "Fast Facts." https://www.census.gov/quickfacts/table/PST 045215/00.

Uvin, Peter. 2008. *Life after Violence: A People's Story of Burundi.* London: Zed Books.

Van Der Kolk, Bessel, MD. 2014. *The Body Keeps the Score: Brain, Mind and Body in the Healing of Trauma.* New York: Viking.

Venkakesh, Sudhir. 2008. *Gang Leader for a Day: A Rogue Sociologist Takes to the Streets.* New York: Penguin Press.

Warner, C. Terry. 1986. "What We Are." *BYU Studies Quarterly* 26 (1): 39–63.

Wheatley, Margaret. 2009. *Turning to One Another: Simple Conversations to Restore Hope to the Future.* Oakland, CA: Berrett-Koehler.

White, Dan. 2012. "Lasting Friendship, Enduring Inspiration: J. Herman Blake and Don Rothman Move Crowd at Forum." https://news.ucsc edu/2012/04/herman-blake-don-rothman-2012.html.

White, Miles. 2011. *From Jim Crow to Jay-Z: Race, Rap and the Performance of Masculinity.* Urbana: University of Illinois Press.

Wiener, Valerie. 1999. *Winning the War against Youth Gangs.* Westport, CT: Greenwood Press.

Wohlleben, Peter. 2015. *The Hidden Life of Trees: What They Feel, How They Communicate.* Vancouver: Greystone Books.

Youth Sentencing and Reentry Project. https://ysrp.org.

Zautra, Alex, John Hall, and Kate Murray. 2009. "Community Development and Community Resilience: An Integrative Approach." *Community Development: Journal of the Community Development Society* 39 (3): 130–47.

INDEX

Keith Morton is professor of public and community service and American studies, and director of the Feinstein Institute for Public Service at Providence College. He received his degrees from the University of Massachusetts and the University of Minnesota. He has worked in the areas of community engagement, nonviolence, and youth development, in both the nonprofit sector and higher education, for more than thirty years. His teaching and scholarship focus on how we learn from experience, on service and nonviolence as practices of community building, and on the historic and present meanings of community and service in people's lives. Much of his work is grounded in the Smith Hill neighborhood of Providence. He and his wife live on a small farm in Warren, Rhode Island.